MW01070125

The publisher gratefully acknowledges the generous contribution to this book provided by the David B. Gold Foundation as a member of the Literati Circle of the University of California Press Associates.

Preserving the Living Past

Preserving the Living Past

John C. Merriam's Legacy
in the State and National Parks

Stephen R. Mark

UNIVERSITY OF CALIFORNIA PRESS

Berkeley / Los Angeles / London

Frontispiece. Sunlight through a stand of coast redwood. (George Grant, National Park Service Historic Photograph Collection.)

Epigraph: Reprinted with permission of Scribner, an imprint of Simon and Schuster Adult Publishing Group, from *The Living Past*, by John C. Merriam. This work is copyright 1930 by Charles Scribner's Sons; copyright renewed in 1958 by Lawrence C. Merriam, Charles W. Merriam, and Malcolm L. Merriam.

University of California Press
Berkeley and Los Angeles, California

University of California Press, Ltd.
London, England

© 2005 by the Regents of the University of California

Library of Congress Cataloging-in-Publication Data

Mark, Stephen R.
  Preserving the living past : John C. Merriam's legacy in the state and national parks / Stephen R. Mark.
      p.   cm.
  Includes bibliographical references and index.
  ISBN 0-520-24167-3 (cloth : alk. paper).
    1. Merriam, John C. (John Campbell), 1869–1945. 2. Fossils—West (U.S.) 3. National parks and reserves—West (U.S.) 4. Paleontologists—United States—Biography. 5. Conservationists—United States—Biography. I. Title: John C. Merriam's legacy in the state and national parks. II. Title.

QE707.M47M37 2005
560'.92—dc22   2004008786

Manufactured in the United States of America

13 12 11 10 09 08 07 06 05
10 9 8 7 6 5 4 3 2 1

The paper used in this publication meets the minimum requirements of ANSI/NISO Z39.48–1992 (R 1997) (Permanence of Paper).

For Larry and Kathie

As I stood once with a group of friends looking into a redwood forest, which we had come far to see, in swift panorama the history of these trees and of their surroundings as I knew them passed before me, stage after stage, from the remote past.

John C. Merriam, *The Living Past*

Contents

Illustrations

Figures

Maps

Acknowledgments

The number of places not significantly modified by humans over the past century or thereabouts is certainly shrinking, so the idea of consciously maintaining a few of them as part of a larger "heritage" for future generations is an attractive one. If budgets reflect the priorities of a society, however, preserving nature as public parks and wilderness areas hardly rises anywhere near the top of government priorities in the United States or elsewhere. That may largely be due to the overriding perception of these places as vacation destinations or as pleasant places to stop for several hours before continuing a longer journey by automobile. This recreational emphasis pushes what could serve as the underlying reasons for preservation into the background while park managers grapple with the concerns of many visitors: the condition of approach roads and rest rooms or the availability of food and lodging.

John C. Merriam saw that parks could do much more than provide basic amenities. He wanted to help those visitors who possess an innate curiosity about nature by making opportunities for education and inspiration paramount, especially as a driving force for managing public (particularly national) parks and wilderness. Merriam left behind some essays and memoranda from the 1930s about how best to do this at Crater Lake National Park, in a file that grabbed my attention as I started work as a historian for the National Park Service in 1988. These writings tracked his thinking as he attempted to find out how visitors could better appreciate stunning natural beauty through some sort of understanding of the forces that produced the lake and its volcanic setting. I became so intrigued by them—mainly because they represented overt attempts to tie preservation to something more than vaguely worded legislation subject to multiple interpretations—that I soon located Merriam's grandson. By an interesting coincidence, he had followed the same career path as his forebear and at that point happened to be an emeritus professor of forestry at the University of Minnesota. Lawrence C. Merriam, Jr., encouraged me to embark on a biography of his grandfather at about the same time that I had begun writing an administrative history of the John Day Fossil Beds National Monument. This assignment allowed me to begin locating source material that benefited both projects, because in the manuscript collections I consulted, I found the elder Merriam's thoughts about the fossil beds over the last third of his life intertwined with his writings on how to foster visitor education and inspiration through nature.

Not only did Larry Merriam play an important early role in providing an impetus for this biography, he also became a mentor and friend as we periodically discussed, over the course of a decade, his grandfather's contributions to parks and to the field of preservation. He gave me access to family papers in his possession that helped to augment correspondence and essays I found in the John C. Merriam Papers at the Library of Congress in Washington, D.C., and the Bancroft Library at the University of California, Berkeley. Ray Bowers and John Strom allowed me to examine files held at the Carnegie Institution of Washington and gave me a thorough tour of the administration building where Merriam presided as head of that research foundation. Elizabeth Potter at the Oregon Parks and Recreation Department also rendered valuable assistance in locating additional file material. I am grateful to librarians Nancy Hori and Mary Ellen Bartholomew at the National Park Service System Support Office in Seattle for obtaining a large amount of published literature for me through numerous interlibrary loans.

I also thank Larry Merriam for his permission to reproduce family photographs. Tom DuRant of the National Park Service supplied several illustrations for this book from agency collections held at the Harpers Ferry Center. I also appreciate the efforts and courtesy of Mary Benterou (Crater Lake National Park), Tina McDowell (Carnegie Institution of Washington), Wil Jorae (California Department of Parks and Recreation), Cathy McNassor (Los Angeles County Museum of Natural History), Valerie Aas and Ruskin Hartley (Save-the-Redwoods League), and Pam Endzweig, Bill and Liz Orr, and Greg Retallack (University of Oregon) for their help in reproducing additional images. Gordon Bettles made some helpful suggestions during the early stages of this project, and I am grateful for the encouragement of John Dewitt, Ron Doel, Joseph Engbeck, Jr., Rick Harmon, and Alfred Runte. Douglas Deur, Ted Fremd, Larry Merriam, and Fred York reviewed the full manuscript and helped me to refine it. My editor, Blake Edgar, saw the potential of this biography, and his belief in the subject proved critical for turning an idea into reality. I should add that the project furnished more than one serendipitous moment when I encountered windows to a living past in those places John C. Merriam wanted to preserve.

FIGURE 1. John C. Merriam in his office at the Carnegie Institution of Washington, about 1935. (Photo by W. F. Roberts, courtesy of Lawrence C. Merriam, Jr.)

Introduction
Beyond Scenic Voyeurism

People have sought meaning in nature for centuries, yet only in the twentieth century did contact with wild settings become both institutionalized and readily available to ever increasing numbers of visitors. John C. Merriam (1869–1945) wanted the national and state parks in the western United States to be more than mere recreational outlets for visitors from an expanding leisure class. These travelers have been described by others more recently as "scenic voyeurs," content with observing sensational landscapes and often validating their journeys through souvenirs and photographs. Merriam associated himself with a movement to save the last coast redwoods in northern California, but he also redefined how other parks centered on remnants of the geological past were perceived. Because he insisted that intellectual curiosity and an individual's search for meaning be the focus behind the public park as an institution, Merriam occupies a unique place in the pantheon of defenders of parks and other wild places.

Although strong willed and highly competitive, Merriam often recalled his boyhood, spent in a small Iowa town, in tones that echo the English romantic poet William Wordsworth's verse about the child being the father of the man. Merriam likened the experiences of his early years to the "natural piety" that Wordsworth so often celebrated, yet they also pushed him toward a career in science. From Iowa he went to the University of California, Berkeley, and eventually to Washington, D.C., first as a professor of paleontology and then as president of a foundation devoted to scientific research. His personality could best be described as austere yet articulate, his climb to national prominence helped less by his scientific credentials than by his capabilities as a man who knew how to seize an opportunity. He frequently turned to nature for reflection and inspiration, such that he could be both loner and leader. Merriam's protégés and associates in the preservation movement frequently wrote about the power of Merriam's ideas and his commitment to bringing about parks managed primarily for the education and inspiration of visitors.

Merriam's efforts on behalf of several national and state parks were part of a desire to continue the teaching he had pursued for twenty-six years as a professor at Berkeley, but in a setting other than a university. Parks made better venues than a lecture hall, Merriam believed, for allowing people to see how nature reflected a divine hand, yet had also evolved from a dimly perceived past. As the most active among three cofounders of a conservation group called the Save-the-Redwoods League, Merriam embraced what he saw as an opportunity to help visitors appreciate how a redwood grove represents continuity between life on earth now and how it was millions of years ago. Even if some ancient plant and animal species had given way to those presently occupying the forest, he said, ancient redwood trees could render the geological time scale comprehensible to visitors who contemplated the past according to a human time scale. This rationale translated into action as the league's program to buy redwoods from private owners (usually lumber companies) became a conduit for establishing a string of state parks in northern California during the 1920s and 1930s. The league's acquisitions gained so much momentum that Merriam, along with league officials based in California, spurred passage of a state bond measure in 1928 by which the state provided money to match private donations to purchase stands of ancient redwoods. This measure laid the foundation for a state park system to grow and eventually rival what entire nations have accomplished in preserving their heritage.

With that bond measure in place, Merriam helped to secure Point Lobos, a site four miles south of Carmel, for California's state park system. This site contained another living remnant of distant geological time, the Monterey cypress, which struggled for survival along a spectacular stretch of coastline. When trampling and disease threatened to damage the small cypress grove at Point Lobos, Merriam secured Carnegie grants to orchestrate the scientific studies needed for more effective management of the new park. The studies represented both a precedent and template for future efforts to preserve particularly sensitive places, and they expanded the scope of planning efforts into new and scientifically grounded dimensions. Instead of merely directing where facilities and other developments might be built, the master plan for Point Lobos, with science as its basis, set a laudable precedent for other parks to follow.

Merriam's paleontological discoveries in the John Day Basin of arid eastern Oregon made him an advocate for the establishment of two state parks there as well. A proposed park in the basin's Painted Hills held fossilized redwoods that made something of a tie to the league's work to save modern redwoods in California.[1] An even greater show-piece of life from the Tertiary period (sixty-five million years ago to two million years ago), Picture Gorge, lay thirty miles east of the Painted Hills. In wanting to underscore the relevance of cooperative research that he and others had undertaken in the basin, Merriam conceived the idea for an oblong park extending from the John Day River all the way to the rimrock that delineated this portion of the valley. Merriam hoped a state park centered on features such as Picture Gorge, Sheep Rock, and the Blue Basin might allow visitors to meet scientists who were working at various fossil localities to reveal the geological past and its meaning. Much of this preservation effort took place after he retired, and it remained unfinished when he died, but Merriam set a precedent for linking Oregon's state parks with its university system: he fostered the creation of an officially sanctioned committee, composed largely of university researchers, that sought to guide land acquisition and educational outreach in the parks by publishing a book that "interpreted" nature in the basin, a guide akin to the one Wordsworth wrote in his effort to preserve his beloved English Lake District.

Merriam's enduring relevance is tied to his contention that merely setting aside an area as a park and prohibiting certain uses within its boundaries—mining, hunting, logging, real estate development—does not make for adequate stewardship in the long run. The "highest values" expressed by each place should be studied, he wrote, so that their contribution toward educating and inspiring visitors could have a lasting impact and would not be obscured by commercial services. Merriam made use of his toehold in the National Park Service to study the educational possibilities in three national parks: the Grand Canyon, Yosemite, and Crater Lake. Each of these parks hosted an experiment to find out how to most effectively reach visitors with what the parks represented as windows on the forces shaping life on earth. Merriam thought that people might truly support the parks if the Park Service could reach them through educational opportunities found nowhere else. By giving preservation this more exact meaning, Merriam also wanted to protect the characteristics that made national parks worth establishing in the first place. He pointed out that allowing commercial development to accommodate more and more people in the parks could lead to distortions in management priorities and ultimately the loss of the primary values that were meant to be preserved.

Paleontologists are not generally known for their work as citizen activists, but this "blueprint" for preservation became Merriam's major focal point, particularly after his research career had reached its zenith, in 1915. He made a name for himself at the University of California, Berkeley, in the field of vertebrate paleontology, largely in fulfillment of a childhood ambition to be both a naturalist and a scientist whose work added to a general understanding of how life on earth had developed. When he moved into preservation work—and especially once he assumed the presidency of the Carnegie Institution of Washington, a privately endowed foundation supporting scientific research—he brought the lessons learned in his field of study with him. Paleontology is heavily interdisciplinary, and Merriam employed a team approach in his efforts on behalf of state and national parks. He appointed committee members to tackle the various facets of preservation that interested him, especially where scientific studies were needed. Because these committees composed of technical experts were external to the agencies that managed the state and national parks, they could function like independent advisory boards whose findings could be implemented by the operational branches of state and national park organizations.

Merriam's insistence on basing his work for the parks on larger meanings assigned to nature reflected not only his academic orientation, but also a personality that valued order. In making intellectual curiosity his foremost aim in the parks, he swam against the current of promotional activity at a time when state and national parks were becoming focal points for mass recreation. This conflict between Merriam's preservationist blueprint and the promotion of natural areas as tourist attractions arose with the increasing mobility of American society during the early years of the twentieth century. Merriam knew that the ability to get around with relative ease on the country's expanded road and rail network allowed more people to enjoy recreational opportunities, but it also made the importance of managing for the higher uses of the parks more acute. He often used the word *primitive* in reference to parks, a term whose meaning was akin to what we call *wilderness* today. It also suggested a ready link to a past that preceded the appearance of humans. The education and inspiration of visitors to the parks thus assumed an even greater importance, since this emphasis could lead to greater numbers of people seeing the primitive and its protection as valuable to understanding, or at least appreciating, the distant past.

Along with words like *pristine* and *restoration,* the term *preservation* is deceptively concrete. Although completely halting biological change is neither possible nor desirable, preservation involves a conscious decision not to extract commodities from a piece of land, much less convert it to agricultural or industrial use. Use may be largely recreational when land is set aside as public property, but there is also tension between the natural values supposedly preserved and the cumulative impacts associated with providing visitor access. How to resolve that inherent conflict deeply concerned him.

Merriam was in the best position to apply his blueprint for preservation while he served as president of the Save-the-Redwoods League, from 1921 to 1944. The organization raised millions of dollars, often in combination with matching funds supplied by state bonds, and formulated plans for four projects—the parks that later became known as the Humboldt Redwoods, Prairie Creek, Del Norte Coast, and Jedediah Smith state parks—as well as a parkway called the Avenue of the Giants. Although he was in Washington, D.C., much of the time, Merriam, as founder and head of the league, directed its course with help from officers such as the secretary, Newton B. Drury. The two men usually corresponded about league projects and other business several times a week, with the diplomatic and affable Drury acting as a sort of foil for the gruff and often uncompromising Merriam. Drury used his experience in the league to good effect, later becoming director of the National Park Service (1940–1951) and chief of the Division of State Parks and Beaches in California (1951–1959).

As league president, Merriam liked the role of philosopher best. He transmitted messages to the league to articulate the highest meanings of the redwoods as a preface to the group's annual meetings. The most famous of these essays initially bore the title "Forest Windows," but with some revisions became "A Living Link in History." The essay stayed in print for more than a half century, becoming part of the league's effort to make the small amount of literature on the reasons for preserving ancient redwoods more readily available to park visitors.[2]

By having a hand in establishing the redwood parks, Merriam used his influence to help shape development and use of the fledgling California State Park System. He helped set the tone for a "rational" system of parks, with each individual site to emerge from a survey of the state conducted by the renowned landscape architect Frederick Law Olmsted, Jr., during 1927 and 1928. After the state acquired each site, Merriam wanted the master plan for each park to be guided by the necessary studies and statements about what constituted their "highest uses," which would guarantee adequate protection. Nevertheless, subsequent administration of the parks has required something of a balancing act by managers, especially in parks where preexisting patterns of use resist the most well conceived changes envisioned in planning documents.

Resistance to Merriam's stance on the preeminence of education and his insistence on not compromising the primitive qualities of the parks' main features was greatest in the national parks. This is perhaps understandable, given how the early national parks, and the National Park Service itself, came into being. As a federal agency created by Congress in 1916 in response to the growing economic importance of recreational tourism, the Park Service, as well as its supporters, cast the national parks as public resorts. To garner and then keep enough political support for annual appropriations to the agency, the Park Service needed to project the idea that tourism in the parks possessed greater net value, even in the short term, than alternative uses such as mining, grazing, and logging. The Park Service had to promote the parks as worthy destinations for tourists, and provide ready access to them, since more visitors meant an increased number of constituents whose support could be demonstrated to Congress.

Still, appropriations for the national parks were lean, which made for a thin field staff with a generalist orientation. Specialists in forestry, landscape architecture, and engineering remained comparatively few and tended to work from central Park Service offices in San Francisco or Washington, D.C. Beginning in the 1920s, Merriam championed the addition of academically trained staff assigned to education and research in the parks. One of his aims was to redirect the main thrust of park operations away from law enforcement, facility maintenance, and regulation of privately run concessions such as hotels and restaurants. The Park Service did accommodate what came to be known as "interpretation," and it tolerated research, but Merriam failed to push recreational tourism and its attendant manifestations out of central position in the agency's mind-set.

Merriam opposed the paradigm characterizing the national parks as primarily public resorts, because tourist amenities like the dance halls,

FIGURE 2. Merriam at Inspiration Point, Yosemite National Park, 1927. (Photo by Carl P. Russell, courtesy of Lawrence C. Merriam, Jr.)

pony rides, and skating rinks in places such as Yosemite Valley impaired the possibility for inspiration to remain at the forefront of visitor experience. In his view, a national park should be a "super-university of nature," where the emphasis of operations lay in the story each place could tell, a story that visitors could retain when they returned home. The explosion in recreational use of the parks came after Merriam's death, though all the preconditions for it existed during the 1930s.

In the post–World War II era, yet another paradigm arose for the parks. Americans now had more leisure time, and that, combined with a soaring population and mass access to automobiles, prompted a perception of nature as a patient whose health had been put at risk by the heavy consumption that comes from affluence. According to this new paradigm, a national park could play a role in warding off impending environmental crises in regional ecosystems by acting as a refuge for endangered biota. Both visitor access and the potential for inspiration took a backseat, in this paradigm, to conservation strategies formulated to maximize potential habitat and allow for wildlife migration corridors. Such biocentric emphasis in management would probably have struck Merriam as too extreme, since he saw parks as valuable primarily for how they inspired visitors.

Merriam's significance in reference to parks is tied largely to his influence on an evolving social institution. It took centuries for American public parks to develop from their European antecedents, whose earliest manifestations were the enclosures privatized from land once held in common and used for a variety of purposes. The rough enclosures where the medieval nobility kept game animals were eventually transformed into "pleasure grounds" during the eighteenth century, when the game park and garden became one in Great Britain and on the European continent. It became fashionable, particularly in England, for large portions of whole estates to imitate the wild so that the landscaped park conditioned a collective response to nature, especially among the elite. In emphasizing scenery, the pleasure ground was perceived according to the rules of artistic composition that governed both paintings and large gardens.[3] Through this sort of cultural lens, the emphasis on perceiving scenery in nature led to the idea that nature could be "preserved" even if it changed on its own through time. Although access to pleasure grounds was limited to the comparatively few within the upper social classes, these parks furnished a model for the eventual appearance of public parks in the nineteenth century, when industrial capitalism concentrated labor in the rapidly growing cities.[4]

Public parks in the United States were inspired by such European antecedents, the first example being Central Park, which opened in New York City in 1857. As they had on the other side of the Atlantic, "landscape architects" played the key role in designing these spaces. Frederick Law Olmsted, who created Central Park, became their dean. Other city parks quickly followed, many of them designed by Olmsted and his assistants, their spread fueled by shared beliefs about the health benefits of fresh air and exercise in "natural" settings.

The idea of creating public parks beyond city limits can be attributed both to the gradual closing of uncontrolled frontier areas and a growing acceptance of the idea of traveling to experience nature. Tourists became essential to this new type of park, once again predicated on the notion of finding landscapes that resembled paintings. By the end of the nineteenth century, many tourists had expanded their pursuit beyond the search for the merely pastoral or beautiful. They sought the sublime, an experience with religious roots that aroused sentiments of awe and reverence beyond full human comprehension. During the nineteenth century, scientific discovery of seemingly harmonious "laws" governing how the earth had formed gave Americans on tour of the western states a geologic focal point. In places such as Yosemite or the Grand Canyon, visitors not only contemplated sublime spectacles, but also could see them as scenery derived from a distant past.

Pursuit of the sublime helped to link nature with American national identity, with one of the earliest manifestations of this coming only a few years after Central Park opened. In 1864, Congress gave the public land embracing Yosemite Valley and a grove of giant sequoias called the Mariposa Big Trees to the State of California, stipulating that the land be held for "public use, resort, and recreation."[5] Commissioners in charge of the new park solicited a report from Olmsted about its use and possible development the following year. Although largely ignored, Olmsted's recommendations centered on restraint: "The first point to be kept in mind is the preservation and maintenance as exactly as possible of the natural scenery; the restriction . . . within the narrowest possible limits consistent with the necessary accommodation of visitors, of all artificial constructions and the prevention of all constructions markedly inharmonious with the scenery or which would unnecessarily obscure, distort or detract from the dignity of the scenery."[6]

In 1872 Congress moved to establish another public park, this one to be managed by the federal government. It contained some two million acres near the headwaters of the Yellowstone River, in Wyoming. Yosemite and Yellowstone possessed striking geological features in abundance, ones that lured visitors to experience firsthand the scenes already scripted by painters and photographers. The government supported tourism to these areas, if only in a tentative way, in large part for economic reasons. Because the parks had been carved from federal land that might otherwise have been sold, it was thought by some that national public parks could—and perhaps should—become self-supporting by charging admission. Moreover, the business of transporting and lodging tourists could have a beneficial overall effect on a fledgling western economy.

In the nineteenth century, images produced by landscape painters and photographers stimulated the interest of the few who possessed the means to travel for pleasure. So did natural history, since this pursuit centered on the notion that knowledge and experience could be broadened by future journeys or reinforced by study at home.[7] Tourists in nineteenth-century America found themselves in need of interpretation in order to decipher the spectacular natural phenomena they saw in person or in photographs. One way to make wild places like Yosemite or Yellowstone intelligible was through the natural history essay, a genre of writing whose popularity largely stemmed from the belief that through the aid of some scientific knowledge, nature could be explained as a story.

Not only could natural history help people make sense of unusual scenery, it also could serve as a forum for the small numbers of preservationists who urged the federal government to retain unusual western landscapes, an idea that included establishing more national parks. John Muir's essays in his book *Our National Parks,* for example, contained a mix of adventure, advocacy, and effusive detail about the natural landscape of Yosemite and wild country in the Sierra Nevada. First published in 1901, this anthology reached a national audience as much of his previous work had—through literary magazines such as the *Atlantic Monthly, Harper's,* or the *Century.* His opening to the book proved popular with large numbers of readers: "Thousands of tired, nerve-shaken, over civilized people find that going to the mountains is going home; that wilderness is a necessity."[8]

Muir remained a compelling figure at the forefront of the movement for nature preservation in the United States. He founded the Sierra Club in 1892, and it had expanded to become a powerful force for preservation by the time Muir died, in 1914. As the club's president, Muir preferred to lead hikes instead of handling the mundane aspects of administration. Other members, such as William E. Colby, could pursue those tasks with greater energy. Muir's considerable personal charisma made him a popular dinner guest, even if he dominated polite conversation with a repetitious mountaineering story or a polemic on the necessity of saving forests in the Sierra. Muir could afford to be a strident preservationist, having acquired a small fortune through shipping fruit grown in California to market in Hawaii.[9] The luxury of remaining an amateur naturalist and writer also freed Muir from the burden of having to maintain his scientific credibility by contributing to scholarly journals.

Merriam, more than a full generation younger than Muir, resembled Muir in only a few ways. Both were prolific writers, though most of Merriam's work appeared in scientific journals, read only by small numbers of practitioners.[10] Muir's advocacy came through his depiction of the Sierra and other mountainous regions as wild gardens where visitors could hike or climb. Merriam focused more on the appreciation visitors could derive from finding evidence of how the geological past influenced the present. Where Muir could describe the Sierra as a resident (he spent all or part of each summer there from 1869 until his death), Merriam's popular writings linked beauty and time with sublime landscapes from the perspective of someone who visited for a few days at most.

Both Muir and Merriam saw expressions of the divine in nature and applied their thoughts about preservation by taking an active role as park makers. Muir led the effort to establish Yosemite National Park in 1890, a reserve containing thousands of acres that surrounded, but did not include, Yosemite Valley. He advocated transfer of the valley to the national park and away from the control of commissioners appointed by the state legislature, whom Muir characterized as weak and even corrupt. It took from 1889 until 1906 to secure the transfer, and when it finally happened he had little time to celebrate, because the city of San Francisco had its eye on flooding a valley within the park, Hetch Hetchy, for use as a reservoir. Muir fought the dam passionately, splitting the Sierra Club over the issue. He took it on himself to form an independent group called the Society for the Preservation of National Parks. Ultimately he lost the Hetch Hetchy fight, and the society itself was short lived.[11]

Merriam, on the other hand, liked the idea of states managing parks that, in some instances, possessed national significance. Although a political conservative, he thought such sites could become part of a state's "educational program" as a kind of open-air university. The national parks had their place, of course, and Merriam emphasized how they could lead the way in adult education with naturalist programs aimed at inspiring visitors. But he disparaged the militancy engendered by "causes," preferring instead to organize committees loaded with technical experts who could then settle important questions of policy and management outside the political arena.

The two men, who knew each other only as acquaintances, each served as head of the preservation group he had started for more than two decades. Some people joined both organizations, but Muir's Sierra Club remained recreational in its orientation, and its scope was broad with respect to the issues the club tackled. Much of the club's work consisted of pressuring government bureaus to preserve areas already in federal ownership. Merriam, as head of the Save-the-Redwoods League, made sure the group kept its main focus on fund-raising so that acquisitions might eventually be transferred to the state as parks. He actively helped the league define its aims and priorities on each park project so that funding could be used the most expeditiously in each negotiation with lumber companies and private owners. A nonconfrontational, ordered approach to building parks became the hallmark of the league's work.

More than almost any of his colleagues and protégés, Merriam personified the aloof, though public-spirited, professional scientist. His demeanor and dress were formal (he sometimes collected fossils wearing a suit), though Merriam retained some quirks, such as repeatedly brushing real or imagined dust from himself. A hat generally covered his balding head, where he took pains to comb over some strands of hair. A graying mustache and a small goatee accentuated Merriam's facial appearance as he aged. His slender build and medium stature did not strike his contemporaries as physically imposing, but Merriam's grave, forceful personality, his intelligence, and his unbending will and determination to succeed impressed many people around him. Those traits alienated some people (he lacked what could be called a common touch), but Merriam also inspired the loyalty of others—generally talented protégés or associates with some political influence.

Merriam's late-blooming interest in preservation came during his second career as an administrator. He remained a scientist and teacher over the course of his life, but Merriam is largely remembered as the long-time president of the Save-the-Redwoods League, a role that gave him an effective public forum, if one without the celebrity status Muir enjoyed. Dedication ceremonies for what became the largest park in the redwoods are thus highlighted in chapter 1, because they allowed Merriam to publicly express his vision as a preservationist. His career in science consumed most of his energy until he reached middle age, so chapters 2, 3, and 4 are presented chronologically. As Merriam's trajectory shifted from research toward administration, however, this profile of the preservationist becomes complex enough to warrant a topical treatment, which begins in chapter 5 with Merriam taking an increasingly active role in saving the redwoods of California. His involvement with parks and preservation widened beyond his focus on state parks and the Save-the-Redwoods League during the 1920s, so it makes sense to keep discussion of Merriam's role in bringing about an educational program in the national parks (chapter 6), separate from his perspective on wilderness (discussed in chapter 7) and his work to establish state parks (the topic of chapter 8). How Merriam articulated a guiding philosophy for preserving nature serves as the conclusion, mainly because it is in this realm that his blueprint has provided a lasting legacy.

Although preservationists have never really dominated the social and political realms of American society, they have helped to set aside an impressive number of parks and other protected areas for the benefit of current and future generations. These places can provide an array of public benefits, not the least of which is stimulating the curiosity of visitors about nature. In this regard, evidence of the geological past can provoke thought and lead to an ever deepening appreciation of nature's intricacies. In realizing what could be achieved through parks, Merriam saw it as his duty to provide guidance. He always aimed high, and Merriam knew he could fail, but Merriam succeeded in providing a vision that gave new meaning to the challenge of preserving nature.

CHAPTER I

Why Save the Redwoods?

Bull Creek Flat lies about twenty-five miles inland from Cape Mendocino on the Northern California coast and is surrounded by the largest remaining stands of old-growth coast redwood *(Sequoia sempervirens)* found anywhere in the world. Its floodplain gives rise to many of the tallest redwoods, their height and bulk enhanced by an ideal climate and a habitat characterized by repeated inundations of silt. Bull Creek itself brings a continuous supply of nutrients and oxygen to the tree roots, stimulating the growth of trunks and branches. So much biomass is produced that the plant material per acre at Bull Creek Flat constitutes the largest amount by volume recorded on earth.

The coast redwood prefers a moist habitat beyond the reach of the ocean's salt air and heavy winds, so the species is confined to a narrow strip of land that corresponds to the reach of inland summer fog. Where the elevation is lower than two thousand feet and year-round temperatures are moderate, the species has optimal growing conditions. Its range extends north from the Big Sur vicinity, in Monterey County, to just over the state border with Oregon. Individual redwoods average more than two hundred feet in height at maturity, and somewhere between ten and fifteen feet in diameter. Despite such great size, the root system of a coast redwood is broad and shallow, with a fragile web supporting even the tallest trees. A redwood can grow from seed, but the species also possesses the ability to regenerate from sprouts on damaged or fallen trees, hence its scientific name *sempervirens,* or "ever living."[1]

On a Sunday morning in September 1931, more than a thousand people crowded together amid the tall trees for the dedication of a new

FIGURE 3. Along the Redwood Highway in Humboldt County, California, 1918. (Photo by H. C. Tibbitts, courtesy of Lawrence C. Merriam, Jr.)

state park. They gathered at Bull Creek Flat, where park supporters likened the towering columns of redwood to an outdoor cathedral. Instead of piercing stained glass, however, the sun's rays filtered through openings in the canopy, illuminating portions of the forest floor where many in the crowd sat. A few visitors reflected on how, just a decade or so earlier, not a single redwood north of Mount Tamalpais, in Marin County near San Francisco, could be counted in public ownership. All ten thousand acres in this new park had since been purchased from lumber companies, although buying back even a modest amount of land containing old-growth redwoods had once seemed difficult to the most optimistic Californians, because redwood fetched good prices even when the supply of sawlogs periodically overwhelmed demand. Logging old-growth redwood on the north coast accelerated once the railroad arrived at Eureka, in 1914, to be followed just a few years later by completion of the "Redwood Highway." The road effectively connected small communities in Mendocino, Humboldt, and Del Norte counties with San Francisco and Oregon, but it also prompted fears among leading citizens that the remaining redwood groves would quickly disappear. Consequently, a "Redwood Empire Association" promoted the region as a tourist destination beginning in the early 1920s, while the Save-the-Redwoods League, established in 1918, took the lead in trying to buy the best groves for preservation as state parks.

Merriam, as one of the league's founders, served as the keynote speaker at the dedication of Bull Creek–Dyerville State Park, an event that represented the culmination of a decade of efforts to save these particular groves. He and his wife, Ada, awoke early that Sunday morning at Benbow, a small resort in southern Humboldt County where they often stayed when in the redwood region. Merriam's secretary, Sam Calloway, drove them north, past Garberville and Redway, toward where they could obtain an occasional glimpse of the Eel River. Just beyond Miranda, the first concentration of redwood groves came into view, and the redwood forest became almost continuous as they reached Weott and the new park adjacent to Dyerville. Much of the forest was shrouded by early-morning fog, so the trees lining the Redwood Highway remained partially obscured until the sun broke through. When it finally did, the light softly illuminated the rough-textured reddish-brown bark of the great trees, their sweeping branches, and an understory of ferns, mosses, and sorrel. That morning Merriam saw the park, still unsullied by the compromises that afflicted places like Yosemite Valley, as a prime venue where contact with primitive nature might give visitors greater insight into and understanding of the often hidden meanings of geological time.

The Save-the-Redwoods League was not a recreational organization like the Sierra Club, which sponsored hikes and focused its lobbying efforts on federal lands. League officials instead concentrated on raising

FIGURE 4. Merriam and his wife, Ada, at Bull Creek Flat, about 1919. The man on the right is unidentified. (Photo courtesy of Lawrence C. Merriam, Jr.)

money to buy tracts of land containing redwoods. But the league did enjoy a broad base of support among civic-minded Californians, some of whom also belonged to the Sierra Club. Even people who lived closest to the burgeoning timber industry in Mendocino, Humboldt, and Del Norte counties could lend their enthusiastic support to the league's preservation effort, because the group had successfully reshaped public discourse by imbuing the largest redwoods with patriotic and inspirational qualities.

The league employed fund-raising methods such as the establishment of memorial groves, where donors literally bought public recognition of loved ones. This idea came about within months of the league's inception and yielded substantial sums, since those memorialized could be recognized in perpetuity: league organizers simply divided the forest into groves and placed a signboard or plaque for each memorial within view of a road or trail. It made the redwoods into awesome living memorials for the affluent by capitalizing on the species name *sempervirens.* Dedications of memorial groves accelerated through the 1920s, and backing from women's clubs and appeals to schoolchildren also helped to broaden the base of league support throughout the decade. By 1931, donations from large contributors of whole forest blocks purchased from private landholders had greatly accelerated the formation of state parks in the redwood belt. Each method of acquisition represented an opportunity to further the preservation effort with substantial publicity.

As a run-up to the 1931 dedication ceremony, gifts from a Humboldt County pioneer family allowed the league to establish an impressive memorial grove across the Eel River from Bull Creek Flat. The heart of the new Bull Creek–Dyerville State Park, however, was purchased largely through donations totaling two million dollars from John D. Rockefeller, Jr. This largesse provided the league with leverage for wresting Bull Creek Flat away from its owner, the Pacific Lumber Company. Voters in California had assisted in the purchase by their passage of a 1928 measure authorizing matching funds from state bonds for buying such lands. Approval of the bond act by referendum represented a major triumph for the league (the measure carried with more than 70 percent of the vote), especially because Rockefeller had made matching funds the main condition of his gift.

Dedicating this state park also represented a victory for preservation in the wake of failed attempts to create a national park in the redwoods. Congress did not provide general authority for the National Park Service to acquire private land (where most of the old growth redwood still stood) until the 1960s, so national parks had to be assembled from existing public land or through donations. The prospect of using an intermediary such as the U.S. Forest Service—league organizers had hoped the Forest Service could negotiate a land swap for private parcels along the nearby lower reach of the Klamath River—fell apart in the early 1920s. The size and complexity of the undertaking was simply too great, and the Forest Service's utilitarian bent had compromised its ability to serve as a conduit for establishing a national park. Thus the league's ability to buy land from private owners for state parks represented the only real hope for saving coast redwoods in any type of preserve.

Preservation-minded Californians rallied to the league for several reasons. One was geographic, since the remnant stands of coast redwood occur primarily in California. Another was related to population. Not only did the state's population almost double during every decade in the first half of the twentieth century, thus heightening the need for more public parks to serve recreational purposes; it also produced a fairly large number of wealthy donors who responded to the league's appeals. New and better roads also allowed increasing numbers of people to see the need for preserving redwoods. The necessity of retaining roadside beauty became greater as visitors multiplied with the dramatic surge in automobile ownership in the 1920s. As the Great Depression took hold of the country in 1929 and leisure travel began to dip from the heights enjoyed just a year or two earlier, expectation and optimism about an economic turnaround still persisted in California. The impact of the Depression did not hit the Golden State as hard as it did other areas; in 1931, two thirds more Californians traveled in other states than residents of other states traveled in California.[2] Consequently, the league continued to acquire redwoods throughout this period and generally benefited from the depressed lumber prices that resulted from the slumping demand for wood products.

The prospect of economic recovery and what it meant for preserving redwoods echoed in the remarks of each speaker at the park dedication in 1931. A local pastor began the ceremonies with an invocation that called for California's newest state park to be protected from any human activity that might destroy its sanctity. Following him was Joseph D. Grant, who chaired the league's executive committee. Grant pointed to the disaster that might have occurred had the group not moved to buy redwood groves along the main road connecting San Francisco with Crescent City, near the Oregon border. Added to the possibility of a Redwood Highway with no redwoods, Grant saw a threat in the form of proliferating roadside stands, advertising signs, and filling stations. He also warned that the most challenging task for preservation-minded citizens was convincing other, less astute visitors to protect what had been so carefully assembled into a park. Grant finished his talk by naming the pioneer family as donors of the memorial grove on South Dyerville Flat. As he put it, surely no memorial to the parents of G. A. and Elinor Dungan could be "more fitting than a grove of their beloved redwoods."[3]

William E. Colby, the longtime secretary of the Sierra Club who also chaired the state park commission, said a few words before Merriam gave a keynote address that lasted roughly twenty minutes. Merriam began by likening the state park dedication to those exercises held at a school commencement, and then revealed that the new park cost roughly three and a half million dollars. He reiterated Grant's message by cautioning that the people of California might find themselves spending at least that much more unless the area was protected from forces that could destroy its native beauty. Saving these groves, Merriam maintained, was an impulse prompted by the tall trees' graceful outlines, immense mass, and great age. To him, the supreme beauty of this forest had been aided by the recognition of its continuity with redwoods that flourished in various parts of the world millions of years before. He also emphasized that the park resulted from the efforts of many individuals and organizations, each of whom had responded to the spiritual significance of the redwoods rather than merely to the recreational benefits made possible through public access to them.[4]

Merriam then presented what he saw as the main reason for preserving the Bull Creek forest. These redwood trees represented "an outstanding result of creative activity arising out of the remote past" and expressed "the greatest forces which we know in nature." What he called primitive elements represented "the hand of God in the world," and he added that they were "the direct result of creation without the influence of human activity." Their antiquity (a redwood can live as long as two thousand years but is also descended from ancestors that date back as far as 160 million years) made the redwoods living expressions of continuity through geological time. Preserving them allowed for their highest use, as a means to link visitors with a past governed by progress and the unity of its components. This, Merriam alleged, could bring about inspiration just by visitors' seeing the undeniable evidence of "creative forces which were in operation before man was placed on the earth."[5]

Standing "silhouetted against the sky," the Bull Creek redwoods ranked with the cliffs of Yosemite Valley, Yellowstone's geysers, and the Grand Canyon as incomparable manifestations of creative power, at least in Merriam's estimation. Much like the trees in the Garden of Eden, he thought, the redwoods were gifts from the Creator, who wanted to see what people might do with them.[6] Now that the area had become a park, Merriam challenged his listeners to consider whether unrestrained use of such a sanctuary was desirable. Might it be best to build hotels and resorts in the midst of a grove, and erect circular ladders around the largest trees? Or could their expression of power and beauty, of grandeur and peace, somehow be preserved? Alluding to the divine power that William Wordsworth revered, Merriam described the grove's influence on the human spirit as stemming from a "source which we describe by devious language but realize we may not fully define."[7] As he finished, a choir made Bull Creek Flat resound with the strains of Handel's "Hallelujah Chorus" before those in the audience dispersed to enjoy their picnic lunches.

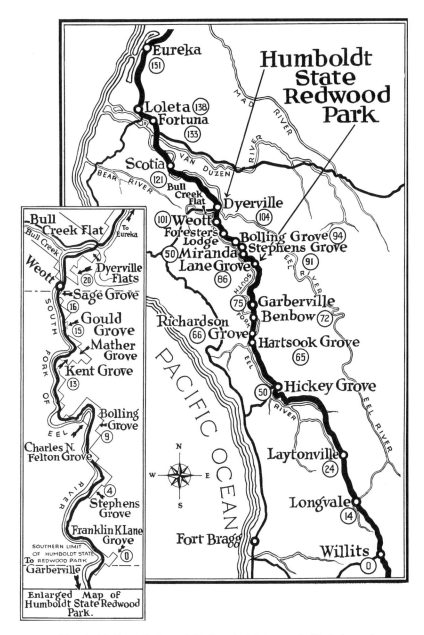

MAP 1. Humboldt State Redwood Park and vicinity, 1928. Circled numbers are mileposts.

The crowd gathered again at 2:30 in the afternoon, this time across the South Fork of the Eel River at North Dyerville Flat. There the tallest tree then known, measured at 364 feet, was dedicated to the three league founders. Merriam gave a short response on behalf of Henry Fairfield Osborn and Madison Grant, his absent colleagues. In August 1917 the trio had set out by automobile from the Bohemian Grove, north of San Francisco, and found themselves appalled by the destruction of the redwood forest along the Redwood Highway. After sounding the alarm, the three founded the Save-the-Redwoods League and easily recruited two other organizers, Congressman William Kent and National Park Service director Stephen T. Mather, as well as influential Californians such as Joseph D. Grant, Robert Gordon Sproul, and Newton B. Drury, to serve as league officers. Osborn and Madison Grant gradually faded from view after the first few years, but Mather and Kent more than took up the slack by securing several key donations. Merriam, meanwhile, regularly took time away from his duties as president of the Carnegie Institution of Washington to maintain an active role as spokesman for saving the redwoods.

On a visit to the forest of petrified trees near Calistoga, California, Merriam noticed how the trunks of ancient redwoods had turned to stone beneath the soil where a mass of living redwoods still grew.[8] Such groves provided a reference point over a far greater span of time than what most people could fathom as "antiquity," so in his advocacy he employed the idea of contrasts. Merriam wrote that through "their seemingly fantastic architecture, ancient castles may tell us of other ages"; similarly, "living trees connect us by hand-touch to all the centuries they have known."[9] Even in fossilized form, the redwoods seemed to express continuity in unusually clear terms. They confirmed that a link existed between human and geological time scales, demonstrating that evolution moved toward unity and progress, often through forms that people can experience as beautiful.

While president of the Save-the-Redwoods League, Merriam attended board meetings and made speeches at memorial grove dedications as part of his summer visits to California. These trips provided a ready opportunity to find new ways to articulate the inspirational value of redwoods. Others built the league's membership base, which boasted more than seven thousand members by 1931. Now bigger than the Sierra Club and collectively the largest preservation group in the United States, the league allowed Merriam to play the role of a strategist who formulated goals while channeling the organization's general direction through policy statements. He made important contacts with business, civic, and governmental leaders and assembled a team of technical experts, usually borrowed from scientific fields, whose collective synergy and individual expertise expedited the league's work—whether it was conducting research or creating new facets of league operations.

Heading both the league and the Carnegie Institution gave Merriam access to the upper echelons of American society. He valued his contacts in government and in 1931 enjoyed many at the highest levels, including the president, Herbert Hoover, who had served as a league counselor and a trustee at the Carnegie Institution. Hoover's secretary of the interior, Ray Lyman Wilbur, had become well acquainted with Merriam once Wilbur became president of Stanford University in 1916. One of the Interior Department's bureaus, the National Park Service, employed several key officials who had been Merriam's students or colleagues at Berkeley. This advantageous alignment of influence allowed Merriam to go beyond saving redwoods in state parks to chair a committee aimed at institutionalizing an educational program in the national parks. The committee's work began in 1928 and culminated three years later, when it released final reports specifying how each of the national parks could best staff and implement a customized plan to educate visitors.

The idea for such programs stemmed from Merriam's belief that the national parks provided an extraordinary venue for adult education. As a professor, he found a large part of all formal education to be based on abstractions such as models and replicas, rather than on visiting sites where students could experience things firsthand. He lectured for many years aided by charts, plaster casts, and a few specimens, but it seemed to him a person's interest could be better piqued by identifying while actually on site the realities upon which a theory rests. Merriam thus wanted to show how to plan an operation that centered on specially prepared literature, museum facilities, and personal "interpretation" of park phenomena by a paid staff of trained naturalists. The idea proved to be so successful that the Park Service used Merriam's committee report on the Grand Canyon as a model for emulation into the 1950s.[10] Merriam's other accomplishments at the Grand Canyon included writing two natural history essays and being the main force behind construction of an observation station on Yavapai Point that would orient visitors to what they saw before them. Merriam also paved the way for hiring the park's first permanent chief naturalist, who had charge of a temporary staff employed to aid visitor understanding of the park.

It seemed perfectly reasonable to Merriam that the Grand Canyon and old-growth redwoods along Bull Creek could be managed with the same fundamental purpose in mind: the spiritual development of visitors through contact with sublime nature. The educational value and inspirational influence of exceptional natural features in both parks could foster what he called "nature appreciation." Merriam came from an era dominated by descriptive fields. As a historicist very much ahead of his time, Merriam believed nature appreciation should be the preeminent concern in managing parks; "educational" and "inspirational" values should take precedence over outdoor recreation, staff housing, or visitor entertainment. Park managers could resolve any conflicts, Merriam reasoned, by using the same logical sequence he and his committees employed to make their recommendations: find or make a clear statement about a park's highest educational or inspirational values, apply that statement to formulate policy governing the park's use, translate the policy into carefully thought-out action, and resist compromises favoring activities that threaten the sanctity of the park.[11]

In addition to this simple and direct way for handling management conflicts, Merriam's idea of complete protection for the parks centered on allowing visitors to visualize and experience the sublime qualities associated with "the primitive." At Yosemite, for example, he became critical of the Park Service for allowing people to take up extended residence in Yosemite Valley, because it led to a host of distractions and impacts that exerted a detrimental effect on wild nature and its ability to educate and inspire. Frivolous "visitor services" interfered with comprehension of the "book" of nature as inscribed through the primitive on the valley walls. If the park's concessionaire (a private business) drew crowds with amusements that had nothing to do with a person's ability to comprehend Yosemite's mountain setting and geological story, it amounted to nothing less than a money changer in one of nature's great temples. Merriam's idea of preservation went beyond simply dedicating an area to public use and banning threats such as logging, mining, and dams; it recognized that without careful planning, mass access threatened to damage the values for which a park had been established.

Merriam had little tolerance for schemes to expand Park Service jurisdiction to encompass areas such as reservoirs, where outdoor recreation, rather than education and inspiration, constituted the dominant value. Merriam believed that dams and scenic roads like parkways should be managed by states and municipalities, or as a legitimate use of national forest land. Expanding Park Service responsibilities to manage these areas would certainly drain precious funds away from the primary purpose of establishing and preserving true national parks, and then would weaken the resolve of the Park Service's staff to combat threats to the parks. By contrast, the agency's efforts to preserve and interpret the nation's most significant historic sites were acceptable, even laudable, provided the endeavor focused on the importance of change over time. "There can be no history without this relation," he wrote, such that change should be interpreted by giving visitors the means to verify truth rather than simply hearing or reading other people's opinions about the past. Solely commemorative sites that served only a local or nationalistic purpose helped to reinforce the assumption that "man of the present is the goal of time."[12] If, on the other hand, visitors could transfer what they had learned about "world questions" toward thinking about future trends, then visiting historic areas could be an impetus to virtuous self-improvement of the kind available in comprehending the story of a "primeval" park such as Yosemite, the Grand Canyon, or Crater Lake.[13]

Merriam's pronouncements about parks and what visitors should be able to derive from their experiences in them reflected the personality of a scientist who saw geology as the background to important events in human history, but who lived as a Victorian romantic fascinated by the sublime. For example, he believed fossil fragments could reveal an omnipotent creative force driving life to progressively higher stages with the passage of geological time. The story they related could be best understood where the primitive held sway, as in a redwood grove or at the rim of the Grand Canyon.[14] Merriam believed that park staff might assist visitors to these places by "interpreting" the site in a concise way and answering questions, provided that the naturalists played the role of guide rather than instructor. If the guides did their job well, visitors might ultimately be able to comprehend a grand natural spectacle by themselves, without continued dependence on the words of another. Park naturalists, as Merriam put it, were to be a group who, "standing in the vivid presence of the Creator, would serve to point out the road."[15]

Such sentiments fit well with progressive ideology, which drove American society during the interwar period, but more than one person might have imagined Merriam born as an adult. A man of fixed ideas, he was once described as stern and distant from other people.[16] Close associates, acquaintances, and even his father-in-law called him "Doctor Merriam." For all his appeals to the sublime, however, he sometimes alienated the people around him by being aloof and domineering, and he exerted a suffocating influence on his family. His eldest son, Lawrence, once replied to a question about why he had joined the Naval Air Service during World War I by saying that it provided the means to get as far away from his father as possible.[17]

If Merriam was overbearing at times, he also possessed a sincere interest in the parks and their potential as vehicles for public education. This avocation found early expression around 1911, when Merriam first became concerned about rapid growth in the cities of the San Francisco Bay Area. He feared the disappearance of open space around Berkeley and responded by working with local officials to establish public parks around Lake Merritt, in Oakland, and in other parts of the East Bay. Acquisition of the remaining forest in the hills above Oakland and Berkeley was his ultimate goal, but he had little time or means to achieve it. The epic trip through the redwoods with Osborn and Grant in 1917 reawakened his passion. It quickly placed Merriam in a position to lead a new type of conservation group, one whose ideals matched his own.

When Merriam finally reached the speakers' stand at the park dedication on that Sunday morning in September 1931, he enjoyed ideal conditions for emphasizing the need to maintain sanctuary in a redwood grove that could be likened to an open-air cathedral. While the sunlight from above pierced through the redwood canopy, Merriam drew from a familiar script as he attempted to provide his audience with greater appreciation for how the supreme grandeur and beauty of the scene arose from its divine source. Better comprehension of the Creator's power, he said, was inseparable from experiencing the pervading sense of mystery inherent to the primeval forest. It had previously inspired him to write in his best-known essay on the redwoods, which concluded: "Standing in this field of shadow, among the living relics of distant ages, in looking out you seem to turn from the clear story of a moving past to see the future rising from it through the miracle of never-failing light—the light that in unnumbered eons has poured down to mingle with the clouds of verdure, and build itself into the unfolding life and beauty of the forest."[18]

CHAPTER 2

To Berkeley and Beyond

The area around Hopkinton, Iowa, is dominated by woodland, representing the last great intrusion of the northern hardwood forest into a
predominantly plains-prairie environment. Among its features are valleys cut through sandstone and limestone formations, occasionally to
depths of several hundred feet. The woodland and valleys around Hopkinton represented the frontier just a generation or so before John C.
Merriam's birth, on October 20, 1869; the first permanent white settlers
from the eastern states reached the Dubuque area in 1832. It took only
five years for a few of them to head southwest toward the Maquoketa
River Valley. About that time, some Highland Scots, emigrants from
Lord Selkirk's Red River Settlement in Manitoba, established themselves in Jones County, about fifteen miles downriver from what later
became Hopkinton. This settlement soon became known as "Scotch
Grove," and before long a few of the settlers advanced up the south fork
of the Maquoketa to found an "Upper Grove" in Delaware County.

Enough of the Highlanders stayed to experience the transition repeated in hundreds of western communities throughout the nineteenth
century: that of isolated frontier farmsteads increasing in density to
eventually support villages containing churches and schools. The Highlanders settling in this part of Iowa could be credited with establishing
the village's most enduring institution, a Presbyterian church, but a mi-
grant from New England renamed Upper Grove Hopkinton in 1850
for the town she had left in Massachusetts.[1] The hamlet sat above the
Maquoketa's floodplain and grew throughout the 1850s. It attracted a
fair number of transplanted Yankees, mostly the landless and younger

FIGURE 5. John C. Merriam (left) with first cousin Frank F. Merriam, the future governor of California, in 1887. (Photo by Boyle of Monticello, Iowa. Courtesy of Lawrence C. Merriam, Jr.)

sons from established families who could expect little in the way of inheritance.

Merriam's withdrawn demeanor and focused outlook had originated in the Calvinist tradition that enveloped both of his parents. His father's family came to Iowa with other New Englanders of Puritan stock, who worshipped as Congregationalists. The surname *Merriam* is Saxon in origin and sometimes spelled *Meriam*, most likely derived from *Merry-ham*—literally, "happy home." Most Merriams resided in the English counties of Kent or Sussex during the medieval period and maintained a

strong tradition as yeomen who owned and worked their small properties. A William Meriam of Hadlow, a village in Kent, grew up a Puritan
and had three sons, all of whom decided to emigrate to the Massachusetts Bay Colony in 1638. The youngest son, Joseph, bought property
near Concord, land that eventually played a role as Meriam's Corner in
the battles of Lexington and Concord during the opening days of the
American Revolution. Joseph's great-grandson Nathan Merriam acquired lands west of Boston and emerged as a proprietor of lands in
Worcester County, at Princeton. Nathan's younger son, Amos, inherited
some of the Princeton property and, among other things, fathered a son
named Marshall. Marshall and his wife, Susan, had three sons: Gustavus,
Henry, and Charles Edward, known as C. E. Marshall's death from ty-
phus in 1845 triggered his family's eventual migration to northeastern
Iowa. Gustavus Merriam established himself in Hopkinton during the
mid-1850s. Soon after, he suffered the misfortune of losing his wife in
childbirth. He and his family needed a housekeeper in the wake of this
tragedy, so his mother, Susan, came to Iowa from western Massachusetts
in 1858. Henry and C. E. accompanied her to Hopkinton.[2]

The domestic arrangement with Gustavus lasted until Susan's death,
in 1860. C. E. Merriam attended Hopkinton's Bowen Collegiate Institute for one year, but the outbreak of the Civil War provided this restless teenager with an opportunity for adventure. He lied about his age
to enlist in the 12th Iowa Infantry, an outfit that the Union Army almost
immediately deployed to help take strategic points in western Tennessee
and Mississippi. Captured at Shiloh, C. E. was imprisoned by the Con-
federates until October 1862. Once released, he reenlisted, served in the
siege of Vicksburg, and found himself in action at Tupelo, where he was
severely wounded on the battlefield.[3] He recovered and eventually enjoyed promotion to the rank of sergeant; he ended the war with the
Freedmen's Bureau in Alabama before being mustered out of the army
in 1866.

On his return to Hopkinton C. E. Merriam talked of going to California, but it was too late in the year for overland travel. Work in his
brother's general store had to suffice that winter, and he abandoned
ideas of California after meeting Margaret Campbell Kirkwood, the
daughter of his brother Gustavus's business partner. Margaret arrived in
town during the spring of 1867, after having spent most of her youth in
Scotland. The Kirkwoods were proudly Presbyterian, like the Highlanders who had settled Hopkinton a decade earlier, but they hailed
from the fiery Covenanter tradition in the Scottish Lowlands. Their sur-

name (literally, "church in the wood") originated in the middle of the seventeenth century at a time when persecution of the Calvinist Covenanters, who resisted the episcopacy of an English king as head of the church, with bishops in authority under him, became so rife that services had to be held in forested areas safe from attack.

Although Margaret had been born on the American side of the Atlantic, in Philadelphia, her parents soon returned to Scotland. Once back in the Lowlands, however, the Scottish couple quickly found that the United States held better prospects, and they decided to have another try at emigrating. They left Margaret behind to be raised by her uncle, John Campbell. As bookkeeper for the Carron Iron Works, east of Glasgow, Campbell had sufficient income to provide Margaret with a good education. Her formal schooling culminated with teacher training, which led her to a position on an estate near Stirling.[4] Although it meant permanent separation from her beloved uncle, Margaret left Scotland in 1867. She wanted to meet the brothers and sisters she had never known. Her immediate family had since settled in Hopkinton, and she joined them there. The Kirkwoods did not have to support Margaret for very long, because she and C. E. Merriam married just a year later. Their union produced three children over the next eight years. They named their first child John Campbell, to be followed by Charles Edward, Jr. (or "Ed," as he was known), in 1874, and Susan Agnes in 1876.

John often referred to his mother's tutelage as the defining feature of his childhood. He possessed her serious self-sufficiency to the point of being a loner, as well as the clarity of direction that marked her personality. His brother believed Margaret intended for her eldest child to enter the Presbyterian ministry, but John never proceeded very far down that path. Margaret did, however, impart the idea that the hand of God could be found in nature, something heavily reinforced by John's early acquaintance with the works of Wordsworth, Shelley, Keats, and Goethe.

Like his siblings, John took reading seriously, though perhaps he linked it more firmly than they did with the discipline he internalized from his mother. Merriam fondly remembered his boyhood training in self-control, recalling a time when, as he read a book with his back to a window, he forced himself not to look out while a band of Indians passed by.[5] Care and precision marked the young Merriam's observations about the local area, so much so that he began to keep notes about what he saw. This practice did not extend to recording his impressions of people, but strange creatures and forms fascinated him. His earliest recollection of spoken words involved standing near two students, boarders in the Merriam residence, who read aloud the name of a strange animal, *Ornithorhynchus anatinus,* the duck-billed platypus of Australia.[6] The students, Thomas H. Macbride and Samuel Calvin, eventually became instructors of botany and geology, respectively, at the University of Iowa. Whereas Macbride evidently stirred the young Merriam's interest in biology during the 1870s, Calvin enlightened him about the odd impressions in the limestone rocks beneath the family house. These happened to be fossil coral, formed on the bottom of an ancient sea; the deposits of alien (or, to use the geological term, *erratic*) rock strewn over the area's limestone plains had been carried there by glaciers. Merriam later reflected that Calvin's explanation led to his early acceptance of the idea that the world had undergone tremendous changes over an immense span of time.[7]

Macbride and Calvin lived in the Merriam house while attending Lenox Academy, the name given the former Bowen Collegiate Institute, the school C. E. had attended in 1860–61. Academies like Lenox, which was run by the Presbyterian synod, grew in number throughout the Midwest after the Civil War and, for all practical purposes, constituted public education during the middle decades of the nineteenth century. The school in Hopkinton consisted of only one building as the Bowen Collegiate Institute, but it had expanded into three by the time Lenox Academy became Lenox College, in 1884. It served a local need for preprofessional training (students could earn a high school diploma and then pursue a bachelor's degree) and provided the initial step for those who wanted to become degree candidates at the state university in Iowa City. The University of Iowa offered further training in law, medicine, and other fields, and it often exchanged faculty with smaller institutions like Lenox. Both Macbride and Calvin, for example, obtained degrees from Lenox and then undertook advanced work at Iowa. Each had a stint as an instructor at Lenox before gravitating back to the university to become tenured professors; Macbride eventually became president of the university.

Next to the Lenox Academy stood the Presbyterian church, where the Merriam family attended services every Sunday. Although he brought a Congregational affiliation with him to Iowa, C. E. Merriam deferred to his wife in matters of religion. He became both a church elder and a board member of the college, a status that reflects the intertwining of religion and education in nineteenth-century Hopkinton. Decisions about the governance of Lenox had to pass through the synod and be approved by the board, composed of local citizens. As secularization began to ripple through midwestern academies during the early 1880s, the Lenox directors approved a synod recommendation to appoint a layman as president of the school. This decision anticipated the name change from *academy* to *college*, hastening the shift away from classics and theology in the curriculum and toward the "practical" and scientific fields that were taking hold in colleges elsewhere.[8] Students with a scientific bent, such as John Merriam, appreciated the changes. He emerged with a bachelor of arts from Lenox at only eighteen years of age, in 1887.

Merriam supplemented his formal education by roaming the surrounding countryside, studying nature firsthand. He often had his younger brother in tow, so Ed did his share of carrying geological specimens back to the house for further examination. Ed also graduated from Lenox, as did their sister, Sue. With a more gregarious personality than his older brother, Ed became as different from John as the family might allow. Ed's penchant for politics pleased his father, who saw a career for him in that field in conjunction with a prosperous law practice. John, meanwhile, made C. E. aware that his main object in life did not concern making money. He sometimes irritated C. E. with his seemingly impractical scientific focus, but that did not result in alienation between father and son.[9] C. E. slowly came to accept that science represented a worthy outlet for John's ambition, eventually realizing that teaching and research could provide his son with a living wage.

Academia, meanwhile, was becoming a conduit for the ascendancy of a middle class in the United States. By the 1880s, greater opportunities in the professions of law and medicine, as well as in industry, increased university enrollment. Posts in new government bureaus helped to make the natural sciences more popular, and with professionalism came greater emphasis on graduate study and publishing original research. Gentleman scientists had once led the fields of botany, zoology, geology, and paleontology, but the professionals with graduate degrees soon began to control the journals, and they even established museums on a few campuses. Funding to support fieldwork came slowly and often with much difficulty, but the appearance of tax-supported public universities greatly accelerated research in the natural sciences. It also allowed science to better serve the broader national transition from an agrarian-based economy to an industrialized one during the latter part of the nineteenth century.

For the son of a barely middle-class storekeeper to entertain thoughts about a career as an academic scientist, expanded access to higher education was critical. That access had been slowly widening since 1850. After the Civil War, American higher education grew from solely church-supported private institutions to include universities run by the states. By the end of the century, the roughly two hundred colleges and universities that existed in 1865 had more than doubled in number.

Despite Hopkinton's seemingly peripheral location in a rapidly industrializing nation, Merriam developed the discipline and support to seek out higher education as a means for advancement. All three children worked in their father's general store, and each commented later in life about how they benefited from the experience. Not only did the store allow them to develop a good work ethic, it also served as a point of contact with the outside world in a town with fewer than a thousand residents. It yielded enough income, along with C. E.'s ventures in lumber trading and land sales, to provide a financial cushion for the family. C. E. slowly attained the status of local entrepreneur, even holding stock in Hopkinton's bank. As testimony to his political connections, he served as postmaster in the years when Republicans occupied the White House and could assure him (in addition to thousands of others of the party faithful throughout the country) of an appointment to that position.

In October 1888, however, several factors led the Merriam family to relocate to California. The move was driven primarily by C. E., who had never truly given up his earlier ambition to go to California. C. E. knew that long-distance train fare had dropped to bargain rates a year or so earlier, and he had since come into contact with a man named James Russell Little, who wanted to set up the Berkeley Bank of Savings and talked of investment opportunities in real estate. When Democrat Grover Cleveland became president in 1885, the position C. E. had held as postmaster for Hopkinton disappeared. There seemed to be little of hope of regaining it in the next election, and the allure of a move west, where the family fancied it would find adventure and opportunity, proved irresistible. Hopkinton remained far from the major travel routes across Iowa, boasting only a spur line on the Chicago and Northwestern Railroad. The town's economic growth seemed sluggish in comparison to that in other parts of the country. As a man facing his forty-fifth birthday, C. E. relished a last chance to seek his fortune in California.

The Merriam family resided in Berkeley, whose population at the time totaled about ten thousand, for a little more than two years. Rapid urbanization jostled land values and capital in the San Francisco Bay Area in ways foreign to those used to the slower pace of northeastern Iowa. It seemed like a different world. C. E. Merriam did not exactly fail at business there; indeed, he had enough confidence in his real estate holdings and the banking venture to return to Hopkinton and put his Iowa property up for sale. He wired his wife about the impending deal, but Margaret understood the message as "Come home at once," so she and her younger children boarded a train for Iowa. It may have been overreaction spurred by homesickness, but Margaret's rheumatism and arthritis had not improved in California, and she missed Hopkinton. The family's living situation in Berkeley had certainly been adequate—they had boarded with a bachelor who taught at the university—but of course, Margaret did not control the nest there.[10]

John had spent the year following his graduation from Lenox College teaching at a country school near Hopkinton. The experience provided him with some money for his graduate studies at the University of California. At Berkeley John did not undertake a degree, preferring simply to "learn something and investigate." He did, however, find himself in the position of having to take exams as part of his coursework, and he was reminded of the necessity of "playing the game" after almost being caught unprepared because he had been more engaged in studies of his own choosing.[11]

As one of several teaching assistants to Joseph Le Conte, Merriam found a mentor in the only geologist on the university's small faculty. Ever increasing enrollment in courses taught by the popular Le Conte demanded that he take on promising students who could help him with tutoring and laboratory work. Most of Merriam's service to Le Conte came in stratigraphy and mineralogy, two subjects where John found himself both confident and proficient. The young man did not, however, confine himself to geology courses; he also sought out a cavalier botanist named E. L. Greene and pursued zoology largely on his own.

Le Conte came to teach at the university in 1869, the year after its doors opened. Born on a Georgia plantation in 1823, he never expressed any doubt about his career choice. The attic laboratory of his father, a gentleman scientist, captivated the young Le Conte, and he conducted scientific experiments there throughout his formative years. After attending Athens College and a medical school in New York, Le Conte found a way to apprentice under the celebrated Swiss geologist Louis

Agassiz in 1850. This lasted only a year but led to a job as a professor in South Carolina. The Civil War brought about the school's closure, and Sherman's famous march to the sea wreaked havoc on the family plantation. Le Conte came to California, as many ex-Confederates did, having lost nearly everything aside from his family.

Beginning with fewer than forty students in 1868, the new university experienced especially slow and painful growth at its temporary site in Oakland. The move to a permanent campus in Berkeley came in 1873, but facilities were makeshift well into the next decade. Despite these disadvantages, Le Conte made the few formal offerings in geology extremely popular and enhanced them with his own exploration. He trekked throughout California in the 1870s and assembled enough material for a textbook based almost entirely on observations he made along the Pacific Coast. Titled *The Elements of Geology,* it soon became one of the nation's most widely used scientific texts and allowed Le Conte to firmly establish California as a worthy center of geological study.[12]

Le Conte also wrote about his trips to the mountains, providing geological and botanical details for general readers who might wish to follow him into what was then largely uncharted territory. He also agreed with John Muir that the alarming disappearance of vast stands of timber in California could be blamed on carelessly set fires and wasteful logging practices. Both men advocated for the federal government to manage and actively protect the forests that remained (at least temporarily) in public ownership in the Sierra Nevada or elsewhere. Le Conte was an early leader in what came to be known as the conservation movement, extending his influence well beyond campus in the 1880s and 1890s to increasingly important debates about the effects of human activities on California's environment.[13]

Despite his popularity as an instructor, writer, and speaker, Le Conte never found a patron who could underwrite the fieldwork necessary to sustain a concerted research effort. He anticipated the appearance of individual benefactors whose endowments came from new opportunities in real estate, industry, and trade, but Le Conte worked before such patrons supported research in American universities to any significant degree. As a way of trying to adapt to the university's chronically inadequate funding, Le Conte established pedagogical conventions such as the field trip. Merriam enthusiastically joined as many outings as he could, and for local excursions that took place while his family resided in Berkeley, he usually enlisted Ed to hold the bag, as had usually been the case in Iowa. Sometimes other faculty members from the university joined these trips around the Bay Area and farther afield. Although largely informal, the field trips helped John decide to focus the direction of his studies on paleontology.

This field, especially the vertebrate side of it, began to emerge from the shadow of geology in the latter part of the nineteenth century. As the evolutionary theory advanced by Charles Darwin and Alfred Russel Wallace gained greater acceptance, paleontology seemed to demonstrate how organisms succeeded one another in a definite and determinable sequence. Fossils could help unravel the complex story of the earth's history once Darwinists formulated a framework for explaining why forms of life change through time. Merriam expressed no qualms about joining a new generation of scientists who believed the fossil record to be directional and nonrepeating, with more complex organisms typically succeeding less complex ones. Even before the work of Darwin and Wallace appeared in the 1850s, geologists had proceeded from the notion that the present is the key to the past. In other words, uniformity between ancient and modern processes, rather than supernatural events, served as a starting point in explaining the story contained in layers of rock—at least for many geologists at that time. Evolution represented a challenge to prevailing interpretations of scripture, though deists and romantics had long seen the earth as a product of natural law imposed by the Creator. For them, "reading from the book of nature" illuminated how progress and unity ordered earthly existence, manifesting God's wisdom. Merriam, for example, wrote that Le Conte considered fossil forms not to be simple curiosities, only of interest because they appear strange; they were instead "sacred remains" left by a limitless succession of generations through which the "germ" of life passed along on an unbroken chain.[14]

O. C. Marsh and Edward Drinker Cope still largely dominated American vertebrate paleontology at the time Merriam attended the University of California. For two decades they had been bitter rivals, each attempting to be the first to name and describe a host of fossil species new to science. This "bone war" became a backdrop to a number of spectacular finds made by both men throughout the western states and territories during the 1870s and 1880s. Discoveries of extinct reptiles, now collectively known as "dinosaurs" or "saurians," generated newspaper coverage and captivated the public's imagination.[15] These creatures lived in the Mesozoic era—divided into three periods by geologists as, beginning with the earliest, the Triassic, Jurassic, and Cretaceous—some 250 million to 65 million years ago. Geologists before Cope and Marsh had long since established that each rock unit, sometimes loosely called a "bed" but often more precisely divided into "formations" or "members," can possess a distinct fossil assemblage. They paid particular attention to certain index fossils, ones widespread geographically but limited to a short span of geologic time. Index fossils are diagnostic: they allow geologists to match rock layers of the same age that occur in different locales. In some cases, index fossils even furnish keys to evolutionary patterns.

Merriam's attention as a graduate student began to center on the fish-shaped reptiles, or ichthyosaurs. These creatures make excellent index fossils and are splendid examples of "adaptive radiation," whereby a land-based reptilian form evolves to live in water to meet the demands of a changing environment. The concept of adaptive radiation is built around the evolution of a certain group of animals, such as Mesozoic reptiles or mammals in the more recent Cenozoic era, that start with a uniform structure. As time goes on, their descendants radiate along numerous evolutionary pathways to fill all habitats open to them. The possibility of adaptation becomes more restricted the further members of a group have carried the process, so the probability of eventual extinction rises. Ichthyosaurs, for example, persisted throughout the Mesozoic, when they evolved to become perhaps the most specialized of the marine reptiles, playing something of the same role presently filled by the mammalian porpoises, dolphins, and toothed whales that appeared in the Cenozoic. As in other cases of adaptive radiation, the appearance of ichthyosaurs during the Triassic period was sudden and dramatic; there are still no clues in pre-Mesozoic sediments as to their probable ancestors.

Merriam, the budding paleontologist, faced some constraints in pursuing his interest in the various species of ichthyosaurs. At the time he was studying at Berkeley, the only North American collection of *Ichthyosauria* came from Nevada and represented Triassic forms; they were housed at Harvard. A greater range of ichthyosaur specimens existed in European museums. Merriam lacked funds to pursue fieldwork, but vertebrate paleontology has always been both a field and curatorial science, with the value of any find depending on the investigator's ability to recognize and conserve fossil fragments that might be of value as specimens. Merriam knew the necessity of training in a museum environment, and when he learned about some Triassic ichthyosaur remains housed in Zurich, Le Conte provided a letter of introduction for Merriam to his Swiss colleague, Alvert Heim. In response, Merriam received an invitation to pursue further study with Heim.

Americans have toured Europe for a variety of reasons since the middle of the nineteenth century. The nation's few paleontologists of that period were mainly affluent scientists representing a few institutions in the northeastern United States. They could draw financial support from fortunes made by their relatives and considered a European trip obligatory in order to make any meaningful contributions to the field. Further study in Europe made sense to Merriam for another reason, however. The future of American higher education lay in the German model of providing graduate and undergraduate instruction, as well as stressing research along with teaching. Most of the larger universities in the United States were still struggling with the initial stages of establishing their own graduate schools. Several European universities, especially the few German-speaking ones connected with state-supported museums, granted degrees in paleontology, and Merriam knew that a doctorate from one of them would allow him to eventually secure an academic position back home.

He left Berkeley for Iowa in the spring of 1890, several months behind the rest of his family. At only twenty-one years old, Merriam could look back on his studies with some satisfaction, even if the University of California was in the process of hiring only its second geologist. A job awaited him as an instructor at Lenox College, where much of his income could be saved for overseas travel and study. He had his first brush with controversy during the following academic year, when he defended the teaching of evolution at the college. Merriam emphasized the contribution of evolution to scientific investigation, and he succeeded in obtaining the administration's support in the face of debate among board members and Presbyterian elders. It was the first of many occasions in which Merriam would articulate his position with evidence and clarity, but always in deference to the prevailing values of those who held power.

His pay for teaching at Lenox did not amount to much, but the job allowed him time for collecting trips. Most of his excursions were confined to the area around Hopkinton, as in his childhood, but some reached as far afield as western Kansas. Chalk deposits there are often exposed in outcrops running along stream channels, and a few of the formations even suggested (at least to whimsical observers) ruins from some ancient civilization. These exposures provided an excellent opportunity for acquaintance with fossil reptiles, especially ones of late Cretaceous age, for those who knew how to find them. The Kansas chalk deposits became a magnet for fossil hunters in 1870, when they yielded the bones of a strange flying reptile that O. C. Marsh called "pterodactyl."

Working two decades later, Merriam did not concern himself with describing new species, but instead with acquiring a better sense of form and structure in some of the organisms that left their imprint in the chalk. In the Cretaceous period, the sea rose and inundated much of what later became the continents of North America and Europe. The chalk formed when the remains of microscopic marine plants and animals continuously settled on the seafloor, where they entombed larger animals that also sank to the bottom. Shells similar in age to the white cliffs of Dover and the chalks of the Paris basin accumulated to a depth of 750 feet in western Kansas.[16] Merriam focused on documenting structural change and attempted to define ancestral and intermediate forms of large marine reptiles called mosasaurs. These creatures possessed a long, snakelike, scaly body, a head resembling that of a lizard with strong recurred teeth (that is, teeth turned back so the reptile could reverse direction in the water), and two pairs of paddle-shaped limbs. Mosasaurs were highly specialized and distributed worldwide, so that their relatively brief appearance in Mesozoic seas, when compared to the longevity of ichthyosaurian species, might be viewed as another manifestation of adaptive radiation.

Merriam surmised that a study built from what he already knew about specialization among extinct marine reptiles had the potential to be a doctoral thesis. In the meantime, he pulled together what he considered to be his first piece of writing worth noting. It appeared in the *Lenox Nutshell,* the college magazine, and had nothing directly to do with his work in paleontology. "Thoughts for Arbor Day" showed that the ruminations about nature that dominated his later writings did not spring from the sense of mortality and obligation to his progenitors that so often accompany middle age. This article, consisting of only three pages, centered on how trees could inspire people; it may have represented a needed diversion near the end of a busy year as an instructor. It also showed, to whatever limited degree, the beginning of his interest in writing for general audiences.

Although the year at Lenox undoubtedly had its difficult moments, it allowed him to pursue his goal of further study in paleontology. With only 250 dollars in his pocket, Merriam left his family and Hopkinton for Europe in the summer of 1891. Careful spending and some borrowing kept him there for the next two years, and he learned German in short order. Upon his arrival in Zurich, where he made some sketches of Triassic *Ichthyosauria,* Merriam was advised by Heim to study under the great Karl Albert von Zittel at Munich for at least one semester.[17] He decided to remain in Munich, where he could combine advanced work in geology, paleontology, botany, and zoology with the invaluable experience of familiarizing himself with von Zittel's collections. It helped Merriam to complete a doctoral thesis called "Ueber die Pythonomorphen der Kansas-Kriede" (The morphology of snake lizards in the Kansas chalk) and eventually publish it in a reputable scientific journal.[18]

Merriam came to admire the German sense of order and discipline, but it seemed to him that too many students in Munich extrapolated Darwinian theory to social contexts, along with attendant notions such as survival of the fittest. Merriam reflected later in life that this attitude presaged the Nazi doctrine of racial superiority that grossly distorted Darwinism. Conversely, his impression of von Zittel, author of the classic text *Palaeontologie* in addition to a massive history of geological study up to that point, remained positive, though the tall and distinguished paleontologist possessed a reserve and aloofness expected of German academics at that time. Von Zittel spoke English and had previously traveled to the United States, and he possessed enough interest in nature on his journey to have endorsed the first proposal to establish Mount Rainier National Park, which came more than a decade before a bill finally passed Congress in 1899.[19] Some colleagues believed that Merriam wanted to match the German's command of taxonomy and the geographic distribution of extinct animals, two areas where the American paleontologist indeed did eventually excel.

Most doctoral students have the circumstances surrounding their oral examinations seared deeply into memory, given what is at stake. Merriam recalled being uninspired after so much study at that particular time, so he decided to buy a tailored dress suit. After hiring a horse-drawn taxi, he proceeded to ride in state through the naturalistic "English" gardens in Munich. The informally landscaped park, with its many groves and plantings intended to engender reflection through interaction with idealized nature, provided him with sufficient stimulation to pass the examination with ease the following day. Merriam donned the same suit again some months later, at which point he added a robe bearing the red and white chevron of Germany. That day in 1893 marked his first great triumph: he graduated with a Ph.D. summa cum laude.[20] He now had a degree in hand, and with philosophical thoughts about nature still largely latent, Merriam set his sights on a job in paleontology.

CHAPTER 3

Paleontologist of the Far West

Despite having the relatively limited options connected with being a doctor of paleontology who possessed only recent credentials, John C. Merriam came home from Europe in mid-1893 feeling fairly optimistic. Pausing in Chicago, he and a more senior colleague named Thomas Chamberlain put together some of the fossil material exhibited at the World's Columbian Exposition held there that summer. Chamberlain had previously held the post of president of the University of Wisconsin; he had come to Chicago the previous year to head the new department of geology at the recently established university there. Merriam and Chamberlain got on well enough for Merriam to remain at the University of Chicago for the following two quarters, but only as a docent at the Walker Museum. Merriam wanted to stay, especially if some money could be found to support his plan to collect fossil whale skeletons in the gulf coastal plain on behalf of the museum. But no more than a modest stipend appeared even though the university existed largely through the benevolence of oil magnate John D. Rockefeller. Frustrated by the lack of research funding, Merriam accepted an offer from the University of California in the spring of 1894.[1]

If Merriam returned to his old stomping ground reluctantly, it was with good reason. He was one of some fifty instructors at an institution with fewer than six hundred students, and one that faced severe financial problems throughout the 1890s. Chronically meager appropriations from the state legislature, constricted even more by financial panic, recession, and a substantial decline in revenue from the federal government as the state's land grant institution, brought serious discussion about whether tuition should be charged to students. Many faculty

Era	Period	Epoch	Began (B.C.)
Cenozoic	Quaternary	Holocene	10,000
		Pleistocene	1,800,000
	Tertiary	Pliocene Miocene Oligocene Eocene Paleocene	5,300,000 23,800,000 33,700,000 54,800,000 65,500,000
Mesozoic	Cretaceous Jurassic Triassic		144,000,000 206,000,000 248,000,000

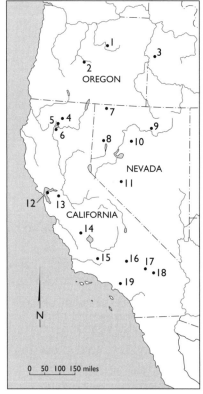

1. John Day Basin, Tertiary mammals and plants
2. Crooked River, Oligocene mammals
3. Payette, Tertiary plants
4. Shasta County limestone, Triassic invertebrates and reptiles
5. Samwel Cave, Pleistocene mammals
6. Potter Creek Cave, Pleistocene mammals
7. Virgin Valley and Thousand Creek, Tertiary mammals
8. Astor Pass, Pleistocene mammals
9. Elko, Tertiary invertebrates and mammals
10. West Humboldt Range, Triassic invertebrates and reptiles
11. Cedar Mountain, Miocene mammals
12. San Pablo Bay, Tertiary plants and Pleistocene mammals
13. Mount Diablo, Tertiary invertebrates and plants
14. Coalinga, Tertiary invertebrates and mammals
15. McKittrick, Pleistocene mammals
16. Ricardo, Pliocene mammals
17. Barstow, upper Miocene mammals
18. Manix, Pleistocene mammals
19. Rancho La Brea, Pleistocene mammals

MAP 2. Localities with fossil remains that appear in Merriam's scientific work.

members still served as both teachers and administrators, yet the board of regents set policy on admissions and curriculum. The result, as one eastern newspaper commented, was a "weak institution with plenty of land, broken-down buildings, and beggarly endowments."[2]

The university president exerted little direct authority to change the overall financial situation until late in the decade, but Joseph Le Conte furnished a bright spot by popularizing geology and attracting an increasing number of students. He had made some headway expanding the course offerings in the earth sciences as early as 1890, but having passed his sixty-seventh birthday that year, Le Conte could not continue with the same teaching load. In the face of continually expanding student enrollment, Andrew C. Lawson was hired as an assistant professor in October of that year. A Scot by birth, Lawson grew up in Canada and received his doctorate from Johns Hopkins, one of the first American institutions of higher learning to establish a graduate school along German lines. Lawson rose quickly at Berkeley, becoming associate professor in 1892 and full professor just seven years later. Along the way he founded the first scientific journal housed at the university, the *Bulletin of the Department of Geology,* and served as its editor until his retirement.

By 1894 Le Conte and Lawson had made a case for hiring an instructor in paleontology, though the successful candidate had to be versatile enough to also teach zoology. The idea was to complement Lawson's emphasis on mineralogy and petrography, the inorganic side of geology. A vertebrate paleontologist could not only help with an increasing teaching load in the ever popular general courses, but also lend credence to a department that wished to promote research and attract more graduate students. Vertebrate paleontology, moreover, filled a void in the curriculum, now that the university had hired its first zoologist, William E. Ritter. The most compelling reason of all, however, was the appearance of a rival institution south across the bay. Stanford University opened its doors in the fall of 1891. Its enrollment exceeded that of the state-supported university in Berkeley during the first term of classes and continued to grow, largely because of a generous endowment from the railroad tycoon Leland Stanford. The new university's president, David Starr Jordan, had a background in paleontology and used his connections at Indiana and Cornell universities to successfully recruit geologists John C. Branner and James Perrin Smith, in addition to some distinguished faculty in zoology and botany.

In returning west, Merriam could claim the status of being the only formally trained and active vertebrate paleontologist situated west of the Rocky Mountains. At first this distinction brought him little more than a cramped office and undersize classrooms in South Hall on the Berkeley campus. The necessity of raising money quickly became evident, because without funding he was limited to local field investigation or describing specimens that others sent him. One of Lawson's graduate students, Charles Palache, led Merriam to a site two miles east of Berkeley soon after the new professor took up his duties. Remains of an extinct beaverlike animal, one representing a new species, were entombed in the rock but easily excavated. Merriam named the rodent after Le Conte and wrote an article about it that appeared in the department's bulletin less than two years later.[3] The intervening period allowed him to develop what eventually became a recurring pattern in his work: precise taxonomy, a synthesis of previous investigation on the particular group of fauna or study area, and descriptions of finds so thorough that they rarely required revision even decades later. The fossil beaver was significant in another respect. It represented Merriam's first serious brush with animals of the Cenozoic era (65 million years ago to the present), in which mammals, instead of reptiles, dominate the top of the food chain. In this instance, the beaverlike *Sigmogomphis lecontei* came from the Pliocene (five million years ago to two million years ago), one of five epochs constituting the Tertiary period, which spanned some sixty-three million years.

Expanding his professional interest to the Tertiary mammals made sense if Merriam had to be content with field excursions limited to the San Francisco Bay Area during those first few years at Berkeley. He made the best of it, among other things collaborating with Lawson to unravel the geological record contained in an area mapped as the Concord Quadrangle, at the north end of the bay. Merriam even contributed to invertebrate paleontology, showing how the evolutionary changes in Tertiary sea urchins could be used to determine the age and correlation of deposits in which these fossils are found.[4]

The remainder of Merriam's written output during his first few years at Berkeley consisted of describing specimens sent to him by other geologists. He authored papers on Tertiary mollusks from Vancouver Island in 1896 and 1897, but he never forgot his interest in marine reptiles of the Mesozoic. Stanford's James Perrin Smith discovered remains of Triassic ichthyosaurs at a remote site in northern California in 1893 and sent the specimens to Merriam for identification. Merriam published a description in 1895, emphasizing that the fossilized vertebrae and other bones found by Smith did not match those of any known genus.[5]

Although heavily burdened by teaching duties and desperate to sink his teeth into expanded fieldwork, Merriam also found time to pursue a romance. Ada Gertrude Little lived on Durant Avenue in Berkeley, close to campus. Her father, James Russell Little, came west by train from New York in 1871 and settled first in Yuba City. There he met Margaret Orr, who had walked across the plains with a wagon in 1865. Their daughter Ada graduated from Berkeley High School in 1892 and went on to study English at the university. She, too, was the eldest among three siblings but a full five years younger than Merriam. Rather diminutive in stature and demeanor, Ada habitually deferred to John and could forgive his occasional eccentricity. She had some prior acquaintance with him, since her entrepreneurial father had induced the Merriam family to come to Berkeley in 1888. That helped in dealing with his apparent aloofness and immersion in his academic work, as did the feeling on both sides that the Littles and Merriams were social equals. Their wedding took place at the First Congregational Church in Berkeley on December 23, 1896, a little more than six months after Ada took her bachelor's degree.

Since the newlyweds could not finance construction of a house, the couple occupied the upstairs apartment in the house where Ada's parents lived. Arrival of their first child in 1898, a son they named Lawrence Campbell, seemed to push John into seeking more active ways to better his position at the university. He joined a formalized discussion group that year, the Outlook Club, and was bold enough to ask Le Conte about the viability of authoring a textbook on paleontology. The elderly professor counseled Merriam against such a project and advised him to write from personal experience instead.[6] Leading an expedition was one way of obtaining that experience, especially if it had sufficient impact to set a research career in motion.

As a paleontologist, Merriam operated at the periphery of scientific inquiry, even at the end of the nineteenth century. Vertebrate paleontology, along with sister fields such as paleobotany, focused then (as it does currently) on the description of structural characteristics and classification of extinct organisms through fieldwork, collections, comparative analysis of organic structure, evolutionary history, and biostratigraphy. Evolution and extinction presented theoretical questions difficult to separate into discrete questions testable through experimentation, so the study of once living animals was fundamentally morphological—

FIGURE 6. Merriam's family on a visit to Hopkinton around 1900. From left: Margaret, C. E., Ada, Susan, Lawrence, and Ed. (Courtesy of Lawrence C. Merriam, Jr.)

dependent on similarities in external characteristics. The rise of experimental biology, an enterprise emphasizing laboratory manipulation of organisms or conditions, allowed scientists working in physics, chemistry, and physiology to obtain answers to problems by testing hypotheses. Although experimental biology did not make the morphological fields redundant, it started to dominate newly established science departments in universities across the United States.

In the late nineteenth century, as the system of American higher education began embracing the German convention of rewarding faculty members' active research, it also adopted utilitarian objectives. Vertebrate paleontology had limited application in medicine and industry, so it gained only a token place in the science curriculum at many schools. Some universities established natural history museums around 1900, but few possessed the financial resources necessary to maintain large fossil collections or to send faculty-led expeditions to recover specimens in the field. Consequently, only a few institutions could support ongoing research (and then mainly through benefactors) that made for regular contributions in scientific journals.[7]

By 1899 military parties and federal surveys had located many, if not most, of the important and accessible fossil-bearing deposits in the western United States. Veteran paleontologists such as Edward Cope and O. C. Marsh had already named hundreds of extinct species new to science and roughed out a number of the scientific problems in the history of life over the eons in North America. Merriam's interests centered not so much on recording new species and genera as on "reading" a geological story in which fragments of earth history in a specific locality could by related to a larger area. As a man who valued synthesis, Merriam's prize lay in placing individual records of this history into proper relation so that broader generalizations might eventually become possible. Facts drawn from vertebrate zoology became useful when they allowed him to fit fossil faunas from different geological periods into their biotic and physical environments, but Merriam kept away from conjecture when presenting evidence. Even in the earliest stages of his career, he liked to stay within the confines of observable fact by deferring final judgment derived from fossil fragments and relative dating until enough material supported more sweeping assessments.[8] Radiometric methods of dating fossils were not available to paleontologists until the mid-twentieth century, so the best Merriam and his contemporaries could hope for rested on a relative sequencing of formations and associated specimens.

For a first expedition, financed largely with a small grant from the university and some donations from several Berkeley residents, Merriam chose to visit the John Day Fossil Beds of eastern Oregon. Cope and Marsh proposed that Tertiary fossil deposits in the West originated through large lakes, but Merriam scanned the scientific literature almost twenty years later and began to doubt the traditionally accepted view. A party of soldiers made the first collections from the John Day Basin in 1864, when several of them brought some fossils to an Irish-born Congregationalist minister then living on the Columbia River at The Dalles. Thomas Condon traveled to that region under army escort the following year and began exploring the basin as much as periodic Indian uprisings allowed.

By 1872 Condon had published an article on the John Day Valley in a literary magazine with national circulation and established rapport with two of the few American paleontologists of the period.[9] One of them was the pompous and bombastic Marsh, who made an important

contribution toward validating evolutionary theory once Condon provided a key specimen.[10] Marsh demonstrated the progression of horse
genealogy through the Tertiary and into the Quaternary, the latter period spanning 1.8 million years ago to the present. He was thus able to
show through specimens a gradual transmutation from four-toed ancestral horses of some fifty million years ago to three- and two-toed genera, down to single-hoofed horses of the Pleistocene epoch (1.8 million
years ago to ten thousand years ago). After visiting the basin in 1875,
Marsh bestowed the name "John Day Fossil Beds" to an area that attracted a number of collectors over the next two decades. Almost a hundred papers had referenced the basin in one way or another by the time
Merriam visited in 1899, but virtually all of them focused on describing
fossil species new to science rather than on placing them in context by
relating how the stratigraphic sequence evident in distinctly different
formations was tied to groups of extinct vertebrates.

The Indian trails Condon and the soldiers traversed had barely been
upgraded to a meandering and often faint "military road" when Merriam and his four companions made the round-trip of several hundred
miles by horseback and wagon from the Columbia River in 1899. Le
Conte, who had accompanied Condon to the John Day Basin a quarter
century earlier, no doubt encouraged Merriam to assemble a modestly
equipped expedition. Funding for it came from several university-
affiliated sources, including some individuals who had become accustomed to contributing to Le Conte's faculty-led field trips, from
friends, and from Merriam's own pocket. Merriam hired Leander S.
Davis of The Dalles, who previously had guided other collectors to fossil localities in the John Day region. Other members of the expedition
included two U.C. students, Loye Miller and Frank Calkins, who had
their expenses covered. The Reverend George Hatch, a friend of Merriam's and head of the Berkeley Congregational Church, helped finance
the trip but came along largely for the fishing.

Members of the party eventually assembled at The Dalles near the
end of May. Merriam first wanted to visit Condon in Eugene, where
Condon had by then become a geology professor at the University of
Oregon. Condon helped Merriam concentrate the expedition on two
localities rich in fossil specimens, where water and time had worked to
strip away the John Day Basin's basalt cap and expose underlying strata.
It took just over a week for Merriam's expedition to reach the Bridge
Creek beds from The Dalles; they made camp on June 1 near where
Condon first collected fossils in 1865. The Painted Hills, so called be-

cause of their alternating red and cream-colored bands, rose not far away, and the group's temporary home came with sagebrush almost as tall as the tent. Calkins found a tooth sticking out of a steep cliff above them the first day at Bridge Creek, at a spot later named for Hatch, but it took a full week before Davis and Miller had the satisfaction of bringing down the fossilized skull of an extinct hoglike entelodont. Merriam knew the specimen to be from an unknown species and named it for Calkins.

Emphasis on the larger scientific questions meant that retrieving the skull paled in comparison to Merriam's observation of how persistently the members of the John Day formation, which possess distinct lithologic characteristics and have considerable geographic extent, were seen over much of the upper basin. These could be linked with discrete assemblages of animals and to a larger framework in geologic time. The brightly colored stratigraphy of the John Day formation represented local divisions, recognized by geologists as "members," in the Oligocene epoch, a roughly thirteen-million-year span of time that ended some twenty-five million years ago. This became patently evident to Merriam as the expedition traveled another forty-five miles east from Bridge Creek, toward a rich exposure in another member of the John Day formation that Condon called Turtle Cove, because of the large number of fossil turtles he found there.

Merriam and the others now experienced more difficult going, largely because they had to overcome the barrier posed by a rugged basaltic ravine known as Picture Gorge, named for the conspicuous Indian pictographs seen in it. This made for some perilous travel with the wagon, but once around the gorge, members of the expedition could spend the last two weeks of June collecting in the cove. Its setting impressed everyone in the party, particularly Miller, who described the spot where the John Day River had cut its way through vast outpourings of lava as a grand theater fit for Titans who could watch from great benches above the valley and occasionally spoke during thunderstorms.[11] Merriam saved his most lyrical prose for the most productive fossil locality:

> The largest outcrop, called by us the Blue Basin, is a veritable labyrinth of canyons, gulches, and coves cut into the soft blue rock of the middle John Day beds by the heavy rains. The coloring of these beds is frequently most wonderful and of the most delicate shades. Passing along the bottom of any of the large canyons, the wilderness of finely sculpted and del-

FIGURE 7. Members of the University of California expedition to the John Day Fossil Beds, 1899. From left: Frank Calkins, Loye Miller, John C. Merriam, and Leander S. Davis. (University of Oregon Department of Geological Sciences.)

icately tinted peaks and pinnacles about frequently causes one involuntarily to pause and gaze, astonished that even nature could produce such magnificent architecture.[12]

Although Blue Basin pulled out the latent romantic in Merriam, his report mostly summarized significant finds and contained the germ of an idea relating to importance of stratigraphy as a framework for understanding the basin's incredible diversity of Tertiary fossils. It ended with a disclaimer about the need to prepare specimens before more exact findings could be published. Merriam and his students arrived back in Berkeley by mid-July, and he read his report to a gathering of university scientists just six weeks later. Interest generated by the expedition not only resulted in his being named the school's outstanding faculty member that year, but also contributed to his promotion from instructor to assistant professor before the fall term began.

With the reconnaissance of 1899 to whet his appetite for more field-work, Merriam began raising money for another trip to the John Day Basin in 1900. This time he took four students along (Vance Osmont, James C. Sperry, H. W. Furlong, and William J. Sinclair), as well as an agent who collected specimens for Karl von Zittel. Merriam again hired Davis to serve as guide, cook, teamster, and fellow excavator. A newly constructed railroad to a depot built to ship wool called Shaniko put them considerably closer to Bridge Creek and Turtle Cove, so this group collected a greater number and variety of specimens than did the expedition of the previous summer. This time Merriam focused his attention on the basin's geological record and, in doing so, could now articulate its significance as a place where more than forty million years of evolutionary change could be appreciated in virtually unbroken sequence. He also named several formations in the basin: the Eocene Clarno Formation, the Miocene Mascall Formation, and the Pliocene Rattlesnake Formation. These designations and his accompanying observations provided the basis for a technical paper—one highly regarded even a century later—that appeared in the university's geology bulletin the following spring.[13]

Merriam also made this return expedition the subject of his first popular article written for a national literary magazine. It appeared in the *Harper's Monthly* of March 1901, in which he outlined a remarkable "history" of life, one where changing environments in each epoch were evident in the distinct stratigraphic layers of the basin. These corresponded to a "splendidly illustrated" succession of fossil faunas representing a much wider region. He noted that deciphering the geological "story" for such a region usually required training and work over a much larger area than the John Day Basin, but here was a place where the "chapters" were distinct in relation to one another and the record open for anyone to view. He concluded with an enthusiasm characteristic of his subsequent writings about the larger meanings of nature: "Probably nowhere in the world does the scientist work amid more impressive surroundings than in this valley, where every cliff has blazoned upon it proof of such immeasurable antiquity of the entombed remains."[14]

Continued success with collecting in the John Day Basin led to another expedition in 1901. Several of his subsequent publications focused on describing finds made there, but Merriam also wanted to determine how the basin's Tertiary faunas related to one another through time. He wisely put off what they meant for larger evolutionary patterns until, as he put it, "all the available evidence should be obtained from several fields of investigation." Merriam waited until 1907 to coauthor his next monograph, this one with Sinclair.[15] Despite producing a broad outline with clear descriptions of both vertebrate fossils and corresponding stratigraphy, Merriam could not make additional headway, limited as he was by the dearth of geological mapping in the region. He lacked the financial resources to pursue such an undertaking on his own, so he took a break from fieldwork in the John Day Basin for the time being.[16]

Raising funds for the first two expeditions to the basin certainly had consumed a great deal of time and energy, even for a man only thirty-one years of age in the fall of 1900. That term, Annie Alexander, heir to a sugar fortune, began attending his lectures. Little in the way of documentary evidence about his teaching style survives, except that decades later one of his students paid tribute to Merriam's ability to bring a "handle" to those attending his beginning course in paleontology. He usually stood at his desk whittling a piece of wood as the students took their seats. Merriam then welcomed them by saying, "This piece of redwood has been buried under the Berkeley Hills for several hundred thousand years, but it is still wood."[17] Such a device probably stirred Alexander's interest in paleontology. The following summer, she financed and organized an independent expedition to Fossil Lake, just south of the John Day country.[18]

Merriam, meanwhile, took part of that summer and traveled to the mountains northeast of Redding to finally make a reconnaissance of the ichthyosaurian locality James Perrin Smith found in 1893. He needed funding for the time-consuming fieldwork; it took painstaking effort to identify skeletal parts whose outlines were often almost obliterated by such long entombment in Triassic-age limestone. Merriam knew proper extrication to be tedious and packing specimens difficult in such rugged terrain, but Alexander readily agreed to fund at least one expedition the following year in exchange for her full participation in it.

Just as she had on her earlier trip to eastern Oregon, Alexander proved to be fully capable of finding ichthyosaur fossils on Merriam's expeditions to Shasta County in 1902 and 1903. Alexander helped to pack specimens for the long trip back to Berkeley, and she also did much of the cooking. After numerous overseas trips in childhood and camping in the mountains of California as a young adult, she possessed abundant stamina for fieldwork in paleontology. She appeared on the scene at a point when U.C. Berkeley had yet to become an important center for paleontology, and Merriam quickly realized that she could provide the kind of patronage that might allow the university's program to blossom. Her offers of financial support were heartily welcomed, and Merriam corresponded with Alexander regularly about the collection of important specimens, eagerly providing salient details about their preparation and to what degree they had broader significance to science.[19]

With Alexander as his benefactor, Merriam described new species of ichthyosaurs found in California and began a series of articles on that reptilian group which culminated with his classic memoir in 1908.[20] In that monograph Merriam provided a formidable contribution on an extinct group of organisms, starting with the geological and geographic occurrences of the Triassic ichthyosaurs. He then discussed their morphological characteristics and the taxonomy of several types of ichthyosaur known from North America, with a succinct presentation of how these forms related to the fundamental questions of the evolution of higher vertebrates in a marine environment.[21]

Alexander funded another expedition to a new ichthyosaur locality once Merriam and some students made a reconnaissance trip to the West Humboldt Range, near Lovelock, Nevada, in 1904. The expedition in May and June of the following year proved to be a spectacular success in a couple of ways. Participants brought back twenty-five ichthyosaur specimens, including some of the largest in the world and the most complete ones ever found in North America. Alexander even found a new type of specimen, which Merriam subsequently described in a published article.[22] The success of this expedition undoubtedly contributed to Alexander's decision to go from periodic financial support of Merriam's work to making regular monthly contributions.[23]

Merriam's research funding did not come solely from Alexander, but her support allowed him to vigorously pursue a variety of field investigations throughout California and Nevada. No less important was the support from university president Benjamin Ide Wheeler. The University of California regents hired Wheeler while Merriam was leading his first expedition to the John Day Basin in 1899, and the new president accepted the post on condition that the regents grant him direct powers to manage university affairs. After gaining the financial support of wealthy patrons in the San Francisco Bay Area, Wheeler eventually convinced legislators in Sacramento to provide the first major infusion of state funding for the school. This support allowed for a dramatic surge in enrollment, more than tripling within a decade the twenty-five hundred students who had attended in 1899, making the University of California the nation's largest institution of higher education by 1910.[24] The university's emergence as a major force among American universi-

ties neatly corresponded with California's ascendancy as a major industrial and economic power during the early part of the twentieth century.

U.C. enrollment kept rising despite more rigorous admissions policies. It had something of a trickle-down effect for the paleontology program by steadily providing Merriam with capable students, especially
ones wanting to pursue advanced degrees. Wheeler could take partial
credit for this development, because he emphasized research, in line
with his German training (he earned his doctorate in philology from the
University of Heidelberg), and greatly elevated its status to that of a
controlling factor in the hiring and promotion of faculty. He rewarded
professors like Merriam who produced a steady stream of publications,
even if a field like vertebrate paleontology had already been shoved aside
by experimental biology on many other campuses (one reason for that
was the cost of fieldwork and curatorial facilities in the absence of external grants or benefactors). Merriam kept Wheeler informed about
each new undertaking. The president had some discretionary funds
that, however meager, could help underwrite fieldwork or allow faculty
members to make occasional visits to the Smithsonian or other museums on the East Coast.

Not long after Merriam attained the rank of associate professor in
1905, one of his graduate students made contact with a man who had
found fossil bones and teeth embedded in an asphalt deposit a few miles
west of Los Angeles. The two collected a number of fragmentary specimens and sent them to Berkeley. Merriam recognized a number of almost perfectly preserved Quaternary mammalian species, some as yet
unreported in California, and hurried to make his acquaintance with a
place called Rancho La Brea. Shortly thereafter, in March 1906, the
University of California obtained permission from the Hancock Oil
Company to begin excavating some promising tar pits on its property.
By August, Merriam had published his first paper about Rancho La Brea
and its fossilized flora and fauna from the late Pleistocene epoch—
roughly thirty-five thousand years ago to the present. He drew his specimens from a site so productive that excavations there quickly yielded
more mammalian remains from that time span than any other single
locality.[25]

Fossilization at Rancho La Brea took place through a combination of
rapid sedimentation and the seepage of crude oil to the surface through
fissures in the earth's crust. Heavy tar remained in sticky pools after the
lighter portion of the oil evaporated. The tar could occur as a nearly bi-
tuminous deposit, but more often it was mixed with sand or clay and

FIGURE 8. Drawing of fossil remains at Rancho La Brea before their recovery from the asphalt. (Carnegie Institution of Washington.)

then was further disguised with a surface coating of leaves and dust. With the pools being as much as thirty feet deep, unwary animals became trapped in the asphalt. As they struggled, carnivores such as the saber-toothed tiger, as well as condors and other scavengers, were lured to their deaths. Bodies decayed, bones became saturated with asphalt, and portions of the skeletons settled in the mire. Winter temperatures solidified the asphalt, and streams deposited new layers of sediments over the exposed bones. Warm summer weather dried the seasonal streams and liquefied the asphalt, thus resetting the trap. Fifty-nine mammal species and 135 bird species were eventually excavated there.[26]

Discovery of what the pits contained, as well as their potential to yield thousands of specimens, had Merriam scrambling to secure an exclusive right to excavate there. He wrote to Wheeler about trying to gently pressure the Hancocks through mutual friends. He also mentioned plans for neutralizing possible opposition to the University of California controlling access to Rancho La Brea (given its position as the "best institution to direct the excavations"), for which he would need time to garner the support of potential competitors.[27] The Hancocks seemed hesitant at first to grant the university an exclusive right to excavate, though Alexander's financing of the work at Rancho La Brea showed them that Merriam meant business. His point man at the site was Loye Miller, who had earned his master's degree at Berkeley in 1904 and had since found employment with the California State Normal School in Los Angeles. Miller specialized in birds and became fascinated with excavating the tar pits. He enlisted the aid of students from Los Angeles High School for the work and regularly reported to Merriam about their progress.

Merriam, meanwhile, sought to further impress the Hancocks by once again venturing outside the accustomed technical outlets for his writing with an article called "Death Trap of the Ages" in the October 1908 issue of the popular *Sunset Magazine*.[28] Photographs accompanied Merriam's account of how the tar pits formed and his short descriptions of the fossils found there. Just so no one could miss the significance of university-sponsored work at Rancho La Brea, a lengthy editorial note dramatizing Merriam's role there prefaced the piece. It drew upon a familiar analogy by opening with, "Geologists turn earth's pages for knowledge—here they have found a three-volume novel."[29] The Hancocks could not fail to notice the favorable publicity, especially when Merriam forwarded Miller's report about fossil material being destroyed while university-sponsored groups were away from the site. They subsequently granted Merriam's request for exclusive rights to collect within a hundred feet of the pits for three years beginning in February 1909.[30]

Miller and other university-affiliated researchers joined Merriam in authoring numerous papers on the extinct fauna of Rancho La Brea over the following decade. By 1909, Merriam, then forty years old, found it increasingly difficult to concentrate on his writing while in Berkeley. He not only coped with a full teaching load, but also contended with a young family. By then it numbered five, with eldest son Lawrence joined by two brothers, Charles W. in 1905 and Malcolm (or "Max," as he was usually known) in 1908. After moving from the apartment on Durant Avenue in 1901, the Merriam family occupied a large wood-frame house on Bowditch Street. It seemed roomy enough, but the elder Merriam liked the idea of a summer place where he could not only write but also spend time with Ada and the children. His father-in-law provided him with the opportunity at Shasta Springs, a retreat north of Dunsmuir popular with Bay Area residents. Merriam built a summer cottage on two acres obtained from the twenty-three that James Little owned. It had the advantage of being close to a train station on the main north-south rail line of the Southern Pacific, and also near to where they could fish for trout on the Sacramento River.[31]

Merriam needed the occasional respite to keep up with his ever increasing workload. More students meant increased administrative duties in addition to preparing specimens, writing, and directing excavations. Personal appearances in the field for any length of time began to fall off significantly after Merriam's promotion in 1905, though he continued to take the lead role in adding to the geographic breadth of the university's paleontological collections. This usually began with colleagues or enthusiasts sending him a specimen from a new locality, on which Merriam followed up by making a reconnaissance in the company of one or more students. If the site looked promising, he arranged with local contacts for provision of transportation or other logistical support for the ensuing field camp. Merriam generally put one of his graduate students in charge of collecting fossil specimens while other participants obtained rock samples. This system allowed him the relative luxury of making only an occasional field visit while an expedition was in progress.

Each collecting trip could also serve a larger purpose, that of correlating one locality's extinct-faunal assemblage with others representing the same slices of geological time. The possibility of correlation furnished much of Merriam's rationale for going to northwestern Nevada in June 1906 to examine the Virgin Valley badlands, a place where he suspected the formations might contain the remains of Tertiary vertebrates similar to those occurring in the John Day Fossil Beds.[32] Annie Alexander organized and funded a three-month expedition to the Virgin Valley in the summer of 1909. The site yielded a wide range of extinct mammals, among them a pair of antelope genera representing the twisted-horn type previously unreported in the Western Hemisphere. Merriam published an article on these animals in December, presenting the find as evidence of a possible relationship to twisted-horn antelopes found in the Old World. In typical fashion, he refused to speculate and instead presented three hypotheses that might account for the presence of twisted-horn antelopes in the Pliocene of North America and left it at that. The more difficult task of correlation found subsequent expression in a comprehensive paper on the Virgin Valley and the adjacent Thousand Creek beds. Merriam published it in two parts, one a geological history (1910) the other on vertebrate faunas (1911), explaining how the fauna of the lower Pliocene (four to five million years ago) at Thousand Creek might relate to the meager number of specimens thus

far found in the John Day Basin's Rattlesnake Formation. He also compared the Virgin Valley beds of the middle Miocene (roughly fifteen
million years ago) with formations of roughly similar age in several
western states, a potentially important one being the Mascall Formation
of the John Day Basin.[33]

The idea of correlating fossil-bearing Tertiary formations found in
such widely separated areas as the Great Plains and the Northern Great
Basin fired Merriam's imagination after 1910, as did some new studies of
Tertiary mammals sparked by specimens he obtained in the Mojave
Desert.[34] Annie Alexander funded several collecting trips led by Merriam's graduate students to some productive fossil localities near Barstow, but by 1912, Merriam was periodically complaining about more
and more administrative duties, with correspondingly less time spent on
research.[35] Part of Merriam's dilemma stemmed from his own ambition, and in a mixed message to Wheeler, Merriam wrote about completing more work in 1911 than in any other year, even while his duties
had doubled.[36] It paid off, at least partially, with his promotion to full
professor in 1912.

Formation of a new department of paleontology had already come
three years earlier, as one of some twenty new departments Wheeler
created during the two decades of his tenure as university president.
Alexander's interest and continuing financial contributions to support
fieldwork throughout California no doubt played a significant role in
splitting paleontology from geology, though mineralogy also achieved
departmental status at the same time.[37] Enrollment in paleontology
courses may have been another factor; the number of students in 1909
was more than double the number reported for 1908. In any event,
Merriam at first served as chair in a two-man department and continued
to teach the occasional course in historical geology, zoology, and even
physical anthropology. He previously had persuaded Alexander to fund
fellowships for promising doctoral candidates, which allowed him to
split his teaching load and in the process have the assistance of future
colleagues such as John Buwalda, W. S. W. Kew, Earl Packard, and
Chester Stock. Slightly older graduates, such as Harold Bryant and
Eustace Furlong, already held positions at Berkeley or, like Miller in Los
Angeles, had taken jobs at other universities where they could be useful
to Merriam in future work.

By 1912 Merriam's name was well known to the handful of American
universities and museums that contributed to the field of paleontology
and in many that lacked the means to do so. He corresponded regularly

with his colleagues on the East Coast, two of the most renowned being Charles D. Walcott (a paleontologist who discovered the celebrated Burgess shale in the Canadian Rockies and headed the Smithsonian) and Henry Fairfield Osborn (longtime professor at Princeton and curator in the department of paleontology at the American Museum of Natural History in New York City). Both Walcott and Osborn actively pursued their interest in parks and scenic preservation, the latter moving to capitalize on the opportunity by becoming president of the American Museum of Natural History in 1910. Osborn assumed the office partly as the result of his impressive research output, but also because of his connection to New York's elite families. With an unparalleled opportunity to enlist philanthropic help for preserving trees and open space around the city, Osborn encouraged Merriam to do similar work by having parks established around the East Bay. The two men began to correspond more frequently, especially after Osborn's visit to Rancho La Brea in 1911.

California's explosive growth between 1900 and 1910 (from 1.5 million people to 2.4 million) furnished another reason for Merriam to take notice of the need for open space and to preserve unique environments. Much of the pressure could be most keenly felt around the San Francisco Bay; Merriam had hunted ducks in the marshes of North Berkeley and for quail around Orinda, in adjacent Contra Costa County.[38] By 1912 he estimated the ducks to be only a tenth of their number of a decade earlier.[39] More alarming was the subdivision of virtually all the available land in the East Bay for housing and business, with virtually no provision made for forested parks and public playgrounds. Merriam saw the area as offering greater possibilities for parks than almost any other metropolis in the country, yet progress toward this end seemed fitfully slow. Like many of his contemporaries, he embraced regional planning as a way to bring about a more civilized society, where education and contact with nature fostered individual self-improvement. In the spring of 1912 Merriam wrote to the recipient of a university fellowship given for the study of urban problems about a need for open space, urging the student to visit eastern cities to see how they crafted their park systems.[40]

Such enthusiasm might have seemed out of character for a man who to this point had expressed little, if any, interest in social institutions other than the University of California. A driving ambition to pursue his research kept Merriam from joining Le Conte or other scientists at Berkeley and Stanford as members of the Sierra Club.[41] He knew the club's president, John Muir, but their interaction had been limited to

Merriam's identifying some fossils that the great naturalist brought back from Arizona.[42] Muir's campaign to save the Hetch Hetchy Valley in Yosemite National Park from being dammed, a battle that raged between 1906 and 1913, elicited surprisingly little comment from Merriam. Building an impoundment there brought the sanctity of national parks into question and remained in the forefront of public debate around the Bay Area, but the dam's supporters pointed to the prospect of freeing San Francisco from the clutches of private water companies that charged residents what the market could bear. Merriam preferred to use what little free time he had to prod authorities in Oakland to be more ambitious in securing Lake Merritt and some other small tracts for public parks.[43] A large expanse of forest in the Berkeley Hills, much of it owned by the East Bay Water Company and not yet subdivided, also beckoned him. Without funding for that more ambitious project anywhere in sight, however, Merriam placed it on hold while his academic career continued to surge toward its zenith.

CHAPTER 4

An Upward Trajectory

Annie Alexander's continuing financial support of collecting expeditions originating from the Berkeley campus provided Merriam with more support than most academic scientists of the time could ever expect. These trips fueled his research output, which centered on fossil material from California and the surrounding states. Merriam published eight articles in the university's geology bulletin in 1913 alone, and exceeded that total two years later with nine contributions to six different journals. These writings consisted of descriptions of new paleontological discoveries and an occasional synthesis of how the work at Rancho La Brea or the extinct faunas of the Mojave Desert fit into the larger geological context of North America.[1] The article possessing the most geographic breadth came in an anthology titled *Nature and Science on the Pacific Coast,* published in March 1915. Merriam called it "Significant Features in the History of Life on the Pacific Coast" and began it with a disclaimer about how little of international interest had resulted as yet from paleontological studies conducted there. Nevertheless, he wrote, the region contained much of interest to visitors. In the space of fifteen pages, Merriam identified the major localities on the West Coast for fossil plants, invertebrates, and the vertebrate groups of fish, amphibians, reptiles, and mammals.[2]

Together, the anthology's contributors, most of them California-based academic scientists, filled the perceived void for a natural-science-oriented travel guide. The book's target audience consisted of the visitors who came to California in 1915 for one or both expositions staged to celebrate the opening of the Panama Canal. *Nature and Science* was also an advertising vehicle for the first West Coast meeting of the Amer-

FIGURE 9. The Redwood Highway in the Franklin K. Lane Grove, Humboldt County, about 1918. (Photo by H. C. Tibbitts, courtesy of Lawrence C. Merriam, Jr.)

ican Association for the Advancement of Science, to be held in the Bay Area over a one-week period that August. The AAAS meeting hitched itself to the larger Panama-Pacific Exposition, held in San Francisco, an event that opened in February 1915 and ran for more than nine months. Other fairs with a national scope had been held on the West Coast, beginning with the 1905 Lewis and Clark Centennial Exposition in Portland, but San Francisco's exposition eclipsed them in grandeur and drawing power. Attendance totaled almost nineteen million people by the time its gates closed in December. By then, the city had successfully projected to an international audience that it had fully recovered from the disastrous earthquake and fire of nine years earlier. Although the fair feted the Panama Canal's August 1914 opening, promoters also wanted to underline how the future lay in the American West. They believed the capital of this new civilization to be California, a place where abundant natural resources, technological power, and optimism would fuel economic progress.[3]

Although it was only a sidebar to the larger exposition, the AAAS meeting loomed large to scientists working on the West Coast. San Francisco was still a four day's journey by train from the eastern seaboard, but the meeting represented an end to regional isolation, because formation of a Pacific Division for the AAAS sprang from the August gathering. This made the association, which started as a society for geologists in 1840 and grew to be the largest organization of its kind in the United States, a truly national umbrella for science. For Merriam and his colleagues in Berkeley, the meeting provided abundant opportunity to display their skill as hosts. It also allowed Merriam to demonstrate his versatility as a scholar; he made six presentations at the meeting, distributed among the sessions for paleontology, zoology, and anthropology. A number of field excursions took place over the following week. On Thursday Merriam attended one led by his doctoral student John Buwalda to the Pliocene geological formation of Ricardo, in the Mojave Desert. On Friday he cohosted a trip to Rancho La Brea, and on Saturday he went farther south, to the San Pedro area, where one of his students, Remington Kellogg, led an examination of remains from marine fauna of the Pleistocene. None of the paleontology field trips were heavily attended (in all cases only five or six scientists went along), but Merriam wrote to Annie Alexander upon his return to Berkeley that his esteemed colleague in the Paleontological Society, Henry Fairfield Osborn, had offered a resolution about this meeting's having been the most important and satisfying that the society had ever staged.[4]

If he looked to Osborn for validation of his program, Merriam had good reason. As president of the American Museum of Natural History, Osborn developed an institution that dominated vertebrate paleontology in the United States and Canada for roughly three decades. Osborn enjoyed the support of wealthy backers, who financed expeditions on a scale unmatched by any other museum or academic institution. International in scope, the paleontology department at the Museum of Natural History possessed sufficient funding and infrastructure to send paid research assistants on extended collecting trips virtually anywhere in the world. In contrast, the support available to Merriam confined his program to a regional focus on the geological past of California and its neighboring states. Merriam depended on Annie Alexander and on small grants from other sources to underwrite the expenses of Buwalda and other students in places such as the Mojave. Osborn could pay a group of fossil hunters to go to Patagonia or other distant destinations.

In playing the role of administrator, Osborn had little time for collecting and the tedium associated with preparing specimens. He could write about taxonomic questions, but he preferred to focus on the broader implications of paleontology for biogeography and inherited biological characteristics. But he also took the lead in translating the museum's acquisitions into spectacular exhibits. One specimen from Montana became especially popular, a dinosaur Osborn named *Tyrannosaurus rex*. Merriam did have the edge over his elder colleague in the rudimentary aspects of paleontology—the collection, identification, and preparation of specimens—if that was any consolation.

The two men had their philosophical differences—Osborn was an adherent of the eugenics movement, he possessed an ideological hostility toward the idea of natural selection, and he routinely dismissed findings from fields such as genetics and experimental biology because they challenged the way science had always been done—but each recognized the need for a good professional relationship. Merriam and Osborn remained on friendly terms because they knew that vertebrate paleontology so often depends on cooperation among investigators and institutions. As a professional courtesy, Merriam thus allowed the Museum of Natural History to make duplicates of specimens he had obtained from Rancho La Brea during the period when he and the University of California enjoyed exclusive rights to excavate there. No one could seriously challenge the museum's position in paleontology anyway, so it made little sense for Merriam and Osborn to become antagonistic toward one another. It did, however, require no small degree of sufferance to interact with Osborn on a personal basis. Known for his pretentiousness even at a time when it was expected of men in his position, Osborn regularly displayed arrogant and condescending behavior toward museum staff. These personality traits may have been why Merriam—at times imperious himself, but to a lesser degree—felt closer to Osborn's assis-

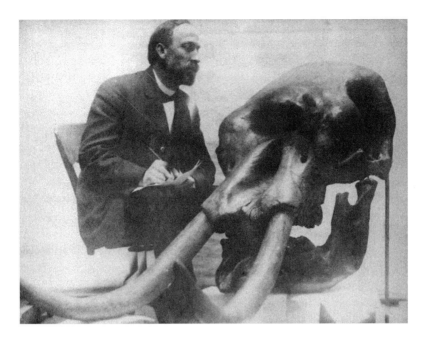

FIGURE 10. Merriam with a Columbian mammoth skull from Rancho La Brea, about 1910. (Courtesy of the George C. Page Museum; J. Z. Gilbert collection.)

tant at the museum, W. D. Matthew, and even invited Matthew to be his houseguest during the AAAS meetings.[5]

Although not exactly birds of a feather, Osborn and Merriam did have much in common not only in their mutual interests but also in their life experiences. For example, Osborn's father also was a merchant who came to accept that his son chose a career in science, not business. Raised a Presbyterian, Osborn entered a bastion of Scottish Calvinism called the College of New Jersey for his university training. The institution's name subsequently changed to Princeton University, where Osborn took his degrees and began teaching in 1881. Osborn even took a leave of absence and went to Munich in 1885–86 for an extended stay at Karl von Zittel's laboratory. The crucial difference between Osborn and Merriam was Osborn's place among New York's wealthy elite. With a fortune in shipping and business dealings with financiers such as J. Pierpont Morgan and Morris K. Jessup, the Osborns remained firmly ensconced in the upper class. They maintained strong ties to powerful people such as E. H. Harriman, president of the Southern Pacific Railroad, and Theodore Roosevelt.

Osborn was in a key position to advance the cause of preserving nature, because the elite who ran the country during the Progressive Era did so through networks of influence. Progressives such as Osborn and his peers played down class distinctions in cultivating social and political reform so that their programs would be supported by the center of the political spectrum. Whether Democrat or Republican, most Progressives fit a middle-class profile, one in keeping with owning a business or being a professional. Adherents to progressivism generally hailed from a small town but lived in a city, had attended public schools, and belonged to one of the mainstream Protestant denominations. Despite their penchant for organizing social and commercial clubs, Progressives supported the regulation of big business to produce a more efficient economy. They also elevated the role of technical experts, initially by commissioning reports from prominent individuals and committees on societal problems, so that reformist politicians could act on the findings of these studies. As long as the investigators shared similar backgrounds and beliefs with those who framed the questions, technical experts were thought to be good candidates for administrative posts or even public office. If an expert like Merriam exhibited a degree of versatility and an ability to handle finances, such prospects might then materialize for him. Joining the small circles of influential people who set the direction of public policy and decided which problems merited study thus made sense. Most significantly for Merriam, doing so could promote the preservation of nature by those not born to wealth.

One of Osborn's achievements, which Merriam sought to emulate at least in part, was the establishment of what later became the Bronx Zoo, in New York City.[6] That park employed the rather novel idea (for the time) of preserving animals in surroundings that resembled their native habitats, and it came about because Osborn enlisted aid from two key sources. One was the elite Boone and Crockett Club, from whose members his friend Theodore Roosevelt secured cash donations and political support. The other was the New York Zoological Society, founded by Osborn himself and other well-connected New Yorkers. It supplied not only financial aid, but also ideological support: most of the zoological society leadership saw the preservation of nature in terms of how it reinforced the identity of those in power—Anglo-Saxon, native-born, upper-class Protestants—and the exhibits at the new park promised to do just that.[7] Merriam's main interest in preservation, by contrast, centered on how a park could be managed to elicit intellectual curiosity among visitors, who might then think about the geological past. Merriam actively distanced himself from any connection with the eugenics movement or social Darwinism, because he believed that neither of those causes possessed any real validity.

Social theories notwithstanding, Merriam knew that Osborn had achieved something significant with the creation of the Bronx Zoo. California still lagged behind the East Coast in the creation of zoos and municipal parks, though the Hancock family's donation of twenty-three acres containing the tar pits of Rancho La Brea in May 1915 did give Los Angeles a distinction that even New York could not claim. This donation came roughly two years after the University of California lost its exclusive privilege to excavate at Rancho La Brea. The Los Angeles County Museum won that privilege so that a collection could be amassed for eventual exhibit.[8] This amounted to only a minor setback for Merriam, because he continued to publish on the fauna of Rancho La Brea and made it a point during the 1915 AAAS excursion to give Osborn an on-site progress report about what had transpired since the latter's last visit.

The two men did not see each other again for more than a year. In the interim, Merriam immersed himself in paleontology and considered 1916 to be his department's most productive year in terms of research output.[9] Graduate students and junior faculty in paleontology worked localities in several western states that summer; Merriam balanced his administrative duties with supervision of this fieldwork, though generally from a distance. The most publicized find came in the John Day Basin, an area Merriam had not seen since 1901. Two of his students, Chester Stock and Clarence Moody, unearthed the remains of a bear several miles south of Blue Basin, in the Pliocene Rattlesnake Formation. It represented an "epoch making" discovery to Merriam, because the fossil matched one previously unearthed in India and implied that Asia and North America had once been joined.[10] He reported the find as lead author of a paper that appeared in November, after which the town newspaper at John Day called for the establishment of a national park in the fossil beds. This proposal, like many from isolated western communities of the time, noted the economic benefits and development that could arise from lands virtually useless for agriculture. For the moment, however, the idea quietly dissipated in the absence of a nearby rail line or roads suitable enough for automobiles.[11]

Osborn, meanwhile, used what little free time he had away from his museum and the zoological park to drum up support for establishing a new federal bureau, the National Park Service. The service came about in August 1916 after four years of concentrated effort by its proponents to push authorizing legislation through Congress. They succeeded largely by promoting the idea that one bureau running the seventeen national parks (and the twenty-two national monuments) assigned to the Department of the Interior was more efficient than each being managed individually under separate appropriations. The Park Service's legislated mandate to "promote and regulate" the parks without impairing them reflected the need for the new bureau to make nature preservation good for business. To get the Park Service legislation passed, proponents had convinced reluctant congressmen not to balk at the prospect of creating an agency that had little prospect of placing receipts from merchantable commodities like timber or minerals back into the federal treasury.

Passage of the Park Service bill took place while the national shift from a predominantly rural population toward one more urban continued in earnest, with the demographic change accompanied by rapidly increasing automobile ownership. The outbreak of World War I also indirectly fostered the creation of the Park Service, because it restricted American tourists from traveling to Europe, thus redirecting some of those dollars to a domestic tourist industry. Debate over whether to build the Hetch Hetchy dam in Yosemite National Park also fueled passage of the Park Service bill, since the dam and its reservoir represented a violation of the sanctity supposedly associated with Yosemite and other national parks. John Muir recruited Osborn for the battle over Hetch Hetchy, but the preservationists ultimately lost because the other side successfully portrayed the project as necessary to ensure public ownership of San Francisco's water supply. Stephen T. Mather, a self-made millionaire raised in California, however, could not help but notice Osborn's support of Muir's vision for Yosemite. Mather had assumed a new post as assistant secretary of the Interior Department in January 1915, mainly because his University of California classmate, Franklin K. Lane, served as secretary of the interior under President Woodrow Wilson. As it turned out, his talent for business promotion (Mather had literally created a market for the borax that made him rich) and his ability to create fresh networks among influential people made the new assistant secretary the critical player in pulling together the necessary backing for creation of the National Park Service.

Mather worked in boardrooms and among his social equals, such as Osborn, but he also possessed a knack for conducting guided tours of existing and prospective park areas. The pack trip he lead from Giant Forest to Mount Whitney through Sequoia National Park in July 1915, for example, proved crucial to winning support for the Park Service legislation. Mather's "Mountain Party" lasted for two weeks and included Gilbert Grosvenor, editor of *National Geographic Magazine,* and E. O. McCormick, vice president of the Southern Pacific Railroad, along with a key congressman, several government officials, and Osborn. Afterward, Grosvenor made sure a special issue of *National Geographic* on the national parks was placed before every member of Congress before they voted on the 1916 Park Service bill. McCormick helped the cause by obtaining large donations from railroad executives to underwrite publication of a picture book titled *The National Parks Portfolio* so that 250,000 copies could be distributed free of charge. Osborn contributed to the effort when he returned home from the AAAS meeting (and the excursions Merriam organized) by rallying preservationists and outdoor enthusiasts on the East Coast to write letters to key congressmen.

In the wake of their successful promotion of the Park Service bill, Mather invited Osborn to an August 1917 meeting of the Bohemian Club at the group's redwood grove, north of San Francisco on the Russian River. Osborn also wanted to see Crater Lake National Park for the first time, so he suggested to Merriam, whom Mather had also presumably invited to the Bohemian Grove, that the two travel together from the grove to Crater Lake.[12] Once they had agreed to a rough itinerary for the trip, Osborn invited Madison Grant, a friend from the New York Zoological Society, to accompany them. Grant relished the opportunity, having never visited California, to examine stands of old-growth redwood along the new Redwood Highway in the company of fellow preservationists. Merriam, meanwhile, made arrangements for a car and anticipated continuing a friendly debate with Osborn over how scientists could best popularize their research.[13]

The trio met Mather's assistant, Horace Albright, who was sent in place of his boss to the Bohemian Grove encampment during the first week of August. As acting director of the newly created Park Service (Mather fell seriously ill in January 1917 and remained incapacitated for more than a year), Albright could not join the party on their journey north through Mendocino, Humboldt, and Del Norte counties—his duties as acting director, and as superintendent of Yellowstone National Park, prevented it. Merriam, Osborn, and Grant found an incredible spectacle among the often fog-shrouded groves of ancient redwoods, yet they quickly recognized the worrisome prospect of the forest's destruction by logging along the newly constructed highway. The drive was slow, on a winding road barely two lanes wide in most places, and the one-lane track north of Crescent City made them finally decide to turn around. Merriam and the others still reveled in the enormous redwood stands located along the Eel River's south fork and found the flats of Bull Creek particularly impressive.

The area around Dyerville so enthralled them that they sent a letter to the governor dated August 9, urging that a state park be established there. Virtually all of Bull Creek and other tributary streams of the Eel were in private hands, but the men cited the example of the Palisades Interstate Park, in the process of being assembled, for which concerned citizens on the East Coast had raised five million dollars from individual subscriptions in order to save the Hudson River corridor between New York and New Jersey. The linear park, they noted, became feasible once the organizers convinced the state to match contributions like the one from J. P. Morgan with public funds from the State of New York.[14] California governor William D. Stephens took no action on the state park proposal for Dyerville Flat, an idea that presumably depended on the existence of an organization that would solicit private donations. Mather, after meeting with Grant in March 1918, established just such a group. Since Merriam had agreed, during the excursion with Osborn and Grant, to serve as secretary to an organization devoted to saving redwoods, Mather thought it timely to send him a letter promising personal funds to aid with initial organization. A total of one hundred dollars arrived in Berkeley shortly thereafter, representing twenty dollars each from Mather, Grant, Osborn, and two other contributors. This signaled the beginning of what Grant wanted to call the "Save-the-Redwoods League," but immediate efforts to formally organize the group stalled while World War I raged in Europe.[15]

In the meantime, Grant traveled to California in August 1918 in an unsuccessful bid to interest state officials in securing timbered strips along the highways. However, he and Merriam started to make headway with organizing the league in October. At that point both went to Washington, D.C., and persuaded Secretary of the Interior Franklin Lane to serve as president of the organization.[16] As Lane assumed a role as the league's presidential figurehead, Merriam's position shifted from secretary to chairman of a provisional executive committee. Without the ability to pay staff members, this committee of "patriotic Californians" remained largely ceremonial. In the absence of formal incorporation Merriam and the secretary-treasurer, Robert G. Sproul (a U.C. graduate and head of the United States Railroad Administration, which continued to finance the *National Parks Portfolio*), handled most of the league's affairs.

Merriam, Sproul, and San Francisco businessman Joseph D. Grant went to work drafting a statement of purpose for the league. The three men also resolved to promote the eventual establishment of a national park in the redwoods, in addition to measures encouraging reforestation of logged parcels once dominated by redwood forest.[17]

Although certainly ambitious, the new organization's agenda drew from several encouraging precedents that made its goals seem achievable to Merriam and other executive committee members. Most of them knew, for example, of the Sempervirens Club, which in 1901 had created enough public pressure on the California legislature to obtain an appropriation of $250,000 to establish a state park in the Big Basin Redwoods, near Santa Cruz. Charles B. Wing, a member of the league's executive committee, had participated in the effort, which preserved four thousand acres from destruction.[18] The next successful effort to save redwoods for a public park had come in 1908, when executive committee member William Kent dodged condemnation of his land in Marin County. Kent foiled a proposed impoundment by a private water company by securing a presidential proclamation under the Antiquities Act for donating to the federal government the land that became Muir Woods National Monument. And Mather had more recently orchestrated another encouraging sign for a group hoping to solicit private donations, in conjunction with state and county bonds, to buy redwoods for parks. He had spearheaded a drive to save some stands of large trees in Giant Forest, within Sequoia National Park, which required raising twenty thousand dollars so that the fifty thousand dollars appropriated by Congress for this purpose could be used before the purchase option ran out, in November 1916. With Franklin Lane's backing, Mather approached Gilbert Grosvenor and the National Geographic Society, whose board of directors then agreed to donate the needed sum.[19]

The first official meeting of the league's executive committee did not occur until August 1919, in San Francisco. Mather meanwhile convinced friends in Congress to pass a resolution authorizing a survey of suitable lands for a national park in the redwoods. The catch was a stipulation that lands or their purchase price had to be donated, but at least the motion signaled some interest from Congress in eventually establishing a park. Logging operations along the Redwood Highway, however, did not allow for the luxury of waiting until Congress might act. Mather and Madison Grant rushed to take a look at the devastation once the meeting in San Francisco concluded.

In the two years since Grant had seen the highway corridor for the first time, the destruction had increased to the point where he and Mather vowed to do whatever they could to stop it. While Grant railed about cutting old-growth redwood for grape stakes or railroad ties (it was like "lighting one's pipe with a Greek manuscript to save the trouble of reaching for the matches," he wrote), residents of Humboldt County arranged a reception and rally for the duo upon their arrival in Eureka.[20] The governor was present, and the festivities included the adoption of resolutions asking the lumber companies to stop cutting redwoods in or near the highway until funds could be raised to save the trees. Large companies such as Pacific Lumber voluntarily agreed to the request, but that kind of delay could mean ruin for small operators. In return for suspending operations and granting options lasting two years on their property, these small-scale lumber operations wanted a total of sixty thousand dollars. Mather leapt at the opportunity to pledge fifteen thousand dollars of his own money, along with fifteen thousand dollars of Kent's. The remainder came when the county issued special bonds.[21]

Everyone connected with the newly organized league saw Mather's action on behalf of himself and Kent as a critical first step. Yet as Madison Grant put it, "Ultimate salvation of these great trees probably will depend upon two factors just entering into active political life—one the automobilists and the other [being] women voters."[22] To build the needed support, the league's executive board decided to hire an advertising and public relations firm. They did so with funds newly generated from members drawn from the general public, but what really provided the necessary boost was a ten-thousand-dollar gift from Mather and Kent. The board selected the Drury Company, an enterprise formed in January 1919 by two U.C. graduates. One of them, Newton B. Drury, formerly served as executive secretary to U.C. president Benjamin Ide Wheeler and for a short time taught English on campus. Small in stature but full of enthusiasm about how to promote the league's aims, Drury understood the art of persuasion. The league quickly made the charismatic Drury assistant secretary, though like everyone else, he served on a volunteer basis.

Board members increasingly looked to Drury for conduct of the organization's daily affairs, especially after he and his brother Aubrey stepped up the statewide publicity campaign. By the end of 1920 the league boasted four thousand members, and the Drury Company even began to secure donations similar to those provided by Mather and Kent, mainly through a program whereby such donors had the privilege of

FIGURE 11. Bolling Grove dedication, August 6, 1921. From left: Madison Grant, William H. Crocker (the man behind them is unidentified), Joseph D. Grant, John C. Merriam, E. C. Bradley, Robert G. Sproul, James C. Sperry, and Newton B. Drury. (Photo courtesy of the Save-the-Redwoods League.)

naming "honor groves." A twelve-thousand-dollar contribution from a Massachusetts donor established another precedent: the donor specified that the grove memorialize his brother-in law, Col. Raynal C. Bolling, the first American officer killed in World War I.[23]

A crisis loomed in late 1920 when league members in Eureka sounded an alarm concerning the resumption of the roadside logging which to that point had been voluntarily suspended by the larger companies. Continued assurances about anticipated funds from the league kept the logging at bay for the time being, but such goodwill seemed to be dissipating fast. Merriam and other board members recognized that they needed to identify some focal points for preservation in order for the lumbermen to defer logging in the best groves. The league consequently targeted four areas where preservation was an absolute priority. They saw twenty thousand acres on the main stem of the Eel River as most imperiled, in addition to redwoods along the Eel's south fork. The most majestic trees in the Eel drainage grew in two "flats," at Dyerville and on nearby Bull Creek. Other localities of special concern lay farther north. These included the immense Redwood Creek stands near Orick, in Humboldt County; groves lining both sides of the lower Klamath River; and an interesting mix of redwoods with other tree species on Mill Creek, near the Oregon border in Del Norte County.[24]

Mather, meanwhile, pointed out to Drury the advantages of incorporating the league, so that donors could deduct their gifts from their federal income taxes. Drafting the articles of incorporation necessitated regular correspondence between Merriam and Drury, in conjunction with several other board members.[25] The two men filed the articles on October 21, 1920, and found that neither of them could simply walk away from the league's activities. Drury wrote to Merriam in January 1921, urging that the league find a leader to secure private subscriptions, since the need to make a living prevented him from spending all of his time saving redwoods.[26] Merriam, who even then always seemed to strike a responsive chord in Drury, convinced the young man to remain as the most active staff member and was aided by a reorganization that took place after the incumbent secretary withdrew from the board. Upon being named the new executive secretary (a position that received nominal compensation, because of the time Drury spent on land acquisition), Drury started dealing with owners of redwood land in addition to soliciting funds, corresponding with members, and directing nationwide publicity for the league.[27] When Franklin Lane died suddenly in January 1921, Merriam found himself elected president of the league. He embraced the position but expressed some reservation about being drawn into the conservation movement much further than he had originally planned to go.[28]

But it was already too late for Merriam to resist the transition from active paleontologist to administrator. Extended periods in the field had long since become a rarity for him, though he still hoped to orchestrate a systematic study of the Tertiary fossil deposits in the John Day Basin. American entry into World War I in April 1917 had brought him more administrative duties. Merriam wanted to persevere, because the 1916 Pliocene bear discovery by Chester Stock and Clarence Moody had rekindled his interest in pursuing a project that had lain fallow since 1907. He failed initially to stir enough interest by the U.S. Geological Survey to map the stratigraphy of the basin, but a decade later Merriam proposed enlisting Stock and John Buwalda so that the three could join forces with geologists from the University of Oregon. Their prospects still looked good near the end of April, but plans for the project began to disintegrate, even after the University of Oregon and the USGS combined to raise almost a thousand dollars to support the work. Buwalda found a job at Yale, and the administrative burden on Merriam became so heavy that it required Stock and Eustace Furlong to assume most of their mentor's instruction and fieldwork duties. By November 1917 Merriam was spending much of his time organizing a wide range of research activities in support of the war effort. Merriam mentioned to Drury (who at that time was secretary to U.C. president Wheeler) that he worked on similar "problems" for the newly formed National Research Council, a body organized by the National Academy of Sciences in September 1916 with wartime funding from the military and President Wilson's Council of National Defense.[29]

World War I struck American society suddenly, like a tornado, affecting its institutional organization more significantly than any event since the Civil War. These changes affected the conduct of research, especially in relation to placing scientific expertise in service of the government. The desire to somehow centralize research activity brought about establishment of the National Academy of Sciences in 1863, but the academy remained a small club that preferred the laissez-faire ideal of gentleman scientists who had their own means of support. Alternatively, the American Association for the Advancement of Science enjoyed an open membership and a broader scientific base. Even though it focused to a much greater extent on popularizing science, however, the AAAS was constrained by chronically poor funding and internal politics from effectively mobilizing scientists for the war effort. President Wilson brought the National Research Council to life by approving a plan for a body that would foster cooperation among all scientific organizations in order to enhance the practical benefits of research to industry, national defense, and the public welfare.

The National Research Council sought to pull scientists away from the nineteenth-century system of patronage, whereby benefactors like Annie Alexander gave individual grants and often continuing support to individual academics. John D. Rockefeller and Andrew Carnegie had begun allocating some of their vast fortunes toward endowing philanthropic foundations. The boards of trustees that ran the foundations consisted of men who believed the good of society rested with efficiency and a businesslike approach to distributing research funds. These foundations wanted to promote science, but they saw the prevailing system of doing research as both inequitable and inefficient. The National Research Council helped to bring the larger scientific community closer to meaningful foundation support by acting much like a trade association or guild; it supplied an administrative buffer between foundation executives and the many university-affiliated researchers seeking support for their work.[30]

An astronomer, George Ellery Hale, served as chairman of the council until 1918, when President Wilson gave the organization permanent status through an executive order.[31] Hale and Charles D. Walcott started at the council in 1916 with only thirty-seven members, but by the end of the first year it had expanded rapidly through their recruiting efforts.[32] Merriam was appointed secretary of the council partly because his organizing abilities at the AAAS meeting in 1915 had so impressed Hale. When Hale stepped down as chairman of the council, Merriam filled the vacancy. He became head of the organization just as it faced a financial crisis brought by sudden demobilization at the end of World War I and the loss of government funding. Without such support, foundation funding represented the only feasible alternative that could perpetuate the council's existence. Hale and several leading scientists convinced the Carnegie Corporation of New York to give four million dollars to an endowment for the council in March 1919. Merriam participated in the negotiations, but insiders such as Henry S. Pritchett and Elihu Root played the key roles in securing the funds.[33]

Merriam's ascendancy at the National Research Council became a source of worry for Annie Alexander, who believed that he might eventually forsake the University of California. She sent Wheeler a letter pledging to increase her support of the paleontology department from twenty-four hundred dollars per year to five thousand (a substantial sum, considering the university allotted only nine thousand dollars to all of its research programs at the time), specifying that the money be used for research under Merriam's sole direction.[34] As had been the case since 1912 or so, the funds Alexander provided largely went to support work undertaken by other members of the paleontology department. After one year as chairman of the National Research Council, Merriam in December 1919 replaced David Prescott Barrows as dean of academic faculties when Barrows was elected president of the university. This came during a period of struggle over control of educational policy among the faculty senate, president, and regents.[35]

As dean and still a department head, Merriam found himself in a changing academic environment rife with more conflict over salaries and working conditions than it had been under Wheeler's iron-fisted presidency. Merriam now drew one of the top salaries at the university—seven thousand dollars per annum—but his choices demonstrated the axiom that those who choose the beginning of a path also choose its destination. In early 1920 one of Andrew Carnegie's foundations, an institution devoted solely to scientific research, began its search for a new president. Headquartered in the District of Columbia, the Carnegie Institution of Washington consisted of ten departments representing fields ranging from plant biology to terrestrial magnetism. Once described as "a university with no students," the departments operated from Carnegie-funded laboratories in various locations across the country.[36] Carnegie endowed the institution with ten million dollars in 1902, and he doubled that amount in 1911 upon visiting Hale, whose operation at the institution's observatory on Mount Wilson near Pasadena, California, so impressed the philanthropist. The endowment allowed for the annual expenditure of more than a million dollars in research funds by 1920. It also paid for overhead, which included the president's salary and the expenses of its board members.

With a vacancy to fill by the end of 1920, the institution's executive committee initially sought out James R. Angell, secretary of the National Research Council. Angell opted instead to head the Carnegie Corporation of New York, whose endowment of 135 million dollars allowed it to dispense 4 million dollars to the National Research Council in 1919.[37] The committee's second choice, Merriam, responded to an official query in January 1920 with an expression of interest in the job. He presented some conditions that would affect his decision whether to accept the post, were it to be tendered. Charles Walcott, as head of the executive committee, contacted him about the forthcoming offer in May. Merriam reiterated those points outlined previously, one condition being an allowance for an extended absence from Washington each year, presumably in the summer, when administrative duties demanded the least attention. Another stipulation was an annual research fund under his control, in an amount that doubled (to ten thousand dollars) the sum he currently received each year from Alexander, to fund the U.C. paleontology department's work.[38] The committee agreed to his terms, and Merriam accepted their offer.

His plans to leave Berkeley came as a shock to Alexander, who had not been informed about his negotiations with the institution. She vented her displeasure at him upon returning from a lengthy collecting trip in California and Oregon.[39] He tried to reassure her that university-sponsored research in paleontology could go on as before. Attempting to ease the blow, Merriam wrote Barrows proposing that Alexander's annual contribution to the department be handled by Eustace Furlong.[40] Once Merriam took up his new duties, Barrows merged the department of paleontology with geology. Prodding from Andrew Lawson and other geologists led to the change, one that Barrows defended on the grounds of efficiency, since a unified department required less overhead and the need to separate Lawson and Merriam, who had clashed for more than a decade (originally over editorial standards for the geology department's *Bulletin*), had now been eliminated. Although disappointed by the move, Alexander could do little more than continue her support for Chester Stock and the paleontologists in a reorganized department, but she arranged for the formation of a new museum of paleontology as a separate entity within the university.[41]

As he departed for the East, Merriam still looked forward to counting paleobotanist Ralph Chaney among his small band of associates and protégés based in California. Chaney had joined expeditions funded by Alexander over the previous two summers, and by doing so he had opened new possibilities for the study of fossil plant localities in the John Day Basin and elsewhere.[42] Although dismayed by having his department merged once again with geology, Merriam planned for his group of investigators to continue working cooperatively throughout the Great Basin and other western localities, subsidized to some extent by a research budget from the Carnegie Institution. Merriam still hoped to actively facilitate and perhaps even direct those investigations, if only from afar.

CHAPTER 5

Redwoods and Research

More than one analysis of the American conservation movement has made the point that an individual's effectiveness is tied to an external means of support.[1] Leaders such as John Muir and Stephen Mather, for example, relied on social networks to promote the establishment and inviolability of national parks. Neither worried about the effect of those efforts on their income, and both men could occasionally draw on personal fortunes to finance projects that they perceived as critical to their objectives. Networks of influential people were even more important to Merriam, since he lacked even a small fortune to draw upon and thus financed his endeavors in parks and preservation with other people's money. A new job as a foundation executive in 1921 did, however, substantially increase his pay from what it had been as a professor and opened new possibilities. For one who wished to keep a hand in research and yet stay active in helping to assemble parks in what remained of the standing redwoods, being president of the Carnegie Institution of Washington gave Merriam the wherewithal to do both.

If the move east bothered Ada and the boys, they tried not to show it. Eldest son Lawrence stayed behind in Berkeley to complete his degree in forestry at the university, while Charles W. and Malcolm, both teenagers, began attending new schools in Washington. Their mother adjusted to the social life of Washington well enough, but she suffered from a nervous disorder that occasionally left her bedridden. Having sold the large residence on Bowditch Street in Berkeley, the family now lived in an apartment within a complex called "Meridian Mansions."[2] It resembled what later came to be called a condominium and demanded less upkeep than a house, but it also seemed to give their stay in Wash-

FIGURE 12. The front of the Carnegie Institution's administration building. (Courtesy of the Carnegie Institution of Washington.)

ington an ephemeral quality, because of their expected summer respites in California. These lasted anywhere from a few days at Benbow or Shasta Springs to several weeks in Berkeley.

The change in living situation dictated a slightly longer walk to the office each day for the new president of the Carnegie Institution. Mer-

riam enjoyed the tree-lined streets of Washington, and at that time the
nation's capital still had more in common with the small university city
of Berkeley than with places like Chicago or New York. The cheap hotels near Union Station made for dramatic contrast with the buildings
lining Northwest Sixteenth Street just two miles away. Among the latter, on a corner lot at P Street, stood the Carnegie Institution administration building. Located a mile or so from the White House, it could
strike anyone who entered it as impressive, though probably not imposing, at least in comparison with the headquarters of the National
Geographic Society down the street.

   Like many office structures in Washington at the time, the Carnegie
Institution building resembled both a Greek temple and an eighteenth-
century manor house. Opened in 1909, it was built of masonry faced
with limestone and situated so that the grand entrance seemed like the
portal to a temple. Supported by six Ionic columns and flanked by two
enormous marble urns, the portico stood at the top of the steps to the
main entrance and was separated from the conspicuous rotunda beyond
by massive bronze doors. The mahogany-paneled boardroom, where
the trustees held their meetings, lay immediately off the rotunda and
adjoined an assembly area for receptions and the occasional dinner. Offices could be found on the next floor, with Merriam's being spacious
compared with the cramped office he had endured in Bacon Hall on the
Berkeley campus.[3]

   The Carnegie Institution's "campus" was more far flung in 1921 than
that of any university. Of its ten departments, three made their headquarters in Washington (Terrestrial Magnetism, the Geophysical Laboratory, and Historical Research). Others stretched up and down the
eastern seaboard, beginning with the Nutrition Laboratory (Boston),
Meridian Astrometry (Albany, New York), Genetics (Cold Spring Har-
bor, New York), Embryology (Baltimore), and Marine Biology (Dry
Tortugas, Florida). Across the continent sat Botanical Research (Tuc-
son, Arizona, and Carmel, California), and George Ellery Hale's
renowned Mount Wilson Observatory in Southern California.

   The institution grew, like the other foundations started by Carnegie,
from a belief in the systematic use of wealth. Part of Carnegie's fortune
went to benevolent purposes (the industrialist gave away 350 million
dollars in his lifetime), and this provided Carnegie with some justification for attaining such great wealth: he used his money to support the
implementation of rationally managed social change. His essay "The
Gospel of Wealth," published in 1889, preached this use of one's for-

tune.[4] Near the end of the essay he listed seven ways in which million-aires could make the most beneficial use of their wealth. The first was founding or contributing to a university, a cause Carnegie did not pursue in earnest until his rival in philanthropy, John D. Rockefeller, provided an endowment to start the Rockefeller Institute for Medical Research in 1901. Carnegie possessed greater means by that time, having made himself some three hundred million dollars richer earlier in the year by selling his steel empire to J. P. Morgan.[5]

One morning while he was still considering the idea of a university, Carnegie supposedly sat down with Charles Walcott for breakfast and asked him about the Smithsonian Institution. Walcott told the story of James Smithson's benefaction so well that he sold Carnegie on starting a foundation whose mission centered on "investigation, research, and discovery; and the application of knowledge to the improvement of mankind."[6] Carnegie did not articulate the foundation's purpose in anything more than general terms, largely because he believed that his philanthropic organizations should possess flexible charters and broad missions, given what might be their unlimited life. He and benefactors like Rockefeller placed their faith and funds in "scientific" philanthropy, in which control of an endowment and its proceeds was left to the judgment of appointed trustees. In the Carnegie Institution's case, business executives and members of government constituted its board, twenty-four men in all.

On the advice of Walcott and Theodore Roosevelt's secretary of war, Elihu Root, Carnegie approved a separation of powers among the board's three elected posts, its executive committee, and its paid president. Although the institution was analogous to the federal government in its trilateral apportioning of power, Root quickly dismissed any notion that Carnegie or his advisors might have had regarding how the institution was destined to become a public body.[7] Root believed that it could better fulfill the research mission if the institution remained under the control of private citizens, rather than elected officials. He, Walcott, and several others thus became the power brokers in the Carnegie Institution over the next three decades. Daniel Coit Gilman, who had served as the first president of the University of California some thirty years earlier, was tapped to be the institution's first president. He quickly ran afoul of the executive committee in a battle over the control of funds, however, and consequently resigned.

The new president, Robert S. Woodward, took office in December 1904 and immediately experienced conflict with the board over disbursements of extramural grants to academic scientists. Merriam even featured among the many grant applicants in 1905, all of whom tried to play up how they fit Carnegie's "exceptional man" criterion, which required that grants be given only to scientists whose research might lead to important discoveries.[8] Since many of the aspirants had advocates on the executive committee, Woodward found himself continually besieged. He feared the financial drain from the grants and battled with the board in his early years as president, while trying to make his point that the eight in-house departments established by the end of 1906 were a better investment than the so-called minor grants program. As an administrator who had formerly managed the much smaller grant programs of the American Association for the Advancement of Science and the National Academy of Sciences, Woodward struck for a compromise involving fewer awards, but ones more lucrative and of longer duration. This arrangement meant more control for the institution executive committee, since recipients became employees with the title of "research associate" but were not attached to any one department.[9]

It took time, but Woodward's relations with the board improved. Carnegie's supplement of another ten million dollars to the institution's endowment in 1911 certainly helped, as did a slow rise in the endowment's real income through its annual proceeds. This allowed for the allocation of a little more than two-thirds of the institution's annual income to support the in-house departments, with the remainder divided among minor grants, publications, and administration. By the time Merriam took over at the institution in 1921, relative peace prevailed between the president's office and the board. With grants to individual scientists now going out of fashion, the administration placed even greater emphasis on the institution's own departments. Merriam characterized the department heads as bringing "exceptional vision and ability" to the "study of great questions," thus allowing groups of scientists to advance knowledge collectively.[10] The theme of cooperation persisted throughout his tenure, partly to assure the trustees that proceeds from the endowment were being expended efficiently, but also as the stamp of a president conditioned by the cooperative nature of a field like paleontology. Minor grants continued, but Merriam placed more emphasis on retaining the services of research associates and running a new program that offered Carnegie Institution fellowships.[11] Both programs allowed him, as chief executive, to direct some of the institution's funding toward special or ongoing geological studies, investigations that did not fit into any of the institution's existing departments.

Merriam knew that Gilman and Woodward had found their relationship with the board to be that of a servant, so he was careful to clear any new initiatives with the trustees first, especially Root and Walcott. In his first year as president he established an interpretive lecture series on major research initiated by the institution, and he assembled an advisory committee for studying earthquakes in California.[12] Merriam acquired some detractors, given his generally distant demeanor and rigidity in dealing with the foundation's finances. Some staff members grumbled about the ban on smoking he imposed in the administration building. But the trustees generally approved of his performance as president. From the beginning, Merriam proved capable of relating the institution's achievements to a general audience. More important, he appeared to be maximizing the effectiveness of the institution's outlays. At times Merriam found additional funding for special projects, usually from the Carnegie Corporation of New York, whose endowment was more than ten times that of the Carnegie Institution. That made finding and retaining talented research associates easier, for example in archeology: Sylvanus G. Morley delved into the ancient Mayan civilization on the Yucatan Peninsula, and his work at Chichén Itzá so captivated the board members that they created a new department of Early American History in 1924.

Although he had left fieldwork and academia behind, Merriam still wanted to oversee the furtherance of the studies he had started at Berkeley, thus his request for annual research support as a condition of assuming the Carnegie Institution presidency. Summaries of this work in paleontology appeared in the institution's yearbooks. Often Merriam's protégés in California were involved, but staff at the American Museum of Natural History, the Smithsonian, and the U.S. Geological Survey also participated. Merriam used his research fund to help cover expenses associated with fieldwork, but he also felt the need to keep Annie Alexander enthused about helping his protégés continue their studies. He wrote a lengthy response to her letter from the Mojave in May 1922, trying to smooth her ruffled feathers by explaining how the Carnegie job put him in a better position to continue the work he had started at Bacon Hall. He opened by noting that U.C. president David Barrows had kindly sent the Merriams a wisp of sagebrush to enjoy in their Washington apartment, but he also made sure to mention the five talks on paleontology he had given the previous month, reminding Alexander that he had not abandoned the field.[13]

Try as he might to patch things up, Merriam could not stop Alexander from redirecting her support elsewhere—to a new museum of vertebrate paleontology on the Berkeley campus. Merriam coauthored a few technical papers over the next few years, generally with Chester Stock, about new finds and how the fossil fauna in one locality fit into broader evolutionary patterns. His protégé could devote the necessary time to fieldwork, mostly at Rancho La Brea, as well as at an asphalt bed in the San Joaquin Valley called the McKittrick locality, which contained fauna similar to that of the tar pits in Los Angeles and made for some interesting comparisons. The breadth of possibilities in the John Day Basin, however, excited Merriam the most, and once he prevailed on two USGS officials in December 1922 to expend part of the agency's appropriation on the long-awaited topographic mapping project, the basin could be explored further.

Starting with completion of the first quadrangle map, Merriam outlined a long-term plan to John Buwalda in early 1923. From that first step, Buwalda could work out the geology, to be followed by monographs from specialists in petrography, paleobotany, and vertebrate and invertebrate paleontology. He fronted Buwalda six hundred dollars for expenses, assuring him that more funds could be secured if necessary. Merriam could not count on the USGS supporting the project beyond the end of that fiscal year, but he wrote Buwalda of "my great desire, by one means or another, to see this splendid study carried out to full realization."[14]

Merriam asserted in a subsequent letter to Stock that all the elements "for not merely a great, but classic, study of the John Day Region" were in place.[15] The beginning of the study provided an excuse for him to visit eastern Oregon for the first time since 1901. This time he bought a car in Portland through his son Lawrence—who went to work there for a consulting firm called Mason and Stevens after graduating from Berkeley with a degree in forestry—and decided to take his youngest son, Malcolm, on the trip. Once they were in the basin, the journey acquired the flavor of a field seminar, since Merriam liked to pause at especially intriguing exposures and point things out. Ralph Chaney observed that the elder Merriam now seemed completely relaxed from the pressures of duties in Washington, indulging himself by shaving with the cold water of mountain streams and sleeping on the ground amid the sagebrush whenever possible.[16] He was moved to anger only once, when Malcolm placed some bottles of soda in his father's coat while

FIGURE 13. A field trip in the John Day Basin, 1923. From left: Malcolm Merriam, Chester Stock, Eustace Furlong, Ralph Chaney, and John C. Merriam. (Courtesy of Lawrence C. Merriam, Jr.)

they traveled. The heat popped the cap from one and soaked the coat, prompting Merriam to stop the car, throw the empty bottle away, and bury the rest alongside the road without uttering a single word.[17]

Chaney produced the most immediate results from the effort through his work in paleobotany. Merriam had induced him to study fossil floras of the John Day Basin beginning in 1920 and was so impressed with the resulting work that he hired Chaney as a Carnegie Institution research associate two years later. Stationed in Berkeley (so he could be close to Stock, Buwalda, and Eustace Furlong), Chaney began studying localities like Rancho La Brea and the Virgin Valley, but the Bridge Creek flora in the John Day Basin gave him an exceptional opportunity to compare forests millions of years apart. Instead of disproportionately emphasizing the differences between fossilized and modern groups of plants, Chaney focused on the numerical representation of the various fossil species he found next to the Painted Hills. Through quantitative methods he found a surprising similarity between the fossilized Bridge Creek flora of some thirty-five million years ago and the range of plant species found in the modern redwood forest at Muir Woods, north of San Francisco. The "redwood" component of the fossil flora, however, turned out to be deciduous *Metasequoia* species rather than the immediate ancestors of coniferous *Sequoia sempervirens*.[18]

Merriam and Stock, meanwhile, pursued the geology of the Pliocene Rattlesnake Formation and studied more bear fragments from the specimen initially found in 1916.[19] The mapping project, which included both a large quadrangle of 750 square miles and a special map of an area dominated by Sheep Rock and Picture Gorge, took Buwalda several summers. He reported its virtual completion in August 1927 in a short notice placed in the journal *Science*.[20] Perhaps more by coincidence than anything else, Merriam wrote Buwalda the day after the article appeared about a man influential in the "scientific, educational and recreational program of Oregon" wanting suggestions for a possible park in the John Day region.[21] Buwalda responded a short time later, emphasizing how the Picture Gorge region displayed the historical geology as no other area did, adding, "One can see the results of the successive events in an unrivaled way." While "scores" of tourists traveled through the vicinity each summer, Buwalda wrote, he believed that they would "gladly stop to accept instructions" if stations with exhibit boards could be constructed.[22]

The only urgency in Buwalda's mind was that "each year passes without the possibilities of instruction being realized," but Merriam sparked some interest in land acquisition for a state park through Robert W. Sawyer. As editor of the newspaper in Bend, a central Oregon town having the largest concentration of people living anywhere near the fossil beds, Sawyer had long promoted the idea of securing land for state parks even in sparsely populated areas. As one who touted scenic preservation in Oregon, he even hosted Stephen Mather and Madison Grant after the two men had rallied residents of Humboldt County in August 1919 to save redwoods along the highway right of way in California. He, Mather, and Grant had hoped to inspire Oregonians to form an equivalent of the Save-the-Redwoods League to preserve their forested roadsides, but the idea never gained sufficient popularity.[23]

State parks made a hesitant start in Oregon, with the first coming in 1920, and it could be rough going when the timber interests voiced opposition. The state's appointed highway commission nevertheless emerged with the power to acquire land along roadways for parks in 1925, in conjunction with passage of a gasoline tax dedicated to road construction and maintenance. When Sawyer was named to the commission in July 1927, he intended to make full use of this power. The highway commission proceeded to double the number of sites it had acquired previously, demonstrating Sawyer's vision for new parks all over Oregon.

Both Sawyer and Merriam knew of federal legislation passed in 1926 that allowed states to buy unallocated lands still under federal control for recreational purposes. Substantial acreage in the Picture Gorge vicinity could be acquired this way, but it would take time, given the priorities for state parks elsewhere in Oregon. Sawyer's support remained critical to the slow, but continual, growth of the parks. He remained behind the scenes after an incoming governor, a longtime political enemy, removed him from the commission in 1930. The goal of assembling a state park in the John Day Fossil Beds inched forward once acquisition of Picture Gorge began in 1931, but for the time being, Merriam had to turn his attention to preservation efforts in California.

Even if saving redwoods represented neither a furtherance of his research nor Carnegie Institution business in the strict sense, this effort had a compelling urgency. The Pacific Lumber Company furnished one reminder of that in 1920, when it removed fifteen million board feet of redwood trees from the periphery of Dyerville Flat. Logging near the highway stopped temporarily, but the Save-the-Redwoods League needed to move while lumber prices remained depressed (overproduction during and after World War I continued to flood the market) and before larger capacity became the rule rather than exception among mills in the region. Acquisition of the redwood groves along the South Fork of the Eel River thus remained a top priority, because of their conspicuous presence along the highway and the very real threat to them.

As league president, Merriam seemed to be a figurehead to some in the organization, because he was so far removed geographically from potential donors and willing sellers of old-growth redwood stands.[24] Keeping Pacific Lumber at bay when estimates for acquiring both Bull Creek and Dyerville flats ranged around five million dollars represented no easy task, and it often fell to Newton Drury and other league officers based in California. Nevertheless, when Merriam in 1925 tried to retire from the presidency because of competing demands for his time, the governing council refused his resignation and asked that he continue for at least another four-year term. Merriam responded with a condition, that being the delegation of some duties, particularly when committees of council members could be formed.[25]

Merriam's most visible role in the league consisted of speaking at ceremonial functions, such as the Bolling Grove dedication in 1921, or presiding at the equally auspicious dedication of the Lane Grove three years later. Another ceremonial function involved sending an annual message to the council. In his first one, Merriam labeled the acquisition of two thousand acres along the Eel River in 1922 a "substantial" accomplishment. He thought it would enable the league to go forward and create a large park system connected with the highways.[26] Such a system could be spurred along by rapid increases in California's human population, which had swelled from 3.4 million in 1920 to 4.5 million by the end of 1927. Expanding automobile ownership likewise fueled a surge in tourism; four times as many Californians traveled by automobile for pleasure in 1923 as had just three years earlier.[27]

League officers, especially Drury and Duncan McDuffie, a Berkeley realtor who rivaled Mather as a promoter, possessed a certain genius for getting tourists to drive the Redwood Highway. They began a promotional campaign at the Pacific Auto Show in 1920. Over the next five years, as tourist traffic swelled, the league issued more than thirty-five thousand windshield emblems with a road map on one side and the league's logo on the other. Businesses along the route organized to form the Redwood Empire Association and recognized the benefits of actively supporting league efforts to preserve roadside beauty.[28] Women's clubs represented another source of support; some staged pageants in the redwoods to raise money for establishing honor groves. Pamphlets issued by the league also promoted travel, displaying black-and-white photographs of mammoth trees in concert with maps highlighting groves saved and their estimated dollar value.

Merriam kept apprised of daily operations by staying in almost constant touch with Drury. A team of prominent and influential people was responsible for the league's successes, though Merriam's role as advisor and tactician had a lot to do with steering the ship. The initial contribution of one million dollars in 1926 from John D. Rockefeller, Jr., for preserving Bull Creek Flat served as just one example. Drury conducted a guided tour for Rockefeller and secured his million-dollar pledge, which was conditional on the eventual appearance of matching funds. Arranging for this trip to the redwoods took more than two years once Madison Grant made the initial contact with Rockefeller in 1923 and the league sent a portfolio of photographs to the philanthropist. Rockefeller provided some assurance of a forthcoming donation about a year later, when Pacific Lumber resumed logging near Dyerville Flat. Merriam and Grant supplied him with information about the crisis so that other league officials could reassure Humboldt County that sufficient funds stood behind the start of condemnation proceedings. The county court also assisted in the effort by ordering Pacific Lumber to halt further logging.[29]

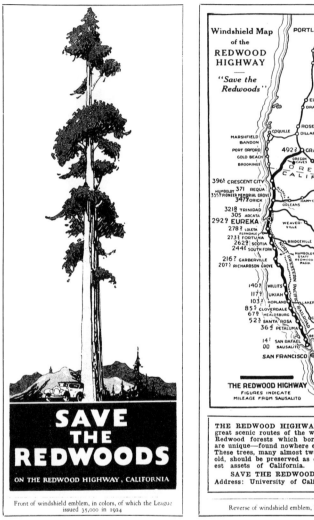

FIGURE 14. Windshield emblem of the Redwood Highway issued by the Save-the-Redwoods League in 1924.

With the most immediate threat to the league's plan for a premier park averted for the moment, Rockefeller delayed a scheduled trip to California. Although condemnation seemed to be the only way Merriam or any of the principals in the league knew to buy time, he routinely advised Drury and other members of the governing council to avoid conflict with the lumbermen, reckoning that more could be accomplished through pleasant negotiations than by coercion.[30] Forcing their hand, even in emergency situations, came with consequences; Humboldt County's action to save Dyerville and Bull Creek flats, for instance, resulted in one donor's withdrawal of the gift of a grove in 1925.[31] It also contributed to the loss of Governor Friend W. Richardson's signature on two bills, one that would have provided for a statewide survey of possible sites for state parks, and another that would have consolidated control of all existing parks under one body and created a state park commission.

Richardson used a pocket veto to kill the bills, even though both passed the state legislature almost unanimously. According to Drury, Richardson did so on the advice of a representative from the lumber companies, despite a personal visit from Drury and Mather.[32] Irrespective of any lobbying by Pacific Lumber and the other timber companies, the park bills were two among some five hundred pieces of legislation that Richardson allowed to die that year as part of his ideological pledge to reduce state spending. In this regard, Merriam did his best to console Drury by predicting that the state park program would carry in time and "much that is important [would be] added to it."[33]

Indefinite though it was, Merriam's prognostication began to be realized in 1926, when lieutenant governor C. C. Young challenged Richardson by announcing his candidacy for the top post. Although Merriam cautioned that the league should not endorse either candidate, he and supporters of state parks found it hard to conceal their delight when Young took the Republican nomination away from Richardson in August. Young, who happened to be McDuffie's close friend and longtime business partner, won the election handily in November. Within six months the new governor had signed one bill creating a state park commission and another authorizing a comprehensive survey of possible state park sites. After some lobbying by McDuffie and others, Young signed legislation authorizing land acquisition through a six-million-dollar bond issue. If passed by the voters in California, these bonds could be used to match, dollar for dollar, those funds contributed by Rockefeller and other donors.

Although Merriam and Drury worried about the league scattering its fire with a headlong push toward a comprehensive state park system, the redwood component of that system could now serve as both a standard and a precedent for a systematic approach to creating state parks. Survey work funded by the league in 1923 and 1924 had proceeded far enough to pinpoint four localities of primeval redwood forest as priorities for eventual acquisition as state parks. Each of the four projects reflected a different set of environmental conditions, starting with the trees at Bull Creek and Dyerville flats, along a river lined by the most majestic groves. Further north, redwood stands in the Prairie Creek vicinity also inspired awe, and they even featured a large herd of Roosevelt elk that frequently grazed and bedded amid giant ferns and lush undergrowth as part of the primeval picture seen from the highway. Although smaller than the inland redwoods, old-growth trees on a rugged coastal strip in Del Norte County provided a sublime contrast against the sea. Virgin forest in the Mill Creek drainage, near the border with Oregon, might never, if cut, return to its primeval condition, because that area lay east of the fog belt usually associated with the redwoods.[34] Acreage in all four localities remained imprecise while Merriam tried to garner support from the landscape architect Frederick Law Olmsted, Jr., to determine boundaries for the prospective parks based on a study of the whole redwood region.[35]

Another of the league's objectives called for creation of a national park with federal aid. Most everyone, Merriam included, conceded that establishing a national park posed significant challenges at a time when Congress was generally refusing to appropriate funds to acquire private lands for parks. Just which area might best serve as the national park piqued enough interest in the U.S. House of Representatives, partly in response to lobbying by the league, the National Geographic Society, and other organizations, that it commissioned a study in 1920. A team of federal and state foresters conducted fieldwork that October and ranked the possibilities, with the lower stretch of the Klamath River emerging as their top choice.

Logging had not yet commenced in an area containing roughly sixty-four thousand acres drained by tributaries on either side of the Lower Klamath, and no roads had yet penetrated this part of the basin. The navigable Klamath could, however, make typical stands of untouched redwood easily accessible to park visitors. Split among various owners, the proposed park area contained tracts with an estimated total of three billion board feet of redwood. The foresters on the team made a compelling case for preserving the forest as one unit, from "River to ridge," as they termed it. Without the entire lower section, they said, "bare and disfigured slopes will greet every person coming up river," so that preservation of the skyline, open glades, and even small bunches of timber would be impossible. They liked the relatively young timber in this area, mainly because it displayed vigorous growth, even if the trees were considerably smaller than the largest trees in the Eel River groves. In combination with the river's breadth and swift current, "exceedingly picturesque" Indian *rancherías* and reservations, and superb fishing, the Lower Klamath, the foresters concluded, probably represented the best area where a large national park could be established.[36]

With Congress decidedly against earmarking funds to buy land for a park, and the possibility of receiving significant donations remote (at least in the study team's view), purchase of tracts through another effective conduit represented the only practical means for assembling a national park on the Lower Klamath River. Groves along the Eel River's south fork remained the league's primary focus, so the only hope for a Klamath park rested with the U.S. Forest Service exercising its authority under the Weeks Act. Passed in 1911, this legislation allowed the agency to trade national forest lands for parcels of equal value in the interest of consolidating public and private ownership. The chief of the Forest Service, William B. Greeley, himself a University of California alumnus and member of the league's governing council, obliged at first. After an extended trip west in the summer of 1922, however, Greeley wrote to Drury about how a coming timber shortage might weaken public confidence in the Forest Service if the agency's budgetary resources were diverted away from actively managing (rather than necessarily preserving) public forests. He saw the authorized exchange of federal stumpage under the Weeks Act as a means of eventually putting cash returns into the federal treasury, rather than using valuable timber on national forest land to, in effect, buy equivalent parcels for transfer to the National Park Service. Establishment of such a national park, he argued, also negatively affected county revenues by permanently removing lands from the tax rolls.[37]

This somewhat reluctant opposition did not completely sink the project, at least in Drury's mind. He solicited numerous opinions about the worthiness of the Lower Klamath as a national park up to 1925 or so, all the while still hoping that complications posed by much of the best redwood forest's being held as Indian allotments could somehow be overcome. The Bureau of Indian Affairs would first have to release the tracts to individual Yurok tribal members, who might then become willing sellers, provided that Congress furnished the funds to acquire much of the eighty-six hundred acres of allotments.[38] Merriam saw little chance for a viable park on the Lower Klamath, given the many complications of orchestrating such a purchase. In any case, the league could take on only one multimillion-dollar project, and that was to be in the

Eel River drainage. Merriam saw the Bull Creek watershed in particular as "finer and more typical" redwood forest than the Lower Klamath, and at the league's annual meeting in September 1925 he called for an endorsement of a large acquisition effort for this land, which would cost upward of four million dollars.[39]

The "more typical" part of Merriam's assessment could be questioned in light of how the foresters in 1920 viewed the South Fork stands. The team found most of the forty-four thousand acres in the Bull Creek tract to be lightly stocked with Douglas fir, with only a few redwoods growing away from the Eel River or its main tributary. The "flats" on Bull Creek and at Dyerville, along with a string of other "bottoms" filled with enormous redwoods on the South Fork, represented what the foresters and league officials perceived as the main attraction. None of the foresters on the study team had ever seen anything rivaling the redwoods on some fifteen hundred acres of Bull Creek Flat, though they cautioned that the entire drainage could not be judged by those groves. Even though they were inferior to some of the timber stands in other portions of the Bull Creek drainage, the slopes had to be included in any park to protect the largest groves from windthrow and flood damage.

Irrespective of having to include some inferior timber growing away from the flats, Merriam and other league officials felt that the Bull Creek project possessed two important advantages over any other localities in the redwood belt: Whether by road or rail, visitors could reach the South Fork groves more easily and quickly than other potentially large redwood park sites. And perhaps more important, all of the South Fork bottoms from Bull Creek to Mendocino County lacked underbrush and displayed very few ferns. These characteristics allowed for better camping or picnicking than did other places in the redwood region, since they provided for recreational use of the groves even in rainy weather.[40] Merriam and other league officials believed that the ability to see into redwood stands from the main highway could also help visitors imagine the impact of logging operations. With this threat clearly evident at Dyerville Flat and several other places along the South Fork, league officials could pitch the idea of trying to save a chain of groves punctuated by pleasing vistas featuring the river, ridgelines, and sky. As a sort of parkway in the making, this section of the Redwood Highway extended south to Richardson Grove, near the Humboldt-Mendocino county line. Motorists coming from San Francisco might first see standing redwoods on a series of flats along the South Fork. Culmination of this drive north through the redwoods would be at Bull Creek Flat, where a forest grew under what two scientists connected with the league regarded as optimal conditions. Its size and splendor also represented an irreplaceable standard from which to study the development of redwood as a forest type.[41]

Although he knew some perils were associated with excluding people from some areas, Merriam advocated leaving certain tracts of redwood absolutely untouched "for all time." That meant preserving some stands without modifications such as trails, which allowed the removal of plants by some visitors and the introduction of nonnative species.[42] The realist in Merriam acknowledged that only 1 or 2 percent of the redwoods standing in 1920 could be saved as primeval forest, and therefore he promoted silviculture studies so that reforestation efforts in the region could be more successful. He urged the league to become the impetus leading to the eventual appropriation of federal money for reforestation research. At his annual address to the league in 1924, Merriam suggested allocating two thousand dollars for studies to be conducted over the following year. He increased his request to a "minimum of $5,000 per year" at the annual meeting in 1925, in order to launch a great study sponsored by the league that would result in a monograph on the coast redwood.[43]

Even if Merriam appeared to be overreaching by suggesting such an ambitious approach to reforestation, it was part of his view that went beyond securing and protecting small tracts of forest. By showing that the league's program extended to continuous production of timber for future generations, he wanted to unite preservation and a more utilitarian approach to conservation of the redwoods under the same banner. Preserving the best primeval forest while also pursuing efficient use of cutover lands gave the league a central position in the battle for good public relations by removing polemics from lumbermen holding redwood stands whose highest use, according to the league, was for parks. Merriam articulated the breadth of the league's agenda again in his message for 1926, at a time when negotiations with Pacific Lumber had reached an impasse over Bull Creek Flat. The standoff required a board of arbitration to step in and set a price of 5.6 million dollars for the main park area of twelve thousand acres.[44]

Despite having Rockefeller's donation of a million dollars more or less in hand, league officials could not raise the balance without the matching funds they hoped a bond issue for state parks might provide. With the statewide referendum to the voters set for November 1928, the

FIGURE 15. Cartoon about the bond issue for state parks, as it appeared in the *San Francisco Examiner* and the league's annual booklet for members in 1928. (Courtesy of the *San Francisco Examiner.*)

league needed to employ as many ways as it could to underline the importance of acquiring Bull Creek and Dyerville flats. It started a publicity campaign early that year to convince voters to support bonds for state parks, then slated the campaign's biggest event for June in San Francisco. After having arranged for the annual meeting of the National Conference on State Parks to be held in California, Mather stood at the center of it.

Mather had founded the conference out of necessity, as a way of deflecting the proliferation of proposals for national parks that so bedeviled him as director of the National Park Service. An organized movement for state parks then began to grow, with a first national assembly of delegates held at Des Moines, Iowa, in 1921. Mather liked beautiful scenery and a comfortable camp, and he even gave the conference the slogan "A State Park Every Hundred Miles," though any distinctions he articulated between parks run by the states and those administered by the federal government often seemed vague at best.[45]

After calling the meeting in San Francisco to order, Mather introduced the first speaker, Governor Young, who expressed support for the bond measure. Merriam, as chair of a body called the Coordinating Commission on National and State Parks, followed Young with a keynote address in which he differentiated between parks supported by city, state, and federal governments. He contended that federal parks concerned the whole nation, whereas cities possessed a local constituency, one primarily interested in having sufficient breathing space and recreational opportunity. Distinctions between state and national roles in parks could be nebulous, he acknowledged, but national parks should embrace exceptional phenomena of importance to the whole country. They should be large enough to include a primitive setting, so as to allow visitors greater opportunity to appreciate the spectacle. State parks went beyond city limits in providing for the needs of residents who needed large, permanent, and even primitive parks for outdoor recreation and enjoyment of nature.[46]

Merriam's talk was emblematic of a shift in general direction, away from a course so well displayed at the AAAS meeting in 1915. Where the budding administrator had displayed his versatility with a multifaceted assault on almost every topic in his bevy of research interests, the league president now focused more narrowly on influencing how and where parks could help people find the larger meanings of nature. His research output had already slowed considerably; what became virtually Merriam's last scientific paper appeared just a month before the National Conference on State Parks meeting, a relatively minor contribution in which he and Stock described the find of a Cretaceous ichthyosaur in marine sediments of the John Day Basin. He still viewed research as something to resume when time allowed and did not consciously surrender to the inevitable ebb of his output of scientific papers, but he allowed it to become secondary to a latent interest that offered new and perhaps greater horizons. One way to bring paleontology together with the importance of preserving nature in the present was through natural history essays, which could synthesize much of his work over the past three decades in a more accessible and popular form while allowing for interpretation of its meaning. He had published this kind of writing before, beginning with the piece on the John Day Fossil Beds in 1901. In the mid 1920s Merriam went back to the essays as a creative outlet and saw this kind of writing as a contribution to public education, now that he no longer taught classes.

The thrust behind natural history was the faith, first expressed during the eighteenth-century Enlightenment, that the average person possesses enough potential to understand and appreciate nature and, by extension, the universe. It also reflected the belief that creation could be ordered, since natural history sought to arrange all life on earth into a single system (the Linnaean emerged as the preferred classification scheme), one that then might illuminate the natural relations among all earth's forms. Natural history reinforced a belief in an underlying unity while fueling a search for beauty and significance in sublime or even ordinary landscapes.[47] Victorians like Merriam pursued natural history as a combination of personal discovery, self-improvement, piety, industry, and recreation. Nature writing represented one facet of natural history, its intent being to induce awe and wonder among readers by presenting the marvels of life and landscape in an accurate, but usually teleological, way. It also served the quest for national or regional identity in settler societies such as the United States and Canada, where newly attached meanings to the land might, in some measure, compensate for being bereft of a past perceived by Europeans as "history."

Reader's Digest contacted Merriam in November 1927 about condensing his story "The Cave of the Magic Pool," which ran in *Scribner's Magazine*. This tale recalled a time almost twenty-five years earlier, when Indian workmen described a cave north of Redding, California, where a maiden once slipped and fell into a dark expanse. Merriam wrote about how his party found a human skeleton there (which they recovered for interment by the local Wintu Indians) amid the bones of extinct animals, an incongruity that eventually led them to find a prehistoric cave entrance. "She fell and struck, and struck again and all was still," he wrote, in the same way that an ancient mountain lion had done eons before, but from a different entrance to the pit, long covered by a "mask" of debris by the time the maiden lost her footing. By joining "the sleeping company of ages past," the girl "opened the way to mysteries which the veil of time had seemed completely to protect," fortuitously leading Merriam and his companions to a place "where we could have a fleeting vision of the world in other days."[48]

Even if the cave essay borrowed elements from three localities in his original report of 1905, Merriam tried to illustrate how inevitable conclusions about ancient life could arise from fragments.[49] It may have been that the Scopes trial of 1925 had a hand in spurring him to write seven feature articles for *Scribner's Magazine* within less than three years. Each of them emphasized the continuity of past with present, generally with some overt reminder that the distant past also represented the Creator's work. He began one essay set in the Columbia Gorge by "reading" a record of ancient lava floods piled high to build a mountain. Through it the Columbia River had exposed a foundation of rocks over which the first lava flow poured, thus representing a way for the past to open, and "for the moment we look through to see the Builder at work."[50]

Chaney found a fossil locality next to the river back in 1916, one situated near Bonneville on the Oregon side about midway through the gorge. Merriam told of visiting the area some years later, at that point asking Chaney about finding evidence of gingko in the exposures below the lava flows. Although gingko was distributed across the Northern Hemisphere millions of years ago, Merriam knew there to be doubt as to whether it still existed in the wild in western China. The deciduous tree commanded a sacred place around Chinese temples, and he remembered the fan-shaped leaves from ornamental plantings around Washington D.C. Chaney told him that finding leaf impressions of the ancient gingko amid rock fragments containing hickory, sweet gum, and oak was rare, but a student in the party had found just such a specimen on a slab from an adjoining cliff face. Malcolm, who happened to be along on this trip, insisted he had seen the very leaf entombed within the rock. At first doubtful, the elder Merriam then saw a brown fragment as he pulled apart the rock layers on which the impression had been made. One of its edges even moved in the wind, giving him pause to reflect on how much time had passed since a breeze last stirred the leaf.[51]

Merriam asked William Greeley to have the Forest Service interpret the gingko locality. He saw to it that a simple metal card marked the cliff where the gingko leaf was found and even arranged to have a gingko planted, so that it might brush the rocks in which the ancient leaves were buried. Merriam told Greeley that such an exhibit close to the highway brought the key elements of living tree, story, fossil specimen, and geological setting together in a place where observers could draw their own conclusions. It therefore represented "the best possible answer to those who may have any doubt regarding the ultimate meaning of geological history."[52]

In a letter Merriam wrote to Drury in late 1927 about league business, he mentioned in his postscript how he had enjoyed writing another article initially titled "Forest Windows."[53] In it Merriam reiterated his theme of continuity, this time with reference to living and petrified redwoods. He related his experience at Garberville, California, where, along its south fork, the Eel River revealed sand and clay strata more than a half mile thick. A boy of eleven took him over a "precipitous wall" to a point where seashells could be found embedded in solid sandstone. Together the untutored child and the paleontologist well into midlife uncovered a whale rib near where a grove of redwoods stood on a slope as a remnant of forests whose "entombed remains lie in the hills upon which they grow."[54]

From that high bluff Merriam then brought readers into a grove where ferns, whose relatives went even further back in time than the redwood, existed in a "zone of shadow." They represented continuation of a "moving region of shade that reached back not for epochs simply, but for eons." Walking toward the deeper shadows, where it seemed harder to distinguish modern from ancient vegetation, one could search the ferns for a dinosaur or see the wings of a flying reptile in the trees. With whatever "turn of fancy" one viewed the forest, Merriam saw it as a living link in an "epic" of history. The "stream of life" through the ages could better be understood in the living redwoods, where "never-failing" light from an infinitely changing sky allowed for a view to the moving past, whose legacy of beauty and mystery unified it with the present.

"Forest Windows" appeared in *Scribner's Magazine* just prior to the National Conference on State Parks meeting and is notable for its articulation of "the deeper reaches of time" as an ultimate value in the redwood parks. It was specially timed for the bond campaign, and Drury sent notices of the article's publication to all six thousand names on the league's mailing list.[55] The article reached seventy-five thousand subscribers to the magazine, so it could have had some effect on the California referendum on bonds for state parks, on which more than a million people voted. Merriam later revised it so that the league could issue "A Living Link in History" as a pamphlet.

Irrespective of the bond measure's outcome, Merriam and other league officials could not ignore the fact that California had experienced an eightfold increase in tourist numbers in the eight years since 1920. The explosive growth in leisure travel came with effects that urgently called into question how parks should be developed to manifest the purposes behind their establishment, regardless of whether they were under state or federal control. Research showed that the trampling of soil and roots by unrestricted concentrations of people and vehicles had already become acute in some places by 1928. Consequently, the league had to do more than simply acquire additional redwood groves. It had to meet challenges posed by further increases in visitation, both by being a catalyst for the state to do better planning in the redwood parks and by diverting those who wanted to carry the pleasures of city life into "the austere temples inherited from past ages."[56]

CHAPTER 6

Interpreting the National Parks

Nature guiding, or "interpretation," as it came to be called, represented another outgrowth of natural history. In the nineteenth century, trained scientists and self-styled naturalists provided the occasional (unpaid) lecture or campfire talk in various outdoor settings throughout the United States. In addition to plants and animals, geological processes (particularly if they were of an unusual or spectacular type) could serve as the subject of such talks, so interpretation was seen as a harmless, if not beneficial, use of the early national parks and monuments.

The fledging National Park Service saw interpretation as part of its survival strategy, especially with Stephen Mather at its helm as director from 1917 to 1929. Government bureaus are especially vulnerable in their first years, given the shifting sands of congressional politics as expressed through annual appropriations. With no way of tapping timber receipts or mining leases as revenue enhancement for its budget, the Park Service relied almost entirely on appropriations to develop a system of parks. To stay relevant to a fickle legislative body, the bureau needed to expand its influence and attract more constituents. Capitalizing on the increased popularity of recreational tourism as a mass activity made sense, especially as ownership of private automobiles and the nation's road network expanded dramatically during the 1920s.[1]

Mather knew he had to publicize the parks during those first years, in conjunction with the park concessionaires and the railroads. Park-Service-sponsored interpretation represented an avenue to drawing crowds to the parks and keeping a steadily growing constituency coming back. The challenge involved finding a way to fund interpretation as a regular part of operations. Quickly recognizing the critical need for a

FIGURE 16. Harold C. Bryant conducting a nature walk for visitors below Yosemite Falls, 1920. (National Park Service Historic Photograph Collection.)

publicist, Mather brought Robert Sterling Yard to Washington in 1915. He even paid Yard's salary from his own pocket, until Congress prohibited such practice three years later, but by that time the Park Service budget had become large enough to include Yard. Yard, who initially met the director when they worked together in the newspaper business during the 1890s and had served as best man at Mather's wedding, started work for the government by producing annual editions of the *National Parks Portfolio*. His ideas about educational possibilities in the parks resulted in a "division" of the Park Service consisting of Yard and a secretary. A nongovernmental "National Parks Educational Committee" headed by Charles Walcott gave the campaign some legitimacy, and in 1919 the committee became a private organization called the National Parks Association.[2]

Assuming the role of executive secretary in the parks association upon its founding provided an effective and face-saving means for Yard to depart from the Park Service but also stay involved with the parks. This separation came about largely as the result of a conflict with Horace Albright in 1917 over who should head the Park Service while Mather was incapacitated by illness. Yard was diminutive in stature and usually quite soft-spoken, but the idealist in him made him ill-suited for life in a bureaucracy because he could come across as inflexible and even abrasive. He also lacked Albright's ability to see an expedient course of action when necessary, though his skill and flair in organizing the National Parks Association impressed Mather. By sharing common objectives such as promoting educational work and encouraging travel, and by insisting on high standards for new units in the national park system, the two organizations could work toward the same goal.

The National Parks Association, like any conservation group, assumed the role of advocate to counter threats to the parks. This meant generating publicity about problems and working on the inside with Congress, things Mather and the Park Service often had to avoid or soften because of their political ramifications. But Yard and Mather had a falling out in 1922 over differences on how far to take opposition by the parks association to a bill that did not prohibit future power development in an expanded Sequoia National Park. Failure to pass the legislation once again frustrated Mather's dream of an enlarged park, and the disagreement with Yard put an end to Mather's financial contributions to the parks association.[3]

Although sometimes shackled as the head of a government bureau, Mather soon found a way to make interpretation part of the Park Service's operations. He brought two of Merriam's protégés, Loye Miller and Harold Bryant, to Yosemite Valley in 1920, and for the next few summers the pair gave talks, led hikes, and prepared educational literature in exchange for their expenses. Ansel F. Hall, a paid full-time ranger, soon began soliciting support for a museum in the valley. Mather, who lacked appropriations for a museum, supported Hall's effort by making him "chief naturalist" of the National Park Service in order to enhance the credibility of the project. The new post also gave Hall the task of coordinating interpretive work in all national parks. Hall concentrated his energy on Yosemite, Mather's favorite park and accustomed testing ground for new ideas, by organizing the Yosemite Museum Association under the auspices of the American Association of Museums, through which he sought grant support for building a permanent museum.

Hall, Chauncey Hamlin of the museum association, and Hermon C. Bumpus, formerly head of the American Museum of Natural History, delivered the goods in 1924 with a seventy-thousand-dollar grant from a foundation called the Laura Spelman Rockefeller Memorial. Bumpus soon took control of the project, stretching available funds to allow for construction of a small lookout on Glacier Point—which he claimed furnished precedent for "trailside" museums—in addition to the main building.[4] These structures opened in 1925 and 1926, respectively. Meanwhile, the Yosemite interpretive program continued to accelerate in popularity through the establishment of the Yosemite Field School of Natural History, which Bryant founded in 1925 to train aspiring naturalists in various aspects of teaching and interacting with visitors. Completion of the museum in Yosemite Valley gave the school a headquarters.[5]

Merriam's participation in any interpretive program within the national parks during the first half of the 1920s had been limited to giving one talk in Yosemite Valley as part of the Le Conte Memorial Lectures, sponsored by the University of California.[6] He captured Mather's attention, however, with a speech at the second National Conference on Outdoor Recreation in January 1926. He focused his talk on the national parks by acknowledging their recreational use, but then asserted that the value of the parks for purely educational purposes far exceeded that of any of the nation's schools. "Not merely places to rest and exercise and learn," he said, the parks embraced "regions where one looks through the veil to meet the realities of nature and the unfathomable power behind it."[7]

Merriam saw national parks as demonstrating the "almost limitless history of earth-making as it is pictured before us," presented in such a way that all might comprehend. In his view, the parks included much of what "represents the unmodified primitive life of the world, both plant and animal, remaining just as the Creator moulded it over the mountains and valleys."[8] If nature could be likened to an open book for those who really wished to read it, however, Merriam also saw grades and shades of meaning that could be hard for many, if not most, people to understand. National parks manifested places where pages were spread wider and contained clearer print than in other portions of the book, but science needed to get a better handle on the story. The main points had to be clarified enough for the casual visitor to read and understand without total dependence on someone else's interpretation. With these places as teachers, supported by guides skilled in the most effective means of presentation, Merriam believed the national parks could become a "super-university" that allowed visitors to "stand upon the highest plane of education."[9]

Nevertheless, he cautioned against picturing the parks solely as venues for understanding science. They also expressed elements of beauty and grandeur beyond the realm of formally associated facts and logic. He characterized the attractiveness of national parks as lying partially in their aesthetic and artistic values, which could stir an individual's emotions, but he also contended that people recognized sublimity in the power and order behind nature. Beauty had an important role, along with recreation and formal education, in attracting visitors and then stimulating "the real appreciation of nature" as the primary use of the parks. The higher educational and spiritual values forming the basis of "real appreciation" could also help to assure complete protection of the natural features in national parks. A good many of the parks held resources of economic value, and Merriam reasoned that recreation as commonly understood, or education in the routine sense, could not of themselves guarantee "unbroken maintenance of primitive conditions." He cited the redwoods, where outstanding groves were in the process of being saved because these higher values drove the urgency to set aside the finest regions as parks. The redwoods also demonstrated how the "problem" of preservation should be viewed from "every possible angle." This was particularly important when planning park developments; every known need had to be judged in light of "the most fundamental requirements."[10]

Mather liked what he heard well enough to enthusiastically write about "educational development" at length in his annual report to Secretary of the Interior Hubert Work. The director first summarized how

MAP 3. Stephen T. Mather and the route of the National Park to Park Highway, 1918. Mather treated the road as a way to promote the parks as a system. (Crater Lake National Park Museum and Archives Collections.)

the number of museums in national parks had increased during the year, with each one helping visitors to understand "the greater museums that are the parks themselves." He also thought it possible for the national park system to tell "wonderful stories of creation while becoming one of the most useful educational institutions in the world." This way of emphasizing how the Park Service managed a *system* also helped to reinforce Mather's earlier promotion of the "National Park to Park Highway," a physical manifestation of linkage (albeit a rugged one in many places) among the system's "crown jewels." At any rate, Mather invoked the phrase "national super-university of nature" and drew the analogy of every national park unit being a building in an exposition of some particular branch of the natural sciences, all enclosed within campus walls. He also credited Secretary Work with having greatly advanced the idea that parks could be both exhibits and teachers.[11]

Although Albright had not attended the conference, he read a transcript of the speech and wrote to one park supporter that Merriam had greatly strengthened "the basis upon which the National Park Service stands."[12] The Park Service had been in existence for a decade, but it still struggled to position itself among federal bureaucracies for increased appropriations. Mather, Albright, and Yard knew the service might benefit from definitive statements forming the foundation of a niche that Congress perceived as the agency's exclusive jurisdiction. The three had previously wrestled with a definition of what should be a national park and found that "everyone knew generally and no one knew specifically," and "a dozen definitions differed radically."[13]

Merriam's speech inspired Yard to devote an entire issue of the *National Parks Bulletin* to the idea of making education the unifying and preeminent force in managing the national park system. He wrote to Merriam in July 1926, and in his usually exuberant way he stated that everyone could grasp the idea behind a "Super-university of Nature," rising to it even if words such as *education* and *museum* left them cold.[14] Having served as a trustee of the National Parks Association since 1924, Merriam had no difficulty convincing Yard that a special committee under the association's sponsorship was needed to help sell the super-university idea. As formally launched in 1927, the Advisory Board on Educational and Inspirational Use of National Parks aimed to concentrate scientific research on "revelations of nature awaiting intensive study" in the parks, then build popular educational activities that stemmed from scientific foundations. This would utilize to the full the system's extraordinary exposition of the great story of Creation, but also serve (just as the National Research Council had) to coordinate effort among "the many agencies now operating from independent and often unrelated courses."[15]

Merriam loaded the board with prominent men drawn from academia and various professional organizations in order to lend influence and prestige to its recommendations. He put himself in the key position as chairman to direct the effort, even though no public or private funds had been earmarked for this purpose. He also effectively co-opted the work of other bodies such as the Yosemite Museum Association, which had so successfully brought about the establishment of a museum in Yosemite Valley and several branch museums at Yellowstone. Merriam simply brought Bumpus on board and then conferred with Hamlin and

Hall about going after another grant from the Laura Spelman Rocke-feller Memorial, this time for an "observation station" on the south rim of the Grand Canyon.

His fascination with the great chasm opened by the Colorado River came, of course, from the idea that rock layers exposed in cross-section by the canyon form a book. To go back in time, one simply looks down-ward toward the river. At the bottom are layers from the Precambrian period, but in between are sections of the book where many pages are missing. Even small pieces of it nevertheless held meaning. For exam-ple, in 1924 two men took Merriam to some ancient tracks made in the layer of sandstone from the Permian period (248 million years ago to 290 million years ago) below Hermit Rest on the south rim. Close by this "trace fossil" were the footprints of a wildcat made just that morn-ing. The tracks prompted Merriam to consider what could be seen and understood at the Grand Canyon. He mused about the formation of the canyon, "when the seconds and minutes of that early time were marked off by rhythmic movement of the feet which made this earlier track." As Merriam and his companions looked upon the two sets of tracks—the two records—they saw continuity: "the prints on ancient sands, preserved through time beyond human understanding, were not less real than were the traces of feet of cat and mule made in the morn-ing of the day which we found them."[16]

The possibilities for interpreting how past related to present drove his interest in building an educational facility at the Grand Canyon. A mile or so from Grand Canyon Village, the center of most visitor ser-vices in the park, a spectacular vista on the south rim encompasses most of the central canyon. Merriam described the view as "a vision of time which is like the opening of a door upon the past," analogous to a win-dow "through which one looks into the Canyon at an unusually favor-able place." As Bryant later recalled, Merriam found people hungry for explanations there about how the canyon had formed and whether the same kinds of plants and animals existed across the chasm.[17] Financed by the Rockefellers, the observation station differed from the enclosed museums in other national parks. The Yavapai Station featured an open porch or "parapet" that allowed unobstructed views of the canyon. High-powered telescopes and a relief model of the canyon enhanced the visual experience. Each of the fifteen exhibits at the rear of the sta-tion corresponded to individually numbered parapet views, so that vis-itors could study them in detail after first acquainting themselves with the features of the canyon through the telescopes and model.

FIGURE 17. A view of the Grand Canyon from the Yavapai Station, 1929. (National Park Service Historic Photograph Collection.)

Merriam intended the Yavapai Station to be self-operating to some degree, but he also stressed the importance of having Park Service naturalists on hand. After giving a brief introductory talk, the naturalists answered questions that arose when visitors examined the parapet views. This job required a considerable knowledge of the region at a time when the Park Service had only begun to employ naturalists at the Grand Canyon. Merriam recognized the necessity of providing special expertise, so in 1927 he made the former chief geologist of the U.S. Geological Survey, David White, a research associate of the Carnegie Institution. The appointment allowed White to reside at the park and accelerated his work identifying plant and animal fossils in the exposed layers of Permian strata. This move also helped the naturalists, most of whom had to work full time giving presentations to visitors.

One of those naturalists happened to be Merriam's son Charles, who was about to graduate with a degree in geology from the University of California in the spring of 1928 when Hall offered him a job on the north rim. His father seemed doubtful that Charles would want the position, even if "the possibilities at the Grand Canyon are perhaps the greatest in the United States" for applying geological and paleontological knowledge on a "very high plane of educational work." If his son should decide to accept the appointment, however, the elder Merriam told him there would be times when "the fact that you are my son will be of advantage, and other times when it will be distinctly disadvantageous."[18] The comment stemmed from Merriam's observation that although he enjoyed "the confidence of Mr. Mather and others leading the work," there were others in the Park Service who did not feel the same way toward him and his ideas. Charles took the job, and his father sent a check for a hundred dollars two weeks later to cover his son's clothing expenses and other incidentals. He also started recommending "fundamental materials bearing upon the history of the Canyon" and made inquiries around Washington about "other bulletins which could be of use to you."[19] No sooner had Charles arrived at the park that summer than a primer of how to give talks to the general public arrived in the guise of a letter. It also contained advice on how a naturalist could use three "principal influences" (magnitude, beauty, and the forces that made the canyon) to help visitors appreciate the place. His father closed the seven single-spaced typed pages by assuring Charles that the letter was "based upon extremely careful study" and represented "the experience of many of us engaged on the problem" of the canyon's ultimate meaning.[20]

Charles did not return to the park for a second summer (he chose to take a field geology course as part of his doctoral work), but the elder Merriam continued visiting the Grand Canyon in 1929 as part of a project that explored the educational "problems" in the national parks. The project had its launch with the opening of the Yavapai Station in 1928, an event that prompted the Rockefellers to cover the expenses of a committee appointed by the secretary of the interior to recommend ways in which the educational potential of the national parks and monuments might best be tapped.[21] At this point the National Parks Association's advisory board on the educational and inspirational use of the parks disappeared in favor of an officially sanctioned committee of six headed by Merriam.

His report on the Grand Canyon took the form of "suggestions," prefaced by a statement of purpose that emphasized how specially prepared literature, museum facilities, and personal interpretation by a well-informed staff of naturalists constituted key components of any educational program in the park. Merriam recognized the challenges of operating such a program, given the demands on staff members to "give information which will be scientifically and philosophically correct and at the same time intelligible to persons of average intelligence." There were likewise difficulties in satisfying "any intelligent person with a purely scientific statement" about something that required "a philo-sophic interpretation, and which at the same time demands the highest type of spiritual appreciation."[22]

Merriam's suggestions for the Grand Canyon and other national parks seemed to be welcomed by Albright, who had replaced Mather as Park Service director early in 1929. Albright even quoted from the com-mittee's preliminary report in his annual narrative to the secretary of the interior. The committee report attempted to tie the importance of ed-ucational work to the basic principles guiding the service's administra-tion of the parks, and Merriam took the lead in drafting the three most significant statements in this regard. All of them were derived from his earlier concern that there had never been full discussion of the aims or purposes of the national parks, and he commented that statements by various officials from time to time were expressed in only general terms, without clear definition of purpose. He acknowledged that the parks were for "use and enjoyment of the people," and that they should be maintained unimpaired, but he concluded, "There has not been precise definition [of] the way in which the parks should be used or enjoyed, or the reasons for their maintenance unimpaired."[23]

Congress had passed the Park Service enabling legislation with only a very general statement about conserving resources and providing vis-itor enjoyment, though the bill made clear that such use was not to im-pair the parks for future generations. Yard and Albright drafted the so-called Lane letter in 1918, on which Secretary of the Interior Franklin K. Lane had supposedly based some of his policy statements for the Park Service. According to the letter, three broad principles for managing the parks had to be the foundation for all future Park Service policy. Main-tenance in absolutely unimpaired form for current and future genera-tions constituted the first. The second specified that use and enjoyment of the parks should include educational activities. The third asserted that the national interest should be paramount in all decisions about private enterprise (such as concessions) in these sanctuaries. The letter concluded with guidelines for expanding the system. Proposals for new national parks, for example, had to meet a vaguely defined standard of national significance, one that was aimed at fending off pressure to in-clude "inferior" areas in the national park system.[24]

Merriam expanded on the Lane letter's guidance by furnishing three statements of principle for the committee report, which Yard and the National Parks Association began to call the "national park standards." The first contended that national parks must clearly possess importance to the nation as a whole; where a park's "special characteristics" were of less than national significance, local interests should support those parks. The second statement attempted to define the "distinctive character" of national parks, given how the "inspirational influence and educational value of their exceptional natural features" expressed the reason why the parks existed. Merriam made the statement more definitive by including, as the third principle, his idea of the primitive. "Outdoor recreation is recognized as an important factor in national park administration," he wrote, but it did not constitute a park's primary purpose, since recreation could "be enjoyed through abundant opportunities furnished elsewhere." He noted that wilderness could not be provided "to an extent sufficient for the future outdoor recreation needs of the whole people," but those primitive areas with features "of especial inspirational significance and educational value" should be protected in fully primitive condition as national parks.[25] This third principle made clear what the first two implied; the primary use of the parks related specifically to their educational and inspirational values. It certainly followed that park administration concerned with appreciation and interpretation would naturally determine the breadth and operation of other activities such as road building, overnight accommodations, and recreational activities.[26]

To make the shift toward more emphasis on education and inspiration, the committee recommended establishing a full educational division within the Park Service, to be directed by a man "with the best scientific and educational qualifications." A key congressman, Louis Cramton of Michigan, made sure this item was included among the appropriations for the Park Service beginning in 1930. It also helped that Ray Lyman Wilbur, formerly president of Stanford University and a member of the National Parks Association's advisory board on educational and inspirational use, had become secretary of the interior with the incoming Hoover administration in 1929.[27] With funding secured, Albright quickly moved to create a "Branch of Education and Research" for the Park Service in Washington in 1930. He made Harold Bryant its chief and one of three assistant directors under him.

Merriam wrote to Bryant in August 1930 about making the recruitment of chief park naturalists for Grand Canyon and Crater Lake a priority. After stating that the needs of the two parks could not be met with the "average scientific man or educator," he described the desired candidate as possessing knowledge based upon original research—someone who held the position of assistant or associate professor at a university.

The candidate should have an acquaintance with a "wide range of facts" in the natural sciences and an ability to make the "human values" of park phenomena clear, as well as administrative acumen. Securing this type of person was absolutely necessary, Merriam warned. If standards fell lower, there was a "large possibility" that a park's educational program would be inadequately handled. The work might then degenerate into "consideration of details" instead of true interpretation.[28] Merriam thus convinced Bryant to try and lure Norman Hinds away from the University of California for the Grand Canyon position; but Hinds chose to remain at Berkeley and continue his field studies (many of them conducted in the park) as a research associate with the Carnegie Institution. Edwin McKee, a historical geologist already serving as a naturalist at the Grand Canyon, filled the job in 1931. Also a research associate, McKee wrote a monograph published two years later by the Carnegie Institution on the origin of the sandstone layer where Merriam had seen the ancient footprints.[29]

Merriam's insider role at the Grand Canyon rapidly faded after McKee's appointment, becoming limited to that of a conduit for funding geological work through the Carnegie Institution. Events followed a slightly different course at Crater Lake, where Merriam conducted what he called "a study in appreciation of nature" for several years. Beauty, rather than time, assumed first place among the educational and inspirational values at the nation's deepest lake. This national park piqued Merriam's interest because Crater Lake sat like an immense "picture" within the physical "frame" formed by a caldera resulting from the collapse of a volcano. That beauty could arise from a cataclysmic eruption several thousand years beforehand captivated him, especially since even a small understanding of the geological story of the lake seemed to produce in visitors "a psychological contrast of great importance" when appreciating a region marked by so much volcanic activity.[30]

Loye Miller established a summer naturalist program at Crater Lake in July 1926, with Merriam paying him a visit the following year to discuss how geological interpretation might be augmented by a proposed observation station. Initial planning for what became the Sinnott Memorial followed a template established by work at the Yavapai Station, in that Merriam's aim was to create a "window through which it is planned to show the visitor things of major interest at the Lake." Active use of the proposed structure should be that of visitors looking outward, with the museum aspect reduced to a minimum through use of materials helpful in development of the window idea.[31]

Construction of the Sinnott Memorial commenced in 1930 with a special ten-thousand-dollar appropriation from Congress. Merriam supplemented this amount with another five thousand dollars from one of the Carnegie Institution's sister foundations, the Carnegie Corporation of New York. Since the Carnegie Corporation's endowment was considerably greater than that of the other Carnegie foundations, Merriam and his peers had a ready source of funds for small projects such as interpretive devices at the parapet and display room. The building occupied a ledge some nine hundred feet above the surface of Crater Lake, yet possessed the virtue of proximity to visitor services at Rim Village. Designed to be nearly invisible to anyone on the lake, it bore a striking resemblance to the Yavapai Station, if slightly smaller in size. The open semicircular parapet allowed for installation of exhibits keyed to telescopes fixed on certain views. If seen in numerical order, the nine views chosen presented "a picture of great forces in the past which have helped to develop the beauty seen today."[32]

Just as he had in the Grand Canyon, Merriam produced a leaflet for visitors on the views from the Sinnott Memorial. It was intended to entice them to go experience these places at closer range, either through a boat tour on the lake or by driving the circuit road, called Rim Drive. In similar fashion to the setup at the Yavapai Station, Merriam intended to have a naturalist give a brief talk while showing visitors the various locations on a relief map in the Sinnott Memorial's parapet. He soon realized that the geological story of Crater Lake might become more meaningful to visitors if they could also obtain some understanding of beauty through exhibits in the adjoining display room. This would help illustrate the earth as a living thing, because the beauty of Crater Lake, set against the power of the volcano that had created it, could be seen in such extreme contrast.[33]

Although Merriam knew the scientific interpretation of Crater Lake to be less complicated than that of the Grand Canyon, the lake's aesthetic features presented new challenges requiring careful thought and study. He and Ada went to Europe in the spring of 1931, with England's Lake District being their first stop after their ship docked in London. After going over "nearly all of the lake country," including "the home and haunts of William Wordsworth," Merriam found the "problem" of Crater Lake to be even more absorbing.[34] In attempting to meld truths derived from scientific study with a compelling presentation, he wanted to go beyond the purely intellectual approach. Merriam knew that artists should have a role in helping visitors toward a profound and perhaps revelatory experience in the park, so the Carnegie funds for the Sinnott Memorial were disbursed to support innovative studies. One involved a team from the University of Oregon, which grappled with how to best present the aesthetic and scientific features of Crater Lake, something more or less complemented by a University of California art professor's evaluation of various view points around the park in relation to their inspirational value.[35]

For exhibits to highlight localities of exceptional interest, the Carnegie money underwrote production of colored glass transparencies, to be placed in the Sinnott Memorial's display room with the hope of enticing visitors to go to the place depicted and see how the sun illuminated its appearance depending on the time of day and weather conditions. Merriam also used the money to acquire artwork illustrating "the point of view of an artist who has studied the Crater Lake region," to help visitors recognize how everyone perceived beauty differently.[36] Foremost among the three paintings and numerous photographs was a stunning watercolor by Gunnar Widforss, who left Hall and perhaps other observers wondering how he could have captured the transparency of Crater Lake so well, and yet have provided a backdrop of deep blue.[37] Widforss painted the scene from a remote spot called Sun Notch, where he could peer over the rim and include a rock formation called Phantom Ship, as set against what seemed to be a limitless expanse of lake, cliff, and sky.

The artist became known as "painter of the national parks" during the 1920s, while working at Yosemite. Monumental landscapes dominated his work; Widforss produced his exceptional realism through disciplined design and an innate ability to harmonize colors. He preferred the delicacy of watercolor as a medium, but bold contour and definition allowed Widforss to clearly interpret each scene. In his best paintings, the foreground was usually pushed to one side so that the viewer could behold the depth and shadows characteristic of a particular spot or time of day. Merriam purchased a number of paintings as gifts for family and friends while Widforss worked in California during the mid-1920s, and he remained part of a circle of devotees that included Mather when the artist subsequently took up semipermanent residence in the Grand Canyon. Although the self-effacing Widforss claimed to know nothing about geology, his watercolors could be seen as an exceptionally careful record of nature and an expression of how the canyon made people feel when they stood at this window on the cosmos.[38]

Merriam believed that the Grand Canyon also allowed visitors to see the unity in nature, because nowhere else, at least in his estimation, were these elements so clearly interrelated. The ability to see this unity depended on the maintenance of primitive character, which Merriam defined as "the uninfluenced remainder of primeval nature as it has come into being through whatever creative power may have been responsible for its existence."[39] Once disturbed, the primitive might never return to its former condition and thus would cease to serve as an exceptionally clear window on the meaning of human existence.[40] As one of his protégés observed in the mid-1930s, a great primitive landscape could be irreparably damaged if only 1 or 2 percent of it were marred by development. Merriam believed that protection should guarantee "maintenance" of the primitive in national parks, with the clear understanding of what was to be protected so that heavy use would not destroy a park's distinctive educational and inspirational values. Promotion of the parks as resorts, where recreational use assumed the predominant or favored role in administration, placed the primitive in continuous jeopardy, since it meant unrelenting pressure for developing more access and facilities.

Park facilities possessed the potential to compromise the primitive unless they were designed and situated to be inconspicuous. In early 1933, Merriam recalled that designers of the Yavapai Station had initially thought about making the structure look like an Indian ruin, but opted instead for a scheme that prevented any projection above the skyline or inclusion of features that could take attention away from the canyon landscape. This type of building contrasted markedly, at least to Merriam's way of thinking, with what the park concessionaire had constructed twenty miles to the east, at Desert View. Norman Hinds had once suggested that another observation station be situated there, since both the landscape and geological features were strikingly different from those seen at Yavapai Point.[41] An "Indian Watchtower," erected in 1932, now occupied the most prominent spot and stood some seventy feet high, in full view of the canyon. It resembled a sham castle more than it did any ruins in the vicinity—least of all one located just three miles distant, at Tusayan. The tower was nothing less than a fraud to Merriam; it had no business in a place like the Grand Canyon, "dedicated as it is by the entire world to the appreciation of truth and sublimity," especially when concession representatives freely admitted their intent was to create a tourist attraction.[42]

The tower quickly became emblematic of Merriam's growing suspicion that education took a backseat to promotion and commerce in the national parks. Over the next year or so, in letters to Yard, Drury, and others, he made frequent reference to this "incongruous combination of features supposed to represent historical data," occasionally adding that it was "not thought possible to introduce such a feature during Mr. Mather's administration."[43] The effusive Yard, who had spent much of 1932 drafting a National Parks Association report on protecting the primitive in national parks, felt the need to give Merriam some additional insight about Mather and the Park Service. In 1933 he wrote that Mather's ideas had been derived from the Sierra Club, though Yard also claimed to have assumed the role of interpreter and mouthpiece in the earliest years of the Park Service because Mather (who died in 1930) was "naturally incoherent." Yard went on to say that Mather had seemed more interested in promoting university summer classes and visits from Boy Scouts during the early 1920s than in institutionalizing museums in the parks. In fact, he wrote, Chauncey Hamlin and the Yosemite Museum Association had faced initial opposition from Mather, Albright, and Arno Cammerer (one of Mather's assistants, who became Park Service director in 1933), who saw the buildings as "stuffy" and "reminiscent of dead things." Once the idea of a "museum system of the primitive American wilderness" had caught fire as a concept, however, Mather supported it. Yard closed his epistle by cautioning that only when legislation defined it would the "major part of our job be completed—our educational system will be safe."[44]

CHAPTER 7

A Voice for Wilderness

From its inception, the National Park Service aggressively pursued expansion of the national park system under Stephen Mather and Horace Albright. Both directors went after new units and additions to existing parks, often locking horns with the U.S. Forest Service over such proposals throughout the 1920s, since most of them would come as land transfers from national forests. Part of the reason Mather and Albright embraced Merriam's super-university idea so readily in 1926 was that the Forest Service retained control of sixteen national monuments that ought, in their view, to be part of a national park system managed by the Park Service. Once government reorganization under the Roosevelt administration had transferred these monuments to the Park Service in June 1933, reference to the super-university in the agency's press releases seemed noticeably absent. Roosevelt's executive order that effected the transfer also included other provisions, such as giving the Park Service responsibility for the city park system of Washington, D.C. A number of historic sites and battlefields also came into the system at that point, an expansion that Merriam thought should be tolerated only if these sites could complement the great natural parks in two ways. The first allowed visitors to see the past in light of "world questions"; the second provided them with the means to make independent discoveries and verify basic truths.[1]

Such pronouncements began to ring hollow with the National Park Service, particularly once Merriam wrote to Arno Cammerer in December 1934 about presenting reality as part of "expressing the lessons of history." The tower at Desert View should be removed, Merriam asserted, in order for the national park system to be "so safely built that

FIGURE 18. Tower at Desert View in Grand Canyon National Park, 1932. (George Grant, National Park Service Historic Photograph Collection.)

its future will secure against every destructive influence." The director's response was typically conciliatory, but firm. Cammerer conceded that Merriam had a point about the tower being both misleading and too prominent, but he did not see how the structure established a precedent for future development. Moreover, he saw no way for the Park Service to require the concessionaire to demolish a seventy-five-thousand-dollar building without compensation, since it seemed to him quite likely that Congress would not appropriate money for this purpose.[2]

Having to watch the Park Service plunge headlong into the field of general outdoor recreation proved more vexing to Merriam than being cast as an impractical idealist. Newton Drury complained to Merriam in early 1934 that the service wanted to become a "Super-Department of Recreation," with the most likely result being a "glorified playground commission."[3] It already supervised work by the Civilian Conservation Corps, a program established by Roosevelt in early 1933 as part of his plan to aid the development of state parks with federal funds. A dual purpose of relieving unemployment and helping the states during the national emergency caused by the Great Depression appeared in many ways understandable, but to Merriam and Drury it came with an objectionable condition. The stipulation that all Civilian Conservation Corps projects in the state parks needed National Park Service approval smacked of an attempt to impose federal control on decisions about recreation that rightly belonged to the states. To both men such a proviso seemed indicative of an effort to centralize the entire recreational park system of the United States and in the process work to "lower the very high standard which has been set up for national parks and monuments."[4]

Further evidence of a fundamental shift in direction came in November 1934, when the Park Service produced a report as part of Roosevelt's national recreation plan. Roosevelt's expansion in Park Service responsibility did include such planning, but Merriam felt that a group drawn from all levels of government should have prepared the report. The Park Service, he believed, "is assumed to be competent in a particular field, which concerns the preservation and use of certain outstanding features," rather than being "expert in the whole field of recreation." He found weak points in the report's section on the national forests, and the discussion of state parks, he thought, was badly informed about past efforts and studies. The suggestion that historical parks could be evenly distributed across the country struck Merriam as odd to say the least, and the recommendation by the Park Service that it be given charge of a national program to study recreation carried the agency "very far from the original plan."[5]

That he had to send this assessment to his brother Ed in hope of influencing the secretary of the interior showed how the shift caused by Roosevelt's election had altered Merriam's influence within the Park Service. For a man who had grown accustomed to an occasional White House invitation during the Coolidge and Hoover administrations, as well as to ready access to the interior secretary, Merriam found the new political landscape left him with a more circuitous route to power. His best contacts now consisted of the president's uncle, Frederic Delano (a trustee of the Carnegie Institution who replaced Charles Walcott after the latter's death in 1927) and his brother Ed. Both had been appointed to Roosevelt's National Resources Planning Board and functioned as advisors to FDR, albeit among many other luminaries in the so-called brain trust. An academic like his older brother, Ed had spent his career as a professor of political science at the University of Chicago. There he made occasional forays into city politics and had long since established a close friendship with Harold Ickes, now secretary of the interior.[6]

The connection with Ickes through Ed worked well enough for the secretary to include Merriam on a committee charged with recommending a new Park Service director when Albright retired, in August 1933. A majority of committee members wanted Drury, but he declined because of his pressing commitments with the Save-the-Redwoods League and as part-time acquisitions officer for the California State Parks Commission.[7] Arno Cammerer, who had assisted both Mather and Albright, emerged as director of a bureau that Ickes wanted to bring in line with his department's general direction. Ickes set the compass toward Interior becoming a "Department of Conservation" and one that also assumed leadership in outdoor recreation. This meant control of all federal recreation programs, including those of the U.S. Forest Service, a bureau in the Department of Agriculture.

Merriam liked what Ickes said about excessive road building in the national parks and refused to believe (at least in the beginning) that the secretary might want to undermine the national park "standards" as set forth in 1929 by endorsing acceptance of inferior areas into the system. But it worried Merriam that the Park Service renewed an effort to have the national forest land around Diamond Lake, an area with a typical offering of recreational activities such as fishing, boating, and camping, transferred to Crater Lake National Park in order to enlarge it. Mather, strangely enough, initiated the campaign to secure Diamond Lake in 1918, but throughout the following decade, the Forest Service successfully rallied local opposition to the proposed transfer each time it surfaced. Merriam saw the latest try as particularly threatening, since it "could easily mean the breaking down of barriers which we have been attempting to build around the primitive values of National Parks." It would mean that the "beauty and wonder of [Crater] Lake are not considered sufficient" for an agency willing to draw away precious staff and funding from its special charge in order to control "general recreational opportunity" in the immediate vicinity.[8]

In regard to the agency's general direction, Merriam frankly "doubted whether the trend was toward betterment," even while Albright served as director. Merriam believed that the decline could be traced to the hiring, back in 1931, of a landscape architect named Conrad Wirth from the National Capital Park and Planning Commission as one of four assistant directors of the National Park Service. Wirth had little use for standards that might serve to separate national, state, and municipal parks from one another. On the contrary, he considered definitions and standards to be impediments to agency expansion and increased budgets. From the time he was hired, Wirth took control of the Park Service's land acquisition program and the study and reporting on proposals for new national parks and monuments. The politically savvy Wirth quickly made the transition to chief of planning for the Park Service, as assistant director, but now with responsibility for all Civilian Conservation Corps work in state and municipal parks.

Drury, meanwhile, arranged to have Merriam's son Lawrence recommended through Albright as a "regional officer" in the CCC. Lawrence had been employed as a consulting forester from the time he took his bachelor's degree from the University of California in 1922, but the Depression greatly reduced the amount of work he could secure from his employer, Mason and Stevens. This new appointment became effective in May 1933, and Lawrence looked forward to supervising state park work in California and five other western states through the CCC.[9] Two years later, as the number of Civilian Conservation Corps camps nationally climbed toward the program's high-water mark, Wirth called Lawrence from Washington, seeking to hire him as an assistant. Lawrence made no immediate commitment, saying that he had to think it over, then turned to his father and uncle Ed for advice.[10]

John was predictably frosty about the idea, wiring back that both Wirth and Cammerer would probably impede free expression of Lawrence's ideas (presumably to Ickes), adding that the small raise in pay might well be consumed by the higher living expenses of Washington over those in Berkeley. Ed waited several days to reply, after first receiving a letter from his brother expressing the view that Wirth represented a "dangerous element," since he possessed considerable political influence and ability; as evidence, John referred to Wirth's having developed a plan for the Park Service to control state parks.[11] After Ed suggested that Lawrence try the new post, John wrote to both brother and son, wondering whether Ickes knew of the machinations within the Park Service and the problems they might cause for Lawrence. John worried that by undermining the relationship of the federal government to the states, Wirth would land in hot water with Ickes, who Merriam believed supported national park standards. Lawrence, if only by association, might be dragged into the morass created by Wirth and his sympathizers in the Park Service. In the end, the younger Merriam found too much uncertainty about the offer to justify a move and decided to stay in Berkeley.[12]

By that time the once-bright prospects for the national park system being a super-university of nature had turned into a "discouraging and disgusting" situation in the view of John C. Merriam. Drury wrote to him in February 1937, asking whether he had seen a "most elaborate booklet" issued by the Park Service for its "Park, Parkway, and Recreational Area Study" authorized by Congress. Passage of this legislation signified to Drury "the entering wedge toward increasing the bureaucratic activity of the Federal Government in local fields."[13] Although he and Merriam felt California was getting along just fine without federal assistance, Drury did not think he could dissuade the governor (Merriam's first cousin Frank) from sending a request for the aid Ickes had made available for studying and planning state park facilities. Merriam wrote to Drury a few days later in a gloomy mood, observing that the Park Service had once possessed "the greatest opportunity that the world has ever presented" for being a leader in the study and appreciation of nature, and it had backed away from that calling to compete with the Forest Service—with the "Conrad Wirth system of general recreation"—very possibly spelling the end of standards and their application to what should be a select group of parks.[14]

There still seemed to be a sliver of hope, if national parks like Yosemite and the Grand Canyon could be recognized as "primitive areas of unusual type" and separated from the city parks and historic sites now under the wing of the Park Service. Merriam believed as early as 1933 that this type of segregation could counteract the danger of more and more recreational use in the "great parks," because maintaining their primitive conditions might then be the overriding objective. Visitors should see great things, but the values of a "primeval" park quickly eroded when up against the "promotional aspect of recreation," with the "large opportunity" it afforded to concessionaires to provide ever increasing commercial services and thereby maintain the atmosphere of a resort.[15]

The most appalling example of the resort scenario could be seen in Yosemite Valley. Managing a place where commercial interests were so firmly entrenched even before creation of the Park Service in 1916 was inherently difficult. Stephen Mather nevertheless thought he could make headway by granting a monopoly to a merger of two rival concessionaires—what became the Yosemite Park and Curry Company, or YPCC—in 1925, and carefully planning the valley's development. The plan revolved around removing the existing Yosemite Village, with its dilapidated buildings and confined spaces, and building a new village across the Merced River, where cliffs formed a backdrop and there was room for eventual expansion. With the museum as a centerpiece, new facilities such as the Ranger's Club (personally funded by Mather as housing for Park Service employees) and an administration building became part of the "New Village," as did a luxury hotel called the Ahwahnee erected by the YPCC. Hotel guests and campers could also avail themselves of a wide array of entertainment slightly farther afield from the New Village, or "civic center," as Mather once called it.[16] These attractions included a zoo, bear shows at the garbage dump, outdoor dances, and a nightly event called the "Firefall," in which flaming embers were pushed over a precipice of fifteen hundred feet from Glacier Point at the same time every summer evening.

Completion of an all-weather state highway to the valley in 1926 coincided with an explosion in automobile ownership among middle-class Californians and hastened the transformation of Yosemite into what Robert Sterling Yard called a "weekend resort" for the multitudes coming from San Francisco and points in between. Visiting within weeks of the road's opening, Yard described Yosemite Valley as "lost," though he concluded his letter to National Parks Association president George Bird Grinnell with the observation that "a healthy reaction" against such a carnival atmosphere "is beginning to be evident."[17] Even if Yard had become too much of a "purist" in Mather's eyes, the director could not ignore the fact that many other prominent people were starting to see the valley in a similar light.

With these perceptions in mind, Mather agreed to Merriam's proposal for a "special commission or group" to develop a plan for the valley floor. Congress sanctioned the Yosemite National Park Board of Expert Advisors largely through Congressman Louis Cramton's efforts. The board consisted of three members recruited by Merriam: John Buwalda, Duncan McDuffie, and Frederick Law Olmsted, Jr.[18] Its purpose centered on helping the Park Service to formulate policies for the

FIGURE 19. Crowded conditions for camping in Yosemite Valley, about 1927. (National Park Service Historic Photograph Collection.)

park, but its insistence on preserving what Merriam called "fundamental values" could also deflect criticism leveled at the agency from a concessionaire eager to expand parking or build a tramway from the valley floor to Glacier Point.[19]

Merriam regularly corresponded with Buwalda about the valley's problems, even though his only official capacity at Yosemite resulted from reporting on educational possibilities there in 1929. Despite lacking funds for facilities like the Yavapai Station or a Sinnott Memorial, Merriam and Buwalda, who at that time taught geology at the California Institute of Technology, devoted considerable attention to interpreting the origin of granite in the Sierra Nevada. This effort, one that included helping visitors to appreciate how the "action of tremendous creative forces" shaped Yosemite Valley, eventually centered on two areas. One was Sentinel Dome, which loomed above the valley; the other was an area in the Merced Canyon west of the park, where the granite and underlying metamorphic rock displayed an obvious contact point along the road. Merriam made periodic trips to assist Buwalda with developing interpretive leaflets during the early 1930s. The view from Glacier Point, however, disturbed him. During the summer of 1932, he could clearly see a "City of Yosemite" with ten thousand people in the valley alone, where scars from road construction remained "almost continuously in sight." Merriam wrote to Buwalda after that trip, bemoaning how the Park Service's desire to show people "things of great wonder and beauty" made it easy to obtain almost unlimited funds for road building. It seemed, however, that little or no money was being allotted for planning ways for visitors to find points of interest without damage. If such provision were made, Merriam optimistically noted, "most of what we wish to see accomplished could be brought about."[20]

Buwalda asked him in the fall of 1933 about the Park Service plan to make the recent addition in the vicinity of Wawona, on the park's southwest fringe, a recreational area. The agency's intent was to relieve Yosemite Valley of the demand for certain kinds of entertainment that presumably brought more visitors into the "city." Merriam feared the precedent such a move might set, since accommodating more visitors lent credence to other proposals for the Park Service to administer sites like Diamond Lake or Boulder Dam, downstream of the Grand Canyon. In lacking superlative expressions of the primitive, these sites' main value, in the eyes of Merriam and his allies, was for recreation instead of education and inspiration. The purely recreational aspect of use "would tend in time to extend itself" over the national park system, overshadowing the idea of having "a relatively small group of National Park areas maintained at a high standard."[21]

The Park Service went ahead with its plan, which included provisions for a golf course and even a place for aircraft to land, but it did little to lessen the demands on Yosemite Valley. Consequently, Merriam saw little possibility of the Park Service's being able to change course by the spring of 1935. He wrote to Buwalda, remarking that "unless outside students of these problems" could have a meaningful impact on the general public, the influence of nature would come from the "smaller things of everyday life, rather than the greater things which ought to have influence, such as the National Parks." Buwalda tried to stay upbeat, relating news of a recently imposed limit of thirty days on camping in the valley. He also observed that "concrete devices which tell their own story," like the Yavapai Station, gave the best results for the purposes of education and inspiration, since they did not depend so much on the personal whims of park employees. For those attempting to help the Park Service, it would be necessary to keep "continuous and watchful contact" with the agency over the course of many years. Buwalda cited the need for repeated proselytizing to new employees in order to make the "ever changing personnel" in parks conscious of some "wiser policies and broader points of view."[22]

Merriam suggested one way around these barriers to institutionalizing education and inspiration as the main aim of the Park Service. The need was evident for clearly articulated principles derived from intensive study of the primitive; if they could be delineated, such principles might be exerted on the government and could eventually influence public opinion. He started writing a paper called "Protection and Use of the Primitive" but found statement of the problem and his aims difficult. The explanation needed when "shifting from the clearly defined regions of research" to the fuzzier realm of "thought concerning human value" proved to be Merriam's main obstacle to making significant progress in his writing.[23] In the meantime, he openly wondered whether such study might come too late, given the tendency, too often pronounced in the parks, for quick decisions to be made on important questions without an opportunity for careful analysis of their impacts. Merriam expressed his displeasure to Buwalda about government officials too quickly giving their approval for roads and other construction, and thus preempting careful consideration of how each development affected the primitive character of a park.[24] The paper lay fallow while Merriam traveled that summer. His writing about the primitive so far lacked the characteristic vitality of his natural history essays compiled by Scribner's and published as *The Living Past* in 1930. While in California during July and August, however, he returned to his frequent practice of writing memoranda as a way of recording events, capturing his thoughts, and formulating a plan of action. In some ways similar to a diary, these pieces were not intended for publication. They furnished a record of his impressions and logic but could stand alone occasionally as expository writing.

Short papers such as "Relation of Landscape Student to Problem of Protecting Primitive" (in late July) and "Memorandum Regarding Yosemite" (in early September) bracketed Merriam's trip to California. The former focused on how landscape architects working for the Park Service should draw on the wide spectrum represented by science and art to protect natural values when designing the means of access or facilities for visitors. In providing clarification for why Merriam stressed seeing a problem from every angle before embarking on major projects in parks, it also gave the rationale for stopping them if necessary.[25] The

memorandum of September 1935 constructed an argument of enumer-
ated points to support his assertion that conditions in Yosemite Valley
were not conducive to preserving the primitive unimpaired for the enjoyment of future generations. It arose from observations made in 1929
that the valley was a resort where the allowance for extended summer
residence compromised opportunities for education and inspiration.
Anyone who cared to weigh the values at stake had to conclude that giving visitors an opportunity for spiritual growth simply outweighed the
option of allowing long-term residence in the valley.[26]

Merriam wrote his most polished essay in late August 1935. Titled
"Memorandum Regarding the Primitive," it placed the problems of
Yosemite Valley into a larger context by giving the need to protect
wilderness in the national parks some philosophical grounding. He believed that of all "students of nature," Wordsworth possessed few rivals
in bringing together currents of emotion, aesthetics, and philosophy in
a unified stream of thought. Selected stanzas from Wordsworth's ode
"Intimations of Immortality from Recollections of Early Childhood"
opened the memorandum, and Merriam attempted to show how the
poet's love of nature grew through his advancing years and as a result
of his personal experience. As a device that drew from what Merriam believed to be among the clearest expressions of nature appreciation, the
poem provided a firm foundation, grounded in the unity of thought, for
the movement to protect the primitive. Merriam used Wordsworth's
poem as a prelude to focusing on how Yosemite Valley served as a symbol where "the original idea of preserving nature in its primitive state
has been so markedly violated" that either Park Service policy must be
changed, or a new procedure must be developed. While in the valley he
put forth what that procedure had to entail. Starting with the indis-
criminate promotion of travel to Yosemite regardless of what resulted,
Merriam thought it necessary to reverse the idea of "fancied greatness"
through records of attendance and through the increased size and
power of the Park Service. In a prescient twist, given his son's appointment to the job less than two years later, he wrote that it would be interesting if a park superintendent administered the valley as a place "for
the sheer enjoyment of nature" rather than promoting commercial
services such as transportation and hotel accommodations.[27]

Merriam concluded the memo, whose distribution was limited to
Drury and a few protégés, such as Buwalda, by observing that the primitive qualities of Yosemite and other national parks could be saved, but
only through intervention by a group of "wise and courageous enthu-

siasts." The scientists, artists, and nature lovers Merriam envisioned in this group could then work out what constituted "protection" and "enjoyment," as well as which "elements" must be turned aside in order for their goals to be reached. If they accomplished their task, Congress might then act on "the desires of those who wish to see the primitive of America protected in its superlative expression."[28]

Strangely enough, Yard had been after Merriam for months to have a hand in guiding such an organization. Yard and several other preservationists launched the Wilderness Society in 1935, though it consisted of only eight board members, with just five of them "known even to small bodies of specialists."[29] Merriam, as a respected scientist and president of the Carnegie Institution of Washington, could have (at least in Yard's estimation) enhanced the group's effectiveness as a political force.

All conservation groups of the 1930s, except for the Save-the-Redwoods League and the slightly smaller Sierra Club, consisted of a few hundred members at most, so the Wilderness Society, in its struggle to exert a meaningful impact on Congress and federal officials, had good company. The idea for a group of preservationists with no "straddlers," who in the past had "surrendered too much good wilderness and primeval [lands] that should never have been lost," came from Bob Marshall.[30] Both Yard and Merriam were impressed after their initial meeting in 1932 with the energetic and financially independent Ph.D. in plant pathology. Marshall publicly attacked what he called "the fake Hopi Watchtower" overlooking the Grand Canyon, and Yard described him as "indomitable" and "daring," perfect to head the Wilderness Society. Ickes, however, did not want Marshall to be "subject to attack" as president of the group while also working in the Department of the Interior for an agency under his control, the Bureau of Indian Affairs. Yard assumed the executive duties, leaving Marshall temporarily out of the line of fire, and turned to Merriam for assistance with striking a higher public profile.

Merriam's national standing as a leader in science made him a logical choice to head an advisory committee, even if, as Yard put it, Merriam never attended a single meeting of the Wilderness Society. But Merriam declined the offer. He did give Yard the benefit of his advice from time to time, but he did not join the group, for several reasons. The one he repeated most often was "other commitments," but the impediments also included the declining health that came with age (he was now in his mid-sixties), Marshall's socialist leanings, and a feeling that his chances of seeing reform in the Park Service were increasingly limited.

Throughout this period Yard continued to apprise Merriam of Wirth's plan to add a new administrative layer in the Park Service by establishing "regions" that would unite national, state, and municipal parks through the Civilian Conservation Corps. At one point Yard issued a communiqué to trustees of the National Parks Association, describing Wirth as unable to distinguish between the various types of parks and quoting Wirth as saying, "All kinds tie together like the rooms of a house."[31] Yard had tried to speak with Wirth "a number of times" about the ideals behind the national park system, but he found Wirth to have "no sense whatever" of why the primitive had value, much less of what bringing national and state parks together might ultimately mean for the system.[32] Wirth, not surprisingly, wanted to be director of the Park Service and took it upon himself to draft a new general goal for the agency in 1936. Taking his cue from Wirth, Cammerer, still director, said the national park system constituted a "progressive step of land utilization," one that "must take its place with other great land-use techniques such as forestry, agriculture, and mining." Cammerer kept any distinctions among these "techniques" intentionally vague, aside from declaring that the system of parks (unencumbered by what Merriam saw as "standards") would encompass less land than that given over to either forestry or agriculture.[33] The director had previously defended the move to incorporate Diamond Lake within Crater Lake National Park in a paper on standards and policies for national parks presented at a 1936 planning conference. He now also endorsed a cooperative agreement for the Park Service to administer recreation at Lake Mead, the water body created by the impoundment of the Colorado River at Boulder Dam.[34]

The Park Service's effective renouncement of the concept of standards for national parks can be better understood in light of any government bureau's need to react to legal requirements and respond to changing political climates if it is to survive. Federal agencies retain a fair amount of discretion in formulating policy but do not, in the absence of legal mandates or regulations, voluntarily restrict their options. They also behave according to a set of organizational values resulting from the social forces that exerted a controlling influence at the time they were created by Congress. Such values form a collective orientation among members of an organization, institutionalizing a set of beliefs that also influence a group's perception of public demands.[35]

The Park Service accepted interpretation as a permanent part of its operations in the national parks but hedged on making educational work the driving force behind park management. In 1916, advocates for the new bureau had to cast the national parks as public resorts to win the support of a broad-based and dispersed group of clients. The parks thus fueled a nascent tourist industry.[36] Irrespective of the legislative requirement that the parks remain unimpaired for future generations, management of these areas needed to reinforce how recreational tourism provided greater economic value than alternative uses such as logging, mining, and grazing. Concessionaires thus became vitally important to park managers, because of their indirect economic contribution in attracting visitors. The Park Service had to take visitor access seriously, since virtually all of the seventeen national parks and twenty-two national monuments it controlled at the end of 1916 were in remote areas away from the few main roads that traversed the western United States. When staff assigned to education appeared in park operations around 1920, they served a need but never really had the chance to push the promotion of recreation away from its central position in the agency's social system.[37]

As the dominant personality in the National Park Service, Stephen Mather tried to impose restrictions on park development in order to prevent chaos. He insisted that the agency's landscape architects take the lead in designing facilities, but withheld final approval until he and his Washington staff could discuss the proposed development with each park superintendent. As more money for improvements became available starting in the early 1930s, the landscape architects produced master plans for each park. The idea was that development could be guided by a carefully conceived circulation system in which existing and proposed facilities were concentrated in relatively few nodes, such as model villages. Many of the park villages, however, predated establishment of the Park Service. The landscape architects were therefore faced with the challenge of reconfiguring and expanding park villages in the face of increasing visitation and commercial pressure; in some cases that meant starting anew by developing adjacent sites to relieve pressure on older ones. With Mather essentially out of the picture after 1928, Merriam and other "purists" saw danger in attempting to accommodate an ever greater number of visitors, because a park's educational values might be harmed if there was no attempt to define what exactly the Park Service intended to preserve.

Every bureaucracy prefers a steadily increasing budget. That can be achieved by growth in its responsibilities, yet the "Lane letter" of 1918 was an attempt by Mather to set limits on future expansion in all national parks and monuments. The letter's emphasis on "scenery of supreme and distinctive quality or some natural feature so extraordinary or unique to be of national importance" could work as a justification for establishing a national park only if Mather's boss, Secretary of the Interior Franklin Lane, did not overrule the Park Service or if Congress concurred with the bureau's assessments.[38] Most of the scenery and natural features meeting the Lane letter's criteria for inclusion within an expanded national park system lay in the national forests. This was especially important if one assumed that Congress would persist in its reluctance to appropriate funds for buying private lands.

As chief of the Forest Service, William B. Greeley hardly relished the prospect of continually losing turf to a competitor who unilaterally decided which of the national forest lands it was better suited to manage. After arguing for a clear distinction between forests and parks in 1921, Greeley maintained that the former should be developed in line with the "traditional" uses (regulated grazing, logging, and mining), as well as for recreation. The Forest Service had already begun developing sites on national forest land in the Columbia River Gorge to demonstrate how it could meet public demand for recreational facilities, and Greeley wanted to capitalize on this precedent. Sensing a threat, Mather convinced several key congressmen to block appropriations for recreational development in the national forests for the following year, but the Forest Service ultimately prevailed in its quest for funding to build campgrounds and other amenities.[39]

Merriam, Yard, and a number of other leading preservationists approved of promoting recreation in the national forests, especially if it could relieve present and future pressure on the national parks. They applauded the idea of setting aside some recreational areas in the forests that might remain free of roads or other modern contrivances. Containing more than twenty times the acreage allotted to the national park system in the early 1920s, the national forests possessed a considerable amount of what their devotees began to call "wilderness." The term lacked the congressional stamp of approval, and the Forest Service continued to hedge on establishing standards to govern permitted uses in large roadless areas of national forest, but national-park advocates saw their value—and so did Greeley. The national forests afforded the luxury of small-scale concessionaires running small resorts at the periphery of areas whose core was intended to remain both scenic and roadless. With most of the logging pressure still on private land, Greeley saw an opportunity for the Forest Service to conduct an inventory of what it administered that might qualify as wilderness, however loosely construed. Although seen internally as a groundbreaking effort when launched in 1926, the inventory represented just one part of the Forest Service's planning for recreational use during that period. The broader effort encompassed locating what might become more intensively developed resorts, with campgrounds and "research reserves" that represented the "virgin conditions" in each of the forest types.[40]

In pitching the concept to their field staff, Greeley and his assistant, Leon F. Kneipp, presented the idea of protecting wilderness as steeped in a romantic past. Kneipp prefaced the outline of the proposed inventory, which was sent to subordinates in the Forest Service, with an essay on the value of wilderness and characterized the national forests as containing the last frontiers of the United States. The national forests included many of the mountain ranges and peaks that in the early days "served not only as landmarks to the pioneers" but also as "spiritual symbols of a new life."[41] Greeley and Kneipp approached prominent citizens, including Merriam, for testimonials and described what they had in mind as maintaining certain undeveloped areas in the United States "as nearly as possible in a state of nature." This might afford posterity "some conception of what the United States was like in its earlier stages of settlement," in addition to providing an opportunity for visitors to pursue outdoor recreation "in a relatively unmodified natural environment."[42] As the two foresters expected, Merriam responded favorably to the idea, urging the Forest Service to consider protecting a large number of areas where primitive conditions could be maintained permanently. He suggested countering objections to the withdrawal of merchantable timber with the view that aggressive reforestation elsewhere should take up some of the slack.[43]

Logging, or even the accelerated pace of building highways through the national forests, did not constitute the most immediate obstacle to launching a credible wilderness program. The threat came in the form of a proposed cable tramway to the summit of Mount Hood, Oregon's highest peak and a landmark for the residents of Portland, the state's largest city. Developers came forward in September 1926 with an ambitious plan for a cog railway on the mountain's northeast side, which would link a new hotel with the top of Cooper Spur. From that point a tower would hold cables, on which a car could run to another tower on the summit. High-powered telescopes were to be located at an observatory planned for the top, with the structure to include rest rooms, a fireplace, and cots for the enjoyment of visitors. The proposal quickly became the topic of serious debate in Portland, with supporters more numerous than opponents.[44]

When faced with having to approve a permit for the scheme, the local forest supervisor deferred to the district forester, who in turn looked to Greeley for a decision. The chief of the Forest Service denied the permit in April 1927, but public pressure soon forced a hearing in Portland at which both sides presented their views. Greeley articulated his position near the end of the hearing and started with a plea for preserving some areas in wilderness condition. He characterized Mount Washington (the highest peak in the northeast, in New Hampshire's White Mountains National Forest) as spoiled from road building on one side and a cog railway on the other. The tramway's similarity to a proposed cable car across the Grand Canyon (an idea Mather had previously killed) went unspoken, though Greeley described the desecration that could result on Mount Hood in a similar way, that of leading to the tawdry atmosphere of Coney Island.[45]

Greeley once again denied the permit, but the developers appealed to his boss, Secretary of Agriculture William M. Jardine. The secretary did not like being placed in the position of having to overrule the head of his largest bureau, so Jardine asked for a committee to make recommendations on the matter. Jardine tried to defuse the tramway question by asking the committee, representing various institutions in Oregon, to study the recreational potential of the Mount Hood region. When the committee issued its report in August 1928, it recommended that the secretary allow the developers to build the tramway.[46] The secretary demurred by appointing a special commission consisting of Merriam, Olmsted, and Frank A. Waugh, a professor of landscape architecture at the University of Massachusetts and a longtime Forest Service consultant, in 1929. Their charge largely consisted of developing "fundamental principles" that might govern the management of features thought to be "of major public importance" in the vicinity of Mount Hood. The secretary justified his action by indicating that the problem possessed national importance, since the "principles" could very well be applied to similar challenges the Forest Service faced elsewhere.[47]

Olmsted's extended illness and the numerous demands on his time in California delayed the commission's report until the spring of 1930. Its members agreed to the idea of having users pay a portion of the costs borne by the government to provide recreational amenities such as campgrounds. They split on the tramway proposal, with Waugh being the lone supporter. By this time, Arthur M. Hyde had succeeded Jardine, and the new agriculture secretary granted the permit in June 1930. As the nation sank into the Great Depression, however, the developers failed to raise sufficient capital for their venture. After all the debates and delays, the tramway project died.[48]

Within a year, the local forest supervisor classified an area of 14,600 acres on the mountain as chiefly valuable for "the maintenance of primitive conditions." This area included the site where the tramway had been proposed and followed from a Forest Service policy drafted by Kneipp in 1929 and that was quickly adopted as Regulation L-20. It permitted forest supervisors to use their discretion in protecting certain tracts in the national forests with the aim of retaining them "in a minimum stage of development in the interest of education, recreation, and inspiration."[49]

Kneipp called these tracts "primitive areas." He took his cue from a conversation with Merriam, who saw the term *wilderness* as a misnomer for places invaded previously by fur trappers, gold seekers, and hunting parties and now bounded by highways or threaded by trails. Merriam advised Kneipp that primitive areas should lack artificial means of habitation, transportation, or subsistence. Visitors were to "sleep out under the stars, and carry a tent," since he envisioned them walking with a pack on their backs.[50] Within two years of their inception in July 1930, primitive areas became a concern to Horace Albright, now director of the National Park Service. He saw them as a parallel system of reserves, already equal in acreage to the national park system, and one with the potential to provide the Forest Service with leverage in arguing that future land transfers for national parks were unnecessary.[51]

Merriam supported Kneipp's efforts, even though he knew that the primitive area classification carried a minimum of restriction on nonconforming uses such as logging, mining, or even road building. In the strongly utilitarian Forest Service, this idea could also seem counterintuitive to managing the national forests in order to avoid future shortages of commodities such as timber. Merriam hoped that the primitive areas might be more widely accepted in time, but in December 1935, he also felt he should check with Robert Sawyer, the newspaper editor in Bend, Oregon, about the tramway's status, after Sawyer sent him a clipping from the Portland newspaper about recreational facilities in the Mount Hood region. Merriam knew that this locality might be a bellwether for areas having "great scenic and recreational value" that were not included in the national park system.[52] Sawyer reassured him that no one planned to build a tram, so the integrity of officially classified primitive areas appeared to be safe for the moment. The predominantly economic function that he and others agreed the national forests should serve, however, worried Merriam. Such an emphasis on commodities like timber, he reasoned, would have an inevitable impact on the largest possibility for primitive recreation on federal land.[53]

CHAPTER 8

Building State Parks

With the decline of primitive conditions in the national forests a virtual certainty, Merriam believed that states carried the primary responsibility for providing "wide, permanent, and if possible primitive areas needed to guarantee the pleasures of outdoor life, physical exercise, relaxation, and enjoyment of nature." States, moreover, could care for natural features possessing national interest and value when they were in a position to more effectively manage them than the federal government could. And where a well-developed state park system possessed "original materials which can teach their own lessons," it aided adult education and thus might benefit from the expertise available in colleges and universities.[1]

That may have been an overstatement, but with such great potential clearly evident in California, Merriam believed that state parks ranked second only to agriculture in their influence on the general welfare of residents.[2] Passage of the 1928 bond measure that led to a spectacular increase in the number of parks (going from eighteen in 1931 to seventy just six years later) helped California stand out among the states. There was also a survey begun in 1927, when the legislature appropriated twenty-five thousand dollars for a systematic examination of potential state parks. It took place over the following two years with Frederick Law Olmsted, Jr., acting as coordinator. He and his assistants recommended 125 sites from the more than 300 initially identified as potential state parks. The final report gave subsequent efforts to build a state park system some focus and direction. It thus represented a more methodical approach than the ad hoc system followed in other states.[3] California also benefited by retaining Olmsted to produce master plans for a

MAP 4. Save-the-Redwoods League map showing its four main park projects and the Avenue of the Giants, about 1940. (Courtesy of Lawrence C. Merriam, Jr.)

number of the state parks that were added to the system during the 1930s. Olmsted's services provided for continuity between the survey and subsequent site planning.[4]

Having an unpaid commission that controlled the state park system gave California another advantage, in the view of Merriam and his associates, since it seemed to function (at least initially) in the same manner as the Carnegie Institution trustees or a similar external board. Like the trustees, California's state park commissioners hired staff, beginning with Charles B. Wing as chief of parks in January 1928, followed by Newton Drury as part-time acquisitions officer once Olmsted finished the survey. The commissioners served at the pleasure of the governor, in contrast to the situation at the Carnegie Institution, and this became a defining difference beginning in November 1934. At that time the newly elected governor, Merriam's first cousin Frank, dumped one of the commissioners, as well as Wing and several state park employees. Merriam intervened at Drury's request and through a telephone call convinced the governor to reinstate the employees, but Wing and the commissioner, Laura E. Gregory, remained as casualties of the spoils system. Aside from the forced resignation of chairman William E. Colby in 1936, no further ousters of commissioners or state park employees took place during the remainder of Frank Merriam's administration. His actions, however, had set a precedent. The next governor, Culbert Olson, for example, replaced the entire commission and the chief of state parks upon taking office in July 1939. Drury somehow survived these upheavals, but he grew increasingly weary of new commissioners whom he considered to be unqualified. He became especially restless once the matching funds supplied by the 1928 bond issue began to dwindle and the formerly rapid growth of the state park system became a thing of the past.[5]

Merriam and Drury maintained their influence on state park policy in California during the decade of the 1930s partly because the Save-the-Redwoods League spent, at least in Lawrence Merriam's estimation, fifteen times as much for state parks per year as the legislature did.[6] An unstated threat of reducing or withdrawing contributions of this magnitude helped to keep Drury in his part-time position and allowed Merriam the opportunity to broker studies in several parks. A new research effort commenced after the Bull Creek–Dyerville State Park dedication in 1931, and it was combined with a small amount of money from the league for Olmsted to produce a master plan that favored preservation over use.[7] Lawrence handled two aspects of what he called a "protection" study in the summer and fall of 1932. It concentrated on fire effects and prevention, but Lawrence also planned a campground in an area of second growth along Bull Creek.[8] Willis Jepson, the renowned University of California botanist, studied plant associations in response to the elder Merriam's desire to avoid unnecessary impact on and destruction of the values that constituted the reason for establishing this park.[9]

Both studies of the redwoods in 1932 built upon earlier recommendations by league committees, such as the one on preservation of redwood groves. Duncan McDuffie led that committee, which in 1929 urged a ban on camping in the groves, along with prohibiting construction of offices or other administrative structures in them. The committee also opposed intentional planting of exotic vegetation and the highway engineer's preference for straightening and widening roads running through old growth stands.[10] Setting the basic policy framework for use was important to the league, but it remained more focused on land acquisition than on additional research needed to assist planners. Merriam wrote to John Buwalda in July 1932 about traveling through the redwoods to study how best to protect their primitive qualities. He wrote about having only a few of the "supposed advantages" enjoyed by the Park Service through more generous federal funding, but he remained optimistic about smaller appropriations from the state legislature to cover more careful review of any development or operation that could ultimately prove destructive to Bull Creek or other parks.[11]

Just a few months later, however, he directed Carnegie grants toward another part of the state park system where research might play an even more crucial role in making visitor use compatible with preserving some living remnants of the geological past. Three miles south of Carmel, on the central coast of California, lies what the Spaniards once called the Point of the Sea Wolves, *Punta de los Lobos Mariños*. It is where the barking of what English-speaking Americans call sea lions can easily be heard, an area along the jagged coastline that also contains several small and isolated stands of naturally occurring Monterey cypress. These trees were once more widespread on the western coast of North America over the last two million years, but climate change forced the species to retreat to a pair of rocky headlands that are often shrouded in fog. Shaped by the wind and occasional storm, the Monterey cypress acquires a gnarled and weather-beaten appearance as it clings to cliffs and crevices above the pounding surf. At Point Lobos, the picturesque

FIGURE 20. Monterey cypress at Point Lobos State Reserve, 1940. (Photo by Earl P. Hanson, © California State Parks, 1940.)

forms of the trees juxtaposed with the sea did not escape the notice of artists, who began flocking to Carmel in the decade prior to 1900. One of them saw the groves of cypress in concert with dramatic seascapes as "the greatest meeting of land and water in the world," a characterization by which Point Lobos became known to visitors throughout much of the twentieth century.[12]

Merriam's scientific interest in the Monterey cypress initially stemmed from finding this species among other fossil plants in the asphalt beds of Rancho La Brea.[13] By the time his childhood mentor Thomas H. Macbride had written a booklet advocating the preservation of the trees and other vegetation on Point Lobos in 1916, there remained only two native stands of Monterey cypress. One was Point Lobos; the other occurred within sight of Point Lobos on Cypress Point, but that grove had already been incorporated within the Pebble Beach subdivision, a development featuring multiple owners, a golf course, entrance gates, and toll roads.[14]

Point Lobos was also in private hands, but most of it remained under the control of one owner, Alexander M. Allan, who fenced off fifteen acres of cypress from grazing. He also charged visitors to enter the enclosure, so this grove and some three hundred acres around it had, in effect, become a private park. By 1926 Allan talked of emulating Pebble

Beach by subdividing his land, though he did not yet control a couple of key parcels. Some angry residents in Carmel disputed the legality of Allan's fences and tollgate, because they claimed previous owners had already donated the grove to Monterey County for a park. Lacking the funds to carry through with condemnation proceedings, one of Allan's neighbors contacted Drury and asked if the league might help rally public support for establishing a state park at Point Lobos. Drury referred the request to Merriam, who agreed. He saw the obvious parallels between rescuing redwoods from destruction and saving the remnant cypress grove, though Merriam knew direct financial aid for land acquisition posed a problem. He attributed the league's great success to its narrow focus, but a local association could work with the state to acquire Point Lobos and remain a constituent group anytime an opportunity or threat appeared on the horizon.

Allan hoped to develop or greatly profit from sale of the Point Lobos property, so he repeatedly rebuffed attempts to negotiate a price closer to standard appraisals when Drury assumed the new role of acquisition officer for the state park commission in 1929. Condemnation proceedings started by the county at the Point Lobos Association's behest effectively stymied the subdivision scheme, and in March 1930, when Allan died, his heirs agreed to sell the land at its appraised value. Even half of the purchase price (six hundred thousand dollars) lay well beyond the reach of the Point Lobos Association; Drury approached Rockefeller for help, but the philanthropist decided not to participate in the project. Although disappointed, Drury soon hit on a solution involving a donation for the Prairie Creek redwoods that the state had not fully matched. In January 1933, once he obtained concurrence from the state attorney general's office to use the unspent matching funds, Drury finalized the purchase of the Allan property.[15]

Even before the sale had been consummated, Merriam wrote to Drury about studying the cypress grove. Lawrence Merriam had observed an almost total absence of young trees the previous fall, presumably because of a combination of past grazing, fires in the stand, and trampling of the forest floor by visitors.[16] The grove represented a challenge of classic proportions for the elder Merriam, a place where protecting the primitive and continued visitor use required a wide range of studies.[17] However, he declined Horace Albright's offer of assigning several National Park Service landscape architects to study the newly acquired land. Merriam distrusted the Park Service's motives in light of one "of the most interesting illustrations in the world of failure to un-

derstand the significance of a magnificent primitive landscape." Although he kept such criticism confidential, Merriam blamed the tower
overlooking the Grand Canyon on the agency's landscape architects.
He knew they had "approved unanimously" its initial design, but he
carefully avoided mentioning Albright's oversight role in the project as
agency director.[18]

Drury and the state park commission asked Olmsted to start a master plan for Point Lobos by the end of 1933. In the interim, Merriam
went after the "necessary talent" to conduct studies funded by a ten-
thousand-dollar grant he obtained from the Carnegie Corporation. Another eighteen hundred dollars came from the Carnegie Institution,
earmarked for publications derived from research that drove Olmsted's
master plan for Point Lobos.[19] The aim, as Merriam put it, was to obtain all the important facts regarding the land's primary aesthetic, educational, and scientific values. He even established a "rule" that all artificial development had to justify itself on the basis of making the area's
outstanding values available for inspiration and education. Merriam also
recognized that constantly changing conditions in an area like Point
Lobos required continued study of trends in growth, in use, and in "destructive factors," so that park policies might be "based on knowledge"
rather than on the whim of individual managers.[20]

Olmsted's master plan, when submitted to the state park commission
in the latter part of 1936, included an inventory of aesthetic values. It
also drew upon an impressive array of studies and reports solicited by
the Point Lobos Advisory Committee, a sort of external board and
funding conduit headed by the former secretary of the interior Ray
Lyman Wilbur. It was charged with deciding how to dispense the funds
provided by the Carnegie Corporation for investigations covering the
local geology, plants, land animals, marine invertebrates, archeology,
history, and weather, but the most urgent studies centered on the Monterey cypress. Just as they had in the redwoods, Jepson furnished a
botanical insight to the species, while E. P. Meinecke, as chief patholo-
gist of the federal Bureau of Plant Pathology, provided recommendations on how to regulate visitor use in the grove. Willis W. Wagener
worked under Meinecke and conducted the most intensive study of all,
in response to a canker that had begun decimating planted cypresses in
many parts of California. When infected plantings were discovered on
the Monterey Peninsula, Wagener and his assistants established a "pro-
tective zone" encompassing a radius of ten miles around the park.
Drury predicted the demise of all cypresses at Point Lobos, but the
canker attacked nursery stock rather than trees in remnant stands.[21]

Drury later cited Point Lobos as an exception to what often happened in many public parks, where recreational pressure forced managers to relegate higher uses (in this case, appreciating a landscape of great beauty and natural interest) to secondary status. The proximity of services in Carmel removed the need for a concessionaire, and the local population's support for measures to preserve Point Lobos certainly helped, as did the decision to provide for camping elsewhere. Pfeiffer–Big Sur State Park, twenty miles south of Carmel on the coast highway, allowed for camping and more intensive development, so that visitor impact on Point Lobos could thus be limited to day use.

Irrespective of whether it represented an unusual set of circumstances, Merriam trumpeted Point Lobos as an example of what could be achieved in protecting the primitive. His annual address to the league for 1936 came from England, where he and Ada were making their second visit to the Lake District. He concluded the letter by stating that the Point Lobos studies held "the largest possibility for good of all [preservation] projects in the world."[22] In the judgment of Merriam and those directly involved, the studies constituted the most thorough investigation ever made of any natural area and how to preserve it. He wrote that Olmsted's final report to the state park commission should be published as an example of how preservation and use could be reconciled through careful study that supported a thoughtful management plan. After Merriam and other members of the Point Lobos Advisory Committee made some minor revisions, Drury later hailed the report as a "counsel of perfection" for how to preserve natural values.[23]

Merriam's disenchantment with prevailing National Park Service attitudes toward the primitive did not prevent him from continuing to pursue the "study in appreciation of nature" at Crater Lake—the only other undertaking comparable to the breadth of the Point Lobos project. Instead of trying to make protection of the primitive compatible with visitor use, the Crater Lake studies aimed to unify interpretation of the scientific and aesthetic features in the park as a means of fostering inspiration among visitors. Just as he had done at Point Lobos, Merriam supplied initial direction in the course of obtaining grants, then proceeded to recruit investigators. Since a geological study could furnish the basis for the naturalist program at Crater Lake, he persuaded Howel Williams at the University of California to settle the question of whether the lake had been formed by the explosion or subsequent collapse of the mountain holding it.[24] Fieldwork commenced in the summer of 1936 and allowed Williams to produce the classic work on Crater Lake, a monograph eventually accompanied by a shorter and more popular version of the study written in both English and Spanish.[25] Two years earlier, Merriam also had recruited astronomer Edison Pettit from the Carnegie Institution to study the lake's optical properties and explain, in a way visitors could understand, why Crater Lake appears so intensely blue.[26]

Aside from Merriam's article on the appreciation of nature at Crater Lake in an art magazine during the summer of 1933, aesthetic studies could not overcome the difficulty of too many variables and dependence upon individual perception of what was beautiful.[27] They never really came to fruition, but Merriam nevertheless experienced the satisfaction of seeing aesthetic appreciation finally take form as an exhibition in the museum of the Sinnott Memorial. This "art room" contained six backlit glass transparencies, each intended to entice visitors to go to the place depicted in color photographs and see the "picture" at various times of day. These were separated from the three paintings that encouraged visitors to question the "type" of beauty seen, and from the black-and-white images in the adjacent "photographic alcove," which emphasized the value of line and form as elements of beauty. Labels were kept to an absolute minimum: wording was limited to a plaque for the art room as a whole and another for the alcove.[28]

Park staff gave Merriam the honor of being the first to see the exhibition at its opening in August 1938. Everyone involved received high praise from him, and Merriam told Buwalda shortly thereafter that the Sinnott Memorial did more to aid nature appreciation than the Yavapai Station, since the elements interpreted were better presented and more intimately related to one another. With the "whole story" connected to how beauty developed in the region, the many years spent on the Crater Lake project yielded what he called "a really important contribution" toward what could be achieved with educational work in the national parks.[29]

Apparent success at Crater Lake made retiring from the Carnegie Institution a little easier, as did opening of the Root Auditorium that fall. Forming an addition to the administration building in Washington, the 410-seat auditorium provided a long-awaited venue for the public lectures introduced during Merriam's presidency.[30] It quickly became a Carnegie Institution showpiece, in conjunction with an adjacent exhibit hall. These facilities helped to make the cloistered world of privately funded research accessible to a public whose only awareness of the foundation's work came through news releases and school bulletins issued in Washington. (Most Carnegie Institution publications went only to selected libraries.) The release of a large testimonial volume titled *Cooperation in Research* marked the close of Merriam's tenure as president. Its formal presentation came at the retirement dinner held for him on December 8, 1938, in Washington.[31]

Merriam wanted to resume his research activities, even though he was sixty-nine years old at retirement. As part of his transition to "president emeritus" of the Carnegie Institution, he received a substantial pension and negotiated for an annual research fund of ten thousand dollars.[32] Much of the latter could go toward the expenses of other investigators, just as such funding had during his presidency, though Merriam also envisioned a more active role for himself, especially in the Great Basin. His own studies there had been on hold for more than a decade, though the prospect of interdisciplinary work in vertebrate paleontology, archeology, and paleoclimate research piqued his interest in light of discoveries in these fields by protégés based in Oregon and California.[33] Apart from a visit to Eugene in June (where Merriam launched a cooperative study that tied Williams's work at Crater Lake with research on the development of ancient peoples in southern Oregon) and a trip through the redwoods in August, Ada's failing health dictated that much of 1939 was spent in Washington. Merriam could still travel, but he could hardly be considered robust. Cold weather gave him greater difficulty than it had before, and Merriam stubbornly refused treatment at the first sign of what later turned out to be prostate cancer, possibly because he feared that treatment would further impede his research.

With a return to the rigors of fieldwork in paleontology out of the question, he continued playing the facilitator's role in pursuing park-related projects. A four-thousand-dollar grant obtained from the Carnegie Corporation during his last few months as Carnegie Institution president for studying "human values of the redwoods" led to the formation of a committee to disburse the funds under league auspices. With the studies at Point Lobos and Crater Lake in mind as templates, Merriam wanted to get at how the "exceptionally grand and beautiful phase of Nature represented by the Redwoods," might best provide "soothing and healing value" as well as inspiration. He praised any sign of progress by other committee members at the league's annual meetings, but his own contributions to the study of how to make the most emotionally and intellectually compelling presentation of the redwoods grew more ragged and brief. The effort languished after several years, with little to show for the expenditures made other than a published compilation of Merriam's annual messages to the league council.[34]

Ada's condition slowly worsened during their visit to California in the first part of 1940. Merriam felt increasingly out of sorts, though a letter from one of Drury's old friends, Freeman Tilden, momentarily lifted his spirits. Tilden had just retired to California from New Hampshire and admired Merriam's address to the league several months earlier. With the onset of World War II in Europe and the Far East, Tilden wrote that a study of human values in the redwoods made a lot of sense for "a world presently bent on suicide." Tilden reassured Merriam that "difficult as it is, I feel the ideas you express *can* be conveyed to a great many people, in terms they can understand." Although some might never quite comprehend, Tilden added, "they will fringe upon understanding, and their vanity will supply the rest."[35] Merriam replied almost immediately and told Tilden that he was one of only five people in the country who fully fathomed the rationale behind the study and protection of the primitive. He expressed the hope that the two of them might work together in a continuation of this effort, something that might go "far beyond the redwoods," even if Merriam admitted being "constantly discouraged and perhaps disappointed with the results so far."[36]

His apparent eagerness to collaborate with Tilden provided yet another reason to be permanently situated in California. Merriam had considered buying a house near Santa Barbara or in the Berkeley Hills when Ada's health problems became severe enough to call for extended rest in 1927, but the couple eventually decided against owning another place. They enjoyed their routine of visiting the west each summer, one that usually involved extended stays at the same hotels. He and Ada could spend several weeks in Berkeley, giving Merriam a chance to conduct league business and visit with Drury, Ralph Chaney, and Mc-Duffie. Then, after excursions to Yosemite and Point Lobos, they usually went south. Merriam's retirement now held the prospect of using southern California as a welcome respite from the winter weather of the east. Chester Stock and John Buwalda were already situated in Pasadena, having moved from their academic positions at the University of California in 1926 to the California Institute of Technology, so the Merriams found it easy to justify an extended stay. Ada's condition took a distinct downward turn during their visit to Pasadena in February 1940, so they rushed back to Washington. Merriam hoped that doctors there might save her, especially since they could draw on the expertise available at Johns Hopkins University in Baltimore, but Ada died of breast cancer on April 13.[37] Charles and Malcolm thought it best to take turns staying with their father at the apartment over the following few weeks, until he could settle his wife's estate. After putting things in storage and dispensing with other household items, Merriam decided he could go west more or less permanently.[38]

His depression lifted a little upon arriving to visit Lawrence and family at Yosemite. The past three years as park superintendent had tested the younger Merriam, given how summer visitation continued to rise (it exceeded five hundred thousand in 1940) and commercial services now extended over a longer season, with downhill skiing and winter sports available at Badger Pass. A flood in December 1937 necessitated substantial rebuilding in Yosemite Valley, though Lawrence did his best to keep a lid on most additional development. Trying to remold the park into a place devoted to "sheer enjoyment of nature" required time, and making headway against entrenched commercial interests like the Yosemite Park and Curry Company was more difficult than it had first seemed from his father's more detached vantage point. Both of his immediate predecessors had succumbed to the stress of the job through heart failure, but Lawrence showed few outward effects of the strain in June 1940 when he welcomed his father at the train station in El Portal.

Drury soon joined them to discuss whether he should to accept the offer from Harold Ickes to become National Park Service director. Several months earlier, doctors had advised Arno Cammerer to take a less demanding position in view of how chronic anxiety had brought him to the brink of cardiac arrest. President Roosevelt refused to accept the secretary's first choice for a replacement, Robert Moses, so Drury now had a second opportunity to accept the appointment. He was inclined to accept, with state park acquisitions winding down as the matching funds supplied by the 1928 bonds approached exhaustion. His other endeavor, the league's acquisition program, was focused almost entirely on buying redwoods in the Mill Creek drainage and along the highway corridor called the Avenue of the Giants, north of Dyerville. It could remain in the capable hands of Drury's brother, Aubrey, while Newton spent a year or two in Washington. In any event, Ickes thought two weeks to think about the offer of becoming director was sufficient. He preempted a formal acceptance by announcing the appointment over loudspeakers in Yosemite Valley as Drury and the two Merriams stood at Glacier Point.[39]

Despite Merriam's extended rest in Yosemite Valley that summer, the disorientation and shock of his wife's death lingered. Lawrence and his brothers agreed that a secretary should be found, if only to keep an eye on their father as he made Pasadena his base for the winter. By November the elder Merriam had divulged to Charles that he intended to marry Margaret Webb, a secretary from Pasadena, in order for her to accompany him to a professional meeting set for the following April in Peru.[40] Although a full generation younger than Merriam, Margaret agreed to his proposal, and the couple were married at her mother's residence in Los Angeles on February 20, 1941. Buwalda served as best man at the ceremony, which Lawrence attended after failing to persuade his father to reconsider.[41]

The marriage disintegrated over the next eighteen months, to some extent because age and infirmity made Merriam more irritable. Merriam also became less disposed toward completing of his own volition what once might have been fairly routine projects. He could even be an obstruction to what others produced after he enlisted their support. Interpreting the story of granite in Yosemite was a case in point. After all the visits and discussions, Buwalda took the lead in drafting text for the signboards planned for Sentinel Dome and the contact point seen from the highway next to the Merced River. Merriam then wanted what he saw as verbiage shortened and simplified, though the full burden of revision fell on Buwalda. With no funding on the horizon, the signboard idea finally died when Lawrence left Yosemite to become a regional director for the Park Service in Omaha during the summer of 1941.[42]

The same pattern unfolded in Oregon, where Merriam wanted to lead an effort demonstrating how state parks might aid education, in line with his thoughts expressed at the 1928 meeting of the National Conference of State Parks. He chose Oregon because associates at the university in Eugene provided him with an introduction to the chancellor of higher education, Frederick M. Hunter. That meeting led directly to establishment of the Committee on Educational Problems of Oregon Parks (CEPOP) in August 1941, an advisory board formally sanctioned by Hunter and others who governed the state's university system.[43] CEPOP consisted of eight of Merriam's academic protégés, two Park Service officials stationed at Crater Lake, and State Parks Superintendent Samuel H. Boardman. For Merriam, CEPOP projects in the John Day region took precedence over resolutions the committee passed for the Columbia River Gorge and state parks along the Oregon coast, mainly because he wanted to produce a guidebook and step up land acquisition for a parkway that followed the road north of Picture Gorge.[44]

Boardman had helped build what became known as John Day Fossil Beds State Park during the 1930s by adding several overlooks and the

Blue Basin locality to acreage near Picture Gorge, which was acquired with Robert Sawyer's help. The parkway proposed by CEPOP would be some twenty-two miles long and roughly a mile wide, and it would encompass a far larger area than any acquisition Boardman and the highway commission had ever attempted to make. Buwalda estimated the price for the arid rimrock and rangeland to be in the neighborhood of seventy thousand dollars, with the more valuable bottomland next to the John Day River to be managed "cooperatively" by local owners and the state. Although the only ready source of funding, Oregon's gasoline tax, had been greatly reduced by wartime restrictions on travel—and Boardman secretly remained dubious of CEPOP's value—Boardman suggested that Merriam pitch the parkway concept to the highway commission. Merriam did so at a luncheon, impressing the chairman with the possibility that a cooperatively managed parkway in the John Day country could work like a national park that was then being assembled in the Lake District of England.

The election of November 1942 brought a new governor into office and thus a clean sweep in the highway commission, which was now much less disposed to consider the parkway proposal as a candidate for the small allotments intended for acquiring and maintaining state parks. Merriam responded to this turn of events in July 1943 by submitting a much less ambitious set of suggestions to Boardman for future acquisitions in the basin. These recommendations largely reiterated what the two had discussed during several previous field trips, though Boardman eventually acquired just two sites on the list. One was a volcanic dike along the parkway route; the other lay some thirty-five miles west at a place near the Painted Hills that Boardman intended to develop for picnicking. He legitimized the latter choice partly because Merriam and his expedition of 1899 had camped at the site for several weeks while they extracted specimens from cliffs a short distance away.[45]

Even less resulted from the guidebook effort, something initially envisioned as a leaflet in discussions with Boardman during their field trip of 1938. Despite having most of a manuscript assembled after Chaney, Stock, and two other protégés contributed chapters in the fall of 1942, Merriam chose to rework and revise the material instead of finding a publisher. By August of 1944 he wanted CEPOP to take responsibility for the book, but none of its members volunteered.[46] His idea for a research arm of CEPOP went the same way. In November 1940, Merriam recruited Buwalda, Stock, and his son Charles (now a paleontologist with the U.S. Geological Survey) to create the John Day Associates, a

FIGURE 21. Merriam (seated left) and Samuel H. Boardman (seated center) accompanied by three Douglas County officials (standing) at Diamond Lake, Oregon, in 1942. The man seated at right is unidentified. (Courtesy of Lawrence C. Merriam, Jr.)

body that would continue the cooperative study of the basin even after his death. However, he did not pursue formal sanction of the group by Oregon's board of higher education until June 1943. At that point the John Day Associates took form as a group dedicated to facilitating research in the basin, but with the intention of also acting as semi-official park custodians. Despite some recurring enthusiasm expressed by CEPOP members at their occasional meetings, lack of funding largely condemned the John Day Associates to being an entity in name only.[47]

CEPOP had its only lasting success as a vehicle for implementing Merriam's suggestion of an annual lecture to interpret specialized scientific research for general audiences, an idea that derived from his time as president of the Carnegie Institution. Named for Thomas Condon, the lectures continued for several decades after CEPOP disbanded and gave rise to publications by Williams, Chaney, and others, which were distributed by the state board of higher education.[48] How effective CEPOP might have been in the state parks, even with funding to implement its recommendations, was questionable in light of Boardman's attempts to undermine the group's credibility. He described CEPOP in a letter to the chairman of the state highway commission as an organization run by "eight doctors of scientific research" who dwelled "in so many years of past history that I was in doubt if I was actually alive." Boardman stated that he could not explain his membership in such a group, and then put forth his objection to Merriam's proposal that would allow the public one place to dig for fossils on the future parkway. He concluded the letter by lampooning another committee member's idea to place concrete replicas of extinct mammals at various localities along the highway north of Picture Gorge.[49]

Why Boardman chose to disparage CEPOP related directly to how he influenced state parks in Oregon. Sawyer could well be considered the system's founder, but Boardman quickly assumed the role of builder upon becoming state parks superintendent in August 1929. Boardman went about the task of acquiring land as a fervent pantheist, railing against overnight camping in the state parks as a form of desecration. His minuscule budget, however, usually did not allow for acquiring service areas away from central features in the parks, so development of visitor facilities both infringed on the primitive and could have disastrous consequences on small areas. He preferred instead to keep much of the system undeveloped, then turned money back on numerous occasions to show the highway commission how expeditiously the tiny allotments given to state parks were being spent. Such a parsimonious attitude also meant that Boardman often parted with timber rights on many parcels in order to acquire them. Boardman nonetheless worked wonders in expanding the system, taking it from slightly more than four thousand acres when he started to more than ten times that size in just a decade. His focus remained on acquiring parcels along the Oregon coast, where more than 70 percent of the visitors to the parks flocked.

Oregon's possession of almost three hundred miles of public beaches (largely thanks to Governor Oswald West, who declared them to be "highways" in 1913) represented what perhaps could be the state's only advantage over California when it came to park development. Because Oregon had only a fraction of the population compared to California, among whom there was widespread reluctance to pass bond measures that could provide even a whiff of the matching funds and donations that Drury had at his disposal, Oregon's park system was largely confined to small areas immediately adjacent to its highways. Administrative fiat molded the state park system in Oregon, one that complemented recreational development by the Forest Service on federal land. A park commission met only once in the state capital of Salem, a month before Boardman was hired in 1929, and there was no discussion of a

survey like the one Olmsted coordinated in California as a guide for future land acquisition.

Despite these defining differences, Merriam wrote to Boardman in
October 1934 about the possibility of holding a meeting to discuss mutual aid and the interrelation of park systems in both states.[50] Drury
doubted the value of such "conferences," but Merriam tried to sell him
and Boardman on the merits of cooperation. For one thing, it might
help defeat attempts to control all recreation at the federal level, because
California and Oregon could show "where the line can be drawn between national and state activities."[51] Prospects for a formal meeting
aimed at such cooperative undertakings were not forthcoming, but
Merriam joined Boardman on several field trips in Oregon throughout
the 1930s. For Merriam's part, two of those excursions were specifically
devoted to the topic of acquiring additional land in the John Day country; Boardman, in turn, looked to Merriam for aid in finding potential
donors who might help with acquisitions on the coast.[52]

With some encouragement from Merriam and others, Boardman
went to California for a working holiday in the early part of 1941. He
downplayed the lavish hospitality from officials in the state and national
parks there by telling his immediate supervisor that the trip represented
belated recognition for what Oregon had accomplished as a leader
among the states in preserving its recreational resources. Whereas Oregon kept "ours as the Creator molded it," the parks in California
seemed overdeveloped to him. Facilities such as buildings, picnic tables,
and fireplaces in many cases injured the scene as "carved by the great
Architect." Politics compromised park standards in California, at both
the state and national levels, whereas Oregon, at least in Boardman's
mind, remained unsullied by resisting pressure to develop camping in
its parks and by repeatedly denying local requests to obtain areas whose
only virtue consisted of their proximity to a town. Entrance fees to parks
galled him, especially the fifty-cent admission charged at Point Lobos
merely for the privilege of walking around a reserve that could not
"hold a candle" to five parks on the Oregon coast he named without
hesitation. Boardman added, however, that he might well prevail on
Merriam to secure grants for studies of those coastal parks, similar to
those conducted for Point Lobos.[53]

Retirement robbed Merriam of the influence needed to direct an
amount like the ten thousand dollars spent on studies at Point Lobos
toward any state park in Oregon. Most of what Merriam had to offer
lay in the realm of interpretation, an activity entirely absent in Oregon's

state parks apart from some signboards built at points along highways by the Civilian Conservation Corps a few years earlier. Not that Sawyer and others in the state lacked an interest in the educational possibilities of the parks, but chronically poor funding meant that maintenance and land acquisition simply had to take precedence. Without money to print booklets similar to the ones distributed by the Save-the-Redwoods League in California since the early 1930s, or the ability to hire naturalists like those who worked in a few of the California state parks, Merriam never really had a chance to make a demonstrable impact.[54]

Oregon nevertheless gave Merriam both respect and a place to withdraw, as his closest associates began to notice by 1943. The state board of higher education bestowed on him the title "Consultant and Lecturer on Human Values of Science and Nature," along with an office at the University of Oregon. He wrote to Drury in December and mentioned the board's request that he take up permanent residence in Oregon, a prospect Drury greeted with both approval and relief.[55] They maintained their correspondence, but with less frequency over the next year, as Drury struggled to run a bureau badly depleted by the manpower needs of the war effort. Merriam, meanwhile, made some token progress on the John Day project from Eugene, and with Stock's assistance, the best part of it went into a progress report for the *Carnegie Institution of Washington Yearbook*.[56]

Merriam invited Charles and Lawrence to visit him on several occasions and by the midsummer of 1944 talked of being lonely and depressed as several university faculty members departed to conduct field studies. Even though the elder Merriam wrote to Charles about making some progress on the John Day guidebook, he divested himself of the editorial role in August and instead opted to write a chapter on human values.[57] The decision gave him a pretext to contact the league and request that he be relieved of his duties as president. Merriam retained a token role as one of twenty councilors, so league officials did him the honor of including his message of some eight pages in the record at the annual meeting on August 31. McDuffie ran the meeting and had already been nominated to be the next president, a move that allowed Merriam to stay in Eugene and "compile data" for his John Day work.[58]

Drury sent a telegram to be read at the meeting. It expressed appreciation for Merriam's longtime leadership of the league, though he knew his mentor was failing. Correspondence between the two men continued, but Merriam now supplied more unsolicited advice about park problems and the general direction of the Park Service, sometimes accompanied by a copy of his weekly letter to Lawrence. Drury's infrequent replies resulted not from irritation, but from his having to swim in a sea of operational details, given how most of the parks were still open but were staffed at only a quarter of the levels achieved in 1941. Being on Capitol Hill with congressmen and their staffers in Washington also demanded time, as it always had for the head of any federal bureau. Drury, however, carried the additional burden of increased train travel, because in 1942 the Park Service headquarters had moved from Washington to Chicago to open up more office space for the military in the capital.

Looking beyond wartime constraints, Drury worried most about the Park Service's renewed involvement directly managing what were essentially local recreation areas rather than focusing entirely on the nation's "great places of nature and great sites of history."[59] Ickes and his assistant secretaries had not wavered in their desire for the Park Service to take over administration of additional reservoir sites developed by the Bureau of Reclamation, including one the latter planned to construct within Dinosaur National Monument.[60] This kind of direction from his immediate supervisor served to weaken the national park "concept" that Drury so often discussed with Merriam, in which the system stood on quality rather than quantity. It also threatened the maintenance of primitive conditions at Dinosaur, a remote unit of the system on the Utah-Colorado border where the prospect of a dam recalled how the sanctity of Yosemite had been violated by the Hetch Hetchy project.[61]

Overcrowding of destinations such as Yosemite Valley before the war posed yet another headache for Drury, because he knew the national parks would face a surge in automobile travel once peace was restored. Like Merriam, Drury's classmate from the University of California Horace Albright did not hesitate to offer counsel. Albright promoted further expansion of the national park system within generally accepted standards of national significance, but in line with his credo of mass access to the parks and relatively few restraints on commercial services offered by concessionaires.[62] Drury turned instead to an old file and found Merriam's "Memorandum Regarding the Primitive" marked confidential. As "a pupil chiding the master," he asked Merriam, "why should truth be held for the select few?" The essay should be distributed widely, Drury contended, and it was "deplorable" how the memorandum had "lain fallow all these years."[63]

CHAPTER 9

What Nature Means

Merriam often referred to his studies as "history," where the change and continuity evident in fossil fragments seemed metaphorical for temporal patterns hidden amid archival records. What Merriam saw as controlling patterns for a history of life on earth derived from the eighteenth-century Enlightenment and was expressed subsequently in the romanticism of Wordsworth and others. It started with discernible natural laws reflecting order imposed by an omnipotent, yet veiled, creative force. Where order represented continuity, "a history of adjustment" brought forth advancement of plants and animals so that progress governed change. This suited a teleological approach to the past, though Merriam's philosophical musings about nature emphasized a larger design in a much stronger and more speculative tone than his scientific writings did. They made frequent reference to modern civilization belonging within a continuum of past and present unified by natural laws "so that all appear as one story."[1]

The validity of directional evolution, particularly where the implied course was progressive, began to be challenged even in the 1930s. Merriam nevertheless thought of the primitive, as the term implies, in reference to progress. As a piece of the past, it also allowed a person to obtain better comprehension of the universe and its basic elements. An observer might even achieve something greater in primitive settings like the Grand Canyon: "When from some commanding point one looks out over the spectacle, not merely is there apparent the true significance in each of a multitude of incidents in order, but the relation of these to each other translates them into an expression of activity extending through time. One sees the mechanism of nature and of history as with

FIGURE 22. Cartoon on the program for the dinner held in honor of Merriam upon his retirement from the Carnegie Institution of Washington, December 8, 1938. (Courtesy of Lawrence C. Merriam, Jr.)

all its parts in operation, and compasses the great complex in a single sweep of vision."[2]

Arriving at this "single sweep of vision" required seeing two fundamental influences in life—truth and beauty—as related, irrespective of their usual separation from each other. Merriam admitted that linking

truth with beauty was hardly new, since the idea could be traced to ancient Greece. Socrates, for example, spoke of a "single science," a unity
of knowledge that made it possible to go from "strength to strength"
to a sudden perception of nature as wondrous beauty, absolute and
everlasting.[3] Merriam often stated that modern science did not elimi-
nate the mystery of nature; as indicative of truth, it only placed "a more
splendid group of elements" within the "picture," thereby adding to
what painters and poets had previously achieved in presenting larger
spiritual meanings.[4] He thought beauty played the dominant role in the
appreciation of nature, because it engaged an individual's imagination
when harmonized through artistic composition. The effectiveness of art
hinged on presentation, particularly if it encompassed the elements of
time, space, power, and movement.[5]

Merriam wrote to Newton Drury at one point about a search for
where the convergence of art, science, and "other attitudes of mind,"
were best displayed. He recalled Mexico City, where the *ahuehuete,* or
"Tule cypress" *(Taxodium mucronatum),* still thrived on the foot of
Chapultepec as living monuments to Aztec civilization. The trees dominated portions of a wide park traversed by paths designed to engage
visitors in contemplation:

> These trails turn in various directions, and so it happens that by a slow
> stream, under spreading cypresses which Montezuma cherished, the way
> of the artists crosses the way of the philosophers. A fountain of excep-
> tional beauty stands near this intersection. Around it are open cases con-
> taining gems of literature. On quiet seats in the shadow of this beauty you
> always find many young adventurers, youths of ten to fifteen years, read-
> ing these books. Each is having through the field of his imagination a
> view of the world of facts and logic described with the artistry and ap-
> preciation of the poet.[6]

The urge to complete a discourse on the influence of nature in
human experience persisted and eventually found expression in a manuscript Merriam started in 1934. He derived its title, *The Garment of
God,* from Goethe's *Faust,* in which, according to the translation by
Thomas Carlyle, the spirit told Faust, " 'Tis thus at the roaring loom of
time I ply and weave for God the garment thou see'st Him by."[7] The
theme of this treatise, published in the early part of 1943, extended the
ideas underpinning his essays in *The Living Past,* but Merriam opted for
examples drawn from his own experience rather than a systematic treatment of its subject. *The Garment of God* thus appeared as a loosely struc-
tured litany about a divine hand in nature, often in reference to a
broader "history" that became most evident through the primitive.

The flat prose and stilted presentation of his main ideas, much of it patched together from previous work, made this second book indicative of Merriam's decline. Sales of the book floundered, yet as late as December 1944 he still hoped to complete two additional manuscripts on the "general movement of evolution as it relates to human progress." He looked to the essays in *The Living Past* as a guide to get himself reoriented while on an extended stay in Pasadena, but he returned to Eugene the following February without making any headway on the manuscripts.[8] Merriam suffered a stroke about six weeks later in combination with uremic poisoning brought on by his worsening prostate condition. Ralph Chaney brought him back to Berkeley, where Charles could take charge of new living arrangements for his father while on leave from his work in Nevada with the U.S. Geological Survey.[9] Merriam began his convalescence in a rest home after a short hospital stay. He lingered for several months, but died in Berkeley on October 30, 1945, from a second stroke.[10]

Memorials by Chaney and Chester Stock appeared in several scientific and humanities journals over the next year or so, each summarizing Merriam's contributions as a scientist, administrator, preservationist, and philosopher.[11] Drury restricted his eulogy, published in *American Forests*, to casting his mentor as a teacher whose place in the conservation movement derived from taking idealism and translating it into concrete action. Many of the achievements of the Save-the-Redwoods League, Drury noted, manifested thoughts about nature expressed by Merriam in his two books. So did the Yavapai Station and Sinnott Memorial, where park visitors gained "a conception of the dramatic story" unfolding before them from a vantage point where "the beholder is guided to see and understand."[12]

Horace Albright wrote to Drury after reading the article in *American Forests* that he felt Merriam had no understanding of the average American traveler.[13] Drury understood the perception behind this comment, given Albright's long-standing advocacy of maximum visitor access to the national parks and his willingness to accommodate a wide range of tastes while he and Stephen Mather ran the National Park Service. If some visitors wanted spiritual uplift, others desired amenities and entertainment. Merriam saw a visit to a national park or a sanctuary such as the redwoods as a fundamentally educational experience with spiritual overtones. He thought the aim of management was to facilitate opportunities for inspiration, so visitors might gain some understanding of, or appreciation for, the great natural forces brought to light by the parks. Perhaps prompted by the qualities of a flower or rock fragment to contemplate the meaning of larger creation, each individual could then find constant delight in nature.

Merriam was adamant that nature could not exert its full influence on people without intellectual or spiritual contact with it. People who spent their time at Yosemite or the Grand Canyon "throwing out from their barren minds projections of monkeys and codfish which they try to see in the marvelously sculptured walls" derived next to nothing from a visit to these places, because their imagination was used in pursuit of trivialities.[14] Preservationists like Merriam are really moralists at heart, as historian Joseph Sax has observed, so visitor behavior has long been a concern to them, because they believe certain types of response to the parks can be redeeming. In his book *Mountains without Handrails*, Sax described preservationists as lay prophets preaching a message of secular salvation; he also pointed out that they must attract at least passive public support to have any effect on park management and policy.[15]

Beginning in the 1920s, Merriam saw the Park Service's tendencies at Yosemite and the Grand Canyon as indicative of a larger organizational trend toward too often emphasizing quantity of visitors instead of the quality of their experience. He wanted to maintain a good relationship with Mather for a number of reasons, but Merriam and Yard fueled a split among the traditional constituents of the Park Service, as the minute number of preservationists diverged from the concessionaires and booster groups who saw national parks primarily in terms of the economic benefits derived from recreational tourism. It may have been an elitist impulse, but for Merriam it had everything to do with the appreciation of nature. Promoting visitation for the sake of exceeding attendance records too often meant damaging the primitive landscapes in parks with more roads and development, since the aim of simply accommodating crowds did not focus on education and spiritual uplift. Merriam could not buy the argument that the Park Service existed to simply protect the parks from logging or other types of extraction, because under that type of management all concerns became equal.

Protecting the primitive so that it might aid the appreciation of nature seemed to remain a higher priority in the redwoods, where Merriam and the league could define what the state acquired as parks and the master plans that shaped their use. In quite another realm of land management, the U.S. Forest Service gained Merriam's blessing for its program to preserve "primitive areas," yet most people assumed that the designation referred to conditions governing access, rather than emphasizing some overriding continuity with the distant past. The larger story Merriam saw in the primitive on Mount Hood or in the Columbia River Gorge did not really factor in passage of the Wilderness Act by Congress in 1964. Public support for wilderness instead centered on the need to save roadless and undeveloped federal land in the national forests from logging and other threats.

President Lyndon Johnson signed the act, which established a National Wilderness Preservation System, on September 3, 1964, but Merriam's advocacy and Forest Service opportunism had created the necessary antecedent. Although primitive areas in the national forests effectively became the parallel system of reserves Albright had feared, and they remained largely immune to land transfers to the Park Service, they also attracted new constituents who liked the idea of a "primitive and unconfined type of recreation" without roads. Their creation through an internal process, however, made primitive areas more susceptible to reclassification (especially once the pressure to cut national forest timber escalated in the 1950s) than the land subsequently protected by legal designation as wilderness. The Park Service, meanwhile, resisted creating its own system of primitive areas largely because Conrad Wirth, who served as director from 1952 to 1963, wanted to retain the agency's discretion in choosing to develop lands placed in his charge. He even opposed passage of the Wilderness Act and thus ran afoul of his boss, Secretary of the Interior Stewart Udall, who drove Wirth into retirement.[16]

Although interpretation did not cause any pronounced shift toward protecting the primitive, it represented Merriam's most pervasive and lasting contribution in the national parks. He helped make interpretation a permanent part of Park Service operations through a committee of distinguished academics, which also represented the forerunner of a permanent advisory board for the national parks, a body authorized by the Historic Sites Act of 1935.[17] Harold Bryant expressed a fair amount of satisfaction with how much the interpretive efforts in the parks had grown after he retired from the Park Service in 1954, even though he believed many employees working in the field settled for dispensing information about park features. As chief naturalist in Washington, D.C., and then superintendent of Grand Canyon National Park, Bryant still lamented that the agency seldom stressed the goal of inspiration, probably because it was so difficult to attain. Even where beauty constituted an overwhelming draw for visitors, as at Crater Lake, it seemed to him that little progress had been made toward helping people come away with a more expansive appreciation of nature.[18]

Freeman Tilden emerged as the genius who formulated "principles" for interpretation and showed how the hidden pattern or revealing generalization constituted a far more effective teaching device than simply communicating facts. His book *Interpreting Our Heritage* became a classic, one whose topical treatment of the subject through examples drawn from the national park system of the 1950s was so successful that Tilden's many admirers considered him to be the "soul" of interpretation.[19] Merriam's link with Tilden was largely that of seeing nature in the same light, as God's "living mantle." They were followers of a literary tradition that reached its height in the nineteenth century and agreed with Shelley (in a line often quoted by Merriam) that "the shadow of some spirit lovelier still" lay behind a tangible and living world that people have not made.[20]

Both men stressed that interpretive presentations had to be delivered in ways that allowed people to judge for themselves what nature meant, but Merriam went further than Tilden in one respect, by orchestrating construction of both the Yavapai Station and Sinnott Memorial. As devices for visitor orientation, these venues were aimed at enhancing the appreciation of nature with the aid of science. Merriam found a place for art in the Sinnott Memorial, yet no one rushed to build similar facilities in other national parks. Visitor centers had arrived by the 1950s, and they became the most recognizable feature in a massive development program called Mission 66, which Wirth successfully promoted throughout the period he served as director.[21] The popularity of visitor centers also corresponded with a more standardized approach to interpretation, one that emphasized efficient handling of general orientation for the crowds that came in ever increasing numbers after World War II.

The Yavapai Station and Sinnott Memorial are listed on the National Register of Historic Places not because they are manifestations of Merriam's ideas about interpretation, but as examples of how to harmonize structures with park landscapes. Although both facilities were deemed worthy of preservation by being listed on the national register, neither attained the higher classification of national historic landmark—one that is far more selective and at least implies greater protection from demolition or unflattering alterations. Ironically, the tower at Desert View achieved this distinction, because of its architecture. In an even greater irony, the national historic landmark status was approved by the permanent advisory board for the national parks—a body descended from the educational committee once chaired by Merriam.[22]

Like many preservationists, Merriam was a self-appointed arbiter of public taste who attempted to mold what society inherited according to his own experience. Research stood at the forefront of this experience, and it represented a third facet of his vision for the parks. Cooperative studies in the John Day Basin during the 1920s provided him with sequels to those collecting expeditions he led more than two decades earlier, but they also provided an impetus for acquiring parkland. Although Merriam touted the basin as a "Mecca" to which many visitors would come "for a vision of time through the ages," state parks in the fossil beds nevertheless languished for three decades after his death.[23] They had little in the way of interpretation for visitors, or even trails, because state priorities for facilities and land acquisition remained fixed on the Oregon coast. Annual visitation at the two state parks in the basin that Merriam helped to instigate never exceeded a combined total of twenty thousand, despite use of Oregon's park system doubling from eleven million visitors in 1960 to more than twenty-two million ten years later. These parks were transferred to the National Park Service in 1975 as part of a new national monument. This move finally brought staff and infrastructure to support interpretation of the John Day Basin and eventually led to a revival of the John Day Associates in 1992. The group quickly emerged as a viable conduit to augmenting ongoing geological and paleontological studies in the basin, mainly because the park superintendent had previously hired a paleontologist who revived the associates and then coordinated the group's work.[24]

Studies made at Point Lobos with Carnegie funding clearly demonstrated how scientific and historical research could serve planning where the need existed to assess impacts or understand threats to the primitive. Like some endeavors that attract foundation support, however, they did not lead to an immediate proliferation of other studies in state and national parks. Agency-funded research in parks did not dawn until the 1960s, and then only in a tentative and piecemeal way. Even Drury, while he served as director, remained skeptical about whether research should have a place in the Park Service, though he expressed this view to Merriam in 1943, four years after the agency lost the few scientists it employed to other federal bureaus through a departmental reorganization ordered by Harold Ickes.[25]

At least Merriam could take solace in the way that studies by Howel Williams and Edison Pettit had exerted their influence at Crater Lake.

Interpretation there even reached beyond park boundaries, once Merriam made some Carnegie Institution money available to Luther Cressman at the University of Oregon for archeological research. Cressman worked in the pluvial lake basins east of Crater Lake, where a discovery of some sandals was made in 1937 at a site roughly eighty miles from the park. Cressman's party unearthed them in Fort Rock Cave, lodged at a point in the stratigraphic column below the layer of volcanic ash originating from Mount Mazama's climactic eruption more than seven thousand years before. This find and others made elsewhere in the region by the University of Oregon group prompted a major revision of the estimates of the length of human occupation in the Pacific Northwest. Conventional wisdom had the presence of ancient peoples stretching back only two millennia, but Cressman made a convincing demonstration through artifacts that Indians had indeed witnessed the cataclysmic event leading to the formation of Crater Lake.[26]

The two CEPOP members stationed at the park had this discovery—and Merriam's facilitation of it—firmly in mind when, shortly after Merriam's death, they began the process of formally naming a viewpoint near the rim in his honor. Merriam had selected the spot years before as the best place for visitors who drove through the park's north entrance to first see Crater Lake, because the point "discloses with explosive suddenness the lake in beauty that is beyond this earth." They would have to walk a short distance to reach it, but the elements of a "stirring story" abounded on all sides so that one's attention would be riveted on "the clear, overpowering picture of force in nature and this conception of time, endless in duration."[27] It seemed a fitting way to honor Merriam, since he did more to "stimulate and further the interpretive program at Crater Lake National Park than any other individual," but the proposed observation platform and trail to it never materialized. "Merriam Point" remains on park maps issued more than a half century later, but it is not marked by signs, much less by any interpretation of the "stirring story" for visitors who reach the spot each summer.[28]

Although a Founders Grove persists in Humboldt Redwoods State Park (where a plaque calls attention to Merriam, along with Henry Fairfield Osborn and Madison Grant), Merriam is not memorialized elsewhere in these great forests. Even his hope that the Save-the-Redwoods League might sponsor research as part of its preservation efforts had to wait until 1997, when the league initiated a grants program.[29] The league nevertheless made his essay "A Living Link in History" available to visitors for more than five decades. As the first in a series of pamphlets

FIGURE 23. An unidentified ranger-naturalist speaking to visitors at the spot later named for Merriam in Crater Lake National Park, 1936. (George Grant, National Park Service Historic Photograph Collection.)

by authorities such as Chaney and Willis Jepson, who were also league councilors, it was sold at cost beginning in 1934. The essay proved to be Merriam's most popular piece, one divided into seven distinct parts, so that each developed a different way to help readers see time in the redwoods. Merriam skillfully blended anecdote with metaphor to reinforce the central theme of continuity with the past, yet he also drew on the simile of light as life in attempting to imbue nature with spiritual meaning. This device allowed him to make his point without labeling it as such, or retreating into abstractions.[30]

Sadly, those virtues did not dominate his subsequent work on the appreciation of nature. The quixotic part of his personality only seemed to get worse with age, all too often leading to the impression of Merriam as opaque or even incoherent.[31] Idealism can be an admirable and effective trait, as Drury attempted to show in an article about Merriam's importance to what the league had achieved, which appeared in the Carnegie Institution testimonial volume of 1938.[32] It recharged Merriam's desire to apply his ideas about the appreciation of nature to the parks, though Tilden was arguably more successful in articulating how to make interpretation relate to visitors' personal experience.[33] Journalists periodically mentioned how Merriam was difficult to approach, let alone interview. As a "highbrow of highbrows," he could push people away rather easily, and those around him soon learned not to ask questions without already having some idea of the answer.[34] Tilden, on the other hand, exhibited a personable demeanor that engaged people and made his audiences feel at ease. It helped him reach the average person, and Tilden also appeared to have a better grasp than Merriam did of what a volunteer could reasonably accomplish in the parks. He chose to restrict his efforts to interpretation, rather than attempting to redirect the focus of management at the same time.[35]

Merriam's importance to the parks may ultimately be tied to his inadvertently raising questions by attempting to supply answers. One of these, for example, has to do with how far definitions go in guiding what a society preserves as its heritage. In the vacuum created by an absence of precise legal language, Merriam tried to apply an ordered and hierarchical structure to public parklands, with the national parks intended to serve a crowning function. Provided they had outstanding educational and inspirational value, exceptional natural features in fully primitive condition were nationally significant. Merriam reasoned that designation of national parks should be restricted to only a few areas, but pressures to expand Park Service jurisdiction during his lifetime brought a variety of new units into the fold. Hot Springs National Park, an area in Arkansas known largely for its public baths, was one; it joined a number of reservoir sites known as "national recreation areas" and the city parks of Washington, D.C., as part of the national park system. Merriam never resolved how to guide the acquisition of state parks (other than to seek a survey like the one Olmsted coordinated in California), but if the federal situation served as any indication, standards rarely governed legislative action.

If what merits preservation is only relative to the shifting winds of politics, then who should control how the parks are run? Merriam saw these places as useful reference points in guiding the thought of average citizens and wanted the advice of technical experts to prevail in planning a national park system that served as a "super-university of nature." He urged that external boards, not staff, formulate policy with the assistance of advisory committees that reinforced the primacy of education and inspiration in the parks. Depending on the threat or opportunity at hand, the composition of such committees would vary, with their carefully considered findings provided for the use of board members who might also be technical experts themselves. Transmuting the practices of foundations and academia has precedent in government, if only in the short run with blue-ribbon panels or commissions that study projected needs, such as outdoor recreation. These commissions' findings can serve as the basis for governmental policy decisions, but inertia and even opposition can govern how bureaucracies respond to decisions made beyond the agency. Group norms and values in the National Park Service, as well as in most state park organizations, favor a line authority vested in a few generalists who can sometimes make policy decisions. This preference reflects the circumstances in which these agencies were born, and that genesis rarely accorded technical experts a leading role.

Perhaps the most compelling question of all concerns just what is preserved in the parks. As a kind of window on the past, the parks epitomized the beauty and order that Merriam—and others stretching back to ancient Greece—thought had always pervaded the world. He also believed these sanctuaries could restore a kind of unity between people and nature, especially if the primitive were patently evident.[36] The vast gulf between a human life span and the past stretching across eons, however, makes it difficult for many people to grasp the primitive in the way he used the term. For them, the idea of seeing a living past in the present seems inconceivable, though Merriam often admitted that experiencing natural beauty constituted reason enough to visit a park, since it also possessed the power to inspire.

Notes

Abbreviations Used in the Notes

CIWF	Carnegie Institution of Washington files, Washington, D.C.
JCMP	John C. Merriam papers, Library of Congress, Washington, D.C.
MMSF	Merriam manuscript file, Crater Lake National Park Museum and Archives Collections
MPBL	John C. Merriam papers (C-B 970), Bancroft Library, University of California, Berkeley
MPBL/A	John C. Merriam additions (mss. 70/100c), Bancroft Library, University of California, Berkeley
OPRD	Oregon Parks and Recreation Department files, Salem, Oregon
RLBL	Save-the-Redwoods League papers (C-A 284), Bancroft Library, University of California, Berkeley
ROHO	Regional Oral History Office interview, Bancroft Library, University of California, Berkeley
SCML	Special Collections, Mazamas Library, Portland, Oregon
SCUO	Special Collections, University of Oregon Library, Eugene

Introduction

1. These fossilized trees were deciduous, or "dawn," redwoods (*Metasequoia* spp.), not *Sequoia sempervirens;* see Ralph W. Chaney, "Ancient Forests of Oregon," in *Ancient Oregon* (Eugene: University of Oregon Press, 2001), 22–33.

2. John C. Merriam, *The Highest Uses of the Redwoods: Messages to the Council of the Save-the-Redwoods League, 1922–1941* (San Francisco: Save-the-Redwoods League, 1941). The essay first appeared as "Forest Windows" in the June 1928 issue of *Scribner's* magazine and was revised and republished as "A Living Link in History," chapter 4 in Merriam, *The Living Past* (New York: Charles Scribner's Sons, 1930).

3. Denis E. Cosgrove, *Social Formation and Symbolic Landscape* (Madison: University of Wisconsin Press, 1998), 142–60.

4. Susan Lasdun, *The English Park: Royal, Private, and Public* (New York: Vendome Press, 1992), 135–86.

5. Act of June 30, 1864 (13 U.S. Stat. 325); for more details, see Alfred Runte, *Yosemite: The Embattled Wilderness* (Lincoln: University of Nebraska Press, 1990), 21–22.

6. Frederick Law Olmsted, "The Yosemite Valley and the Mariposa Big Trees: A Preliminary Report" (1865) in *Landscape Architecture* 43 (October 1952), 17, 22–23; the passage is also quoted by Alfred Runte, "Prospect," *Landscape Architecture* 81, no. 3 (March 1991): 136.

7. Paul Shepard, *Man in the Landscape: A Historical View of the Esthetics of Nature* (New York: Knopf, 1967), 136.

8. John Muir, *Our National Parks* (Boston: Houghton Mifflin, 1901), 1.

9. Thurman Wilkins, *John Muir: Apostle of Nature* (Norman: University of Oklahoma Press, 1995), 159–68.

10. A full bibliography of Merriam's work can be found in Chester Stock, "Memorial to John Campbell Merriam," *Proceedings Volume of the Geological Society of America, Annual Report for 1946* (Washington, D.C.: The Geological Society of America, 1947), 183–97.

11. Stephen Fox, *John Muir and His Legacy: The American Conservation Movement* (Boston: Little, Brown and Company, 1981), 144.

1. Why Save the Redwoods?

1. John B. Dewitt, *California Redwood Parks and Preserves* (San Francisco: Save-the-Redwoods League, 1985), 4–6.

2. *Touring Topics* 24 (August 1932), p. 9, cited in Earl Pomeroy, *In Search of the Golden West: The Tourist in Western America* (Lincoln: University of Nebraska Press, 1990), 223.

3. Frank F. Flaherty, "Thousands See Bull Creek Park Dedicated," *Eureka Standard,* September 14, 1931, 1–2.

4. Ibid.

5. Ibid.

6. As published in John C. Merriam, *The Highest Uses of the Redwoods: Messages to the Council of the Save-the-Redwoods League, 1922–1941* (San Francisco: Save-the-Redwoods League, 1941), 17.

7. Flaherty, "Bull Creek Park," 2.

8. Newton B. Drury, "Transmuting Science into Conservation," in *Cooperation in Research,* publication 501 (Washington, D.C.: Carnegie Institution of Washington, 1938), 762.

9. John C. Merriam, "A Living Link in History," in Merriam, *The Living Past* (New York: Charles Scribner's Sons, 1930), 58.

10. John C. Merriam, "Suggestions Regarding Educational Program of Grand Canyon," in *Individual Reports of Members of the Committee on Educational Problems in National Parks* (Washington, D.C.: W. F. Roberts, 1932), 17–23.

11. Drury, "Transmuting Science," 756.

12. John C. Merriam, "National Policy on Historic Sites," excerpt from remarks at the meeting of the American Association for the Advancement of Science in Boston, December 28, 1933, 1, MMSF.

13. Ibid.

14. Chester Stock, "John Campbell Merriam as Scientist and Philosopher," in Staff Members and Research Associates, *Cooperation in Research,* publication 501 (Washington, D.C.: Carnegie Institution of Washington, 1938), 776.

15. John C. Merriam, *Parks: National and State* (Washington, D.C.: W. F. Roberts, 1932), 9, revised from an address before the National Conference on Outdoor Recreation, Washington, D.C., January 30, 1926, which appeared as "The Responsibility of Federal and State Governments for Recreation," *National Parks Bulletin* 7, no. 49 (March 1926): 5–8.

16. Harold C. Bryant, "John Campbell Merriam—A Biography" (c. 1960 typescript), 16, MMSF.

17. Speech by Lawrence C. Merriam, Jr., at a ceremony marking the seventy-fifth anniversary of the Save-the-Redwoods League, in Humboldt Redwoods State Park, October 3, 1993.

18. Merriam, *The Living Past,* 70.

2. To Berkeley and Beyond

1. William E. Corbin, *A Star for Patriotism: Iowa's Outstanding Civil War College* (Monticello, IA: published by the author, 1972), 3–6.

2. Lawrence C. Merriam, Jr., "The Merriam Family in the United States," and "The Meriam/Merriam Family to JCM," typescripts, MMSF; see also Charles Henry Pope and John Merriam Kinsbury, *Merriam Genealogy in England and America* (Ithaca, NY: Bullbrier Press, 1988).

3. See Corbin, *A Star for Patriotism,* 208–70, for details about Hopkinton's contribution to the war effort.

4. Susan Agnes Merriam Gearhart, handwritten narrative on Margaret Kirkwood Merriam, ca. 1945, in possession of Margaret Gearhart Johnston, Springville, Iowa.

5. John C. Merriam, "Educational Values of Recreation," *Educational Record* 13, no. 4 (October 1932): 253.

6. John C. Merriam, "The Place of Research in the Progress of the Next Generation," *University of Iowa Studies,* n.s., 194, Series on Aims and Progress of Research, no. 33, January 31, 1931, 75.

7. John C. Merriam, "The Inquiring Mind in a Changing World," *Rice Institute Pamphlet* 21, no. 3 (July 1934): 197; William S. Barton, "Mt. Wilson's Unknown Man," *Los Angeles Times Sunday Magazine,* July 25, 1937, 7.

8. Barry D. Karl, *Charles E. Merriam and the Study of Politics* (Chicago: University of Chicago Press, 1974), 18–19.

9. Ibid., 20.

10. Ibid., 14–16.

11. "John Campbell Merriam," autobiographical typescript dated September 1, 1944, 15, MMSF; John C. Merriam to Charles W. Merriam, November 27, 1929, 1–2, MMSF.

12. Michael L. Smith, *Pacific Visions: California Scientists and the Environment, 1850–1915* (New Haven: Yale University Press, 1987), 43–45.

13. Ibid., 157–58.

14. John C. Merriam, "The Geological Work of Professor Joseph Le Conte," *University of California Magazine* 7 (September 1901): 214.

15. Alfred Romer, "Cope versus Marsh," *Systematic Zoology* 13, no. 4 (December 1961): 201–7; David Rains Wallace, *The Bonehunters' Revenge: Dinosaurs, Greed, and the Greatest Scientific Feud of the Gilded Age* (Boston: Houghton Mifflin, 1999).

16. Frank Wilson, "Landscapes: A Geologic Diary," in *Kansas Geology,* ed. Rex Buchanan (Lawrence: University Press of Kansas, 1984), 33.

17. Merriam to Heim, November 17, 1905, Box 1, MPBL.

18. John C. Merriam, "Ueber die Pythonomorphen der Kansas-Kriede," *Palaeontographica* 41 (1894), 1–39.

19. Theodore Catton, *Wonderland: An Administrative History of Mount Rainier National Park* (Seattle: National Park Service, 1996), 47–48.

20. "John Campbell Merriam," 16–17.

3. Paleontologist of the Far West

1. "John Campbell Merriam," autobiographical typescript dated September 1, 1944, 17, MMSF.

2. Utica (N.Y.) *Observer,* October 4, 1901, quoted in John A. Douglass, "Shared Governance at UC: An Historical Review," p. 2, University of California, Santa Barbara, October 23, 1995, AAD Web site, http://aad.english.ucsb.edu/ucgovern (accessed May 17, 2004).

3. Merriam, "Sigmogomphis Le Contei, A New Castoroid Rodent from the Pliocene near Berkeley, California," *University of California Bulletin of the Department of Geology* 1, no. 13 (February 1896): 363–70.

4. Chester Stock, "John Campbell Merriam as Scientist and Philosopher," in Staff Members and Research Associates, *Cooperation in Research,* publication 501 (Washington, D.C.: Carnegie Institution of Washington, 1938), 766.

5. John C. Merriam, "On Some Reptilian Remains from the Triassic of Northern California," *American Journal of Science,* 2nd ser., 50, no. 395 (1895): 55–57.

6. "John Campbell Merriam," 17.

7. Ronald Rainger, *An Agenda for Antiquity: Henry Fairfield Osborn and Vertebrate Paleontology at the American Museum of Natural History* (Tuscaloosa: University of Alabama Press, 1992), 19–20.

8. Stock, "Merriam as Scientist and Philosopher," 769–70.

9. Thomas Condon, "The Rocks of the John Day Valley," *Overland Monthly* 6, no. 5 (May 1871): 393–98.

10. O. C. Marsh, "Notice of New Equine Mammals from the Tertiary Formation," *American Journal of Science and Art,* 3rd ser., 7 (March 1874): 251–54; see also Ellen T. Drake, "Horse Genealogy: The Oregon Connection," *Oregon Geology* 6 (October 1978): 587–91.

11. Loye Miller, *Lifelong Boyhood: Recollections of a Naturalist Afield* (Berkeley: University of California Press, 1950), 123.

12. John C. Merriam, "Report on the Expedition to the John Day Fossil Beds," *University Chronicle* 2, no. 3 (August 1899): 224.

13. John C. Merriam, "A Contribution to the Geology of the John Day Basin," *University of California Bulletin of the Department of Geology* 2, no. 9 (April 1901): 269–314.

14. John C. Merriam, "The John Day Fossil Beds," *Harper's Monthly Magazine* 102, no. 60 (March 1901): 590–91.

15. John C. Merriam and William J. Sinclair, "Tertiary Faunas of the John Day Region," *University of California Bulletin of the Department of Geology* 5, no. 11 (1907): 171.

16. He made several unsuccessful pleas to the U.S. Geological Survey beginning in 1907; Merriam to George Otis Smith, USGS Director, May 7, 1907, Box 1, MPBL.

17. David T. Mason, "Time to a Forester," *Oregon Historical Quarterly* 58, no. 4 (1957): 360.

18. Barbara R. Stein, *On Her Own Terms: Annie Montague Alexander and the Rise of Science in the American West* (Berkeley and Los Angeles: University of California Press, 2001), 24–29.

19. "Annie Montague Alexander, Benefactress of UCMP," biographical narrative portion of the finding aid for the Alexander Papers, University of California Museum of Paleontology, Berkeley, 1998.

20. John C. Merriam, "Triassic Ichthyosauria, with Special Reference to the American Forms," *University of California, Memoirs* 1, no. 1 (1908): 1–196. For more about Alexander's benefaction to Merriam, see Stein, *On Her Own Terms,* 29–30 and 165–66.

21. Stock, "Merriam as Scientist and Philosopher," 767–68.

22. "Saurian Expedition of 1905," UCMP Web site, www.ucmp.berkeley.edu/archives (accessed January 29, 1999); John C. Merriam, "The Skull and Dentition of a Primitive Ichthyosaurian from the Middle Triassic," *University of California Bulletin of the Department of Geology* 5, no. 24 (1910): 381. For an ac-

count of the expedition from Alexander's diary, see Janet Lewis Zullo, "Annie Montague Alexander, Her Work in Paleontology," *Journal of the West* 8 (1969): 185–96.

23. Alexander to Merriam, October 23, 1905, and Merriam to Alexander, January 22, 1906, Box 1, MPBL.

24. Douglass, "Shared Governance at UC," 2–3.

25. John C. Merriam, "Recent Discoveries of Quaternary Mammals in Southern California," *Science,* n.s., 24, no. 608 (August 24, 1906): 248–50.

26. J. M. Harris and G. T. Jefferson, eds., *Rancho La Brea: Treasures of the Tar Pits* (Los Angeles: Natural History Museum of Los Angeles County, 1985); John C. Merriam, "The Fauna of Rancho La Brea: Part I. Occurrence," *University of California, Memoirs* 1, no. 2 (November 1911): 197–213.

27. Merriam to Wheeler, January 21, 1907, Box 1, MPBL.

28. John C. Merriam, "Death Trap of the Ages," *Sunset Magazine* 21, no. 6 (October 1908): 465–75. This periodical was started by the Southern Pacific Railroad to promote tourism on the West Coast, especially in California.

29. Ibid., 465.

30. Merriam to Miller, January 16, 1909; Merriam to Hancock, January 29, 1909; Merriam to Miller, February 19, 1909, all in Box 1, MPBL.

31. Merriam to James Perrin Smith, July 7, 1909, Box 1, MPBL; Stock, "Memorial to John Campbell Merriam," 187; Lawrence C. Merriam, Jr., interview with the author, February 6, 1999.

32. John C. Merriam, "The Occurrence of Middle Tertiary Mammal-Bearing Beds in Northwestern Nevada," *Science,* n.s., 26, no. 664 (September 20, 1907): 380–82.

33. John C. Merriam, "Tertiary Mammal Beds of Virgin Valley and Thousand Creek in Northwestern Nevada, Part II: Vertebrate Faunas," *University of California Bulletin of the Department of Geology* 6, no. 11 (September 1911): 199–304.

34. John C. Merriam, "A Collection of Mammalian Remains from Tertiary Beds on the Mohave Desert," *University of California Bulletin of the Department of Geology* 6, no. 7 (April 1911): 167.

35. Merriam to Harry Torrey [Reed College, Portland], December 23, 1912, Box 3, MPBL.

36. Merriam to Wheeler, March 11 and March 13, 1912, Box 3, MPBL.

37. Verne A. Stadtman, *The University of California, 1868–1968* (New York: McGraw-Hill, 1970), 207.

38. Harold C. Bryant, "John Campbell Merriam—A Biography," 3, MMSF.

39. Merriam to Bryant, December 2, 1912, Box 3, MPBL.

40. Merriam to Francis H. Bird [Madison, Wis.] April 27, 1912, Box 3, MPBL.

41. Michael L. Smith, *Pacific Visions: California Scientists and the Environment, 1850–1915* (New Haven: Yale University Press, 1987), 144–50.

42. Merriam to Muir, October 2, 1906, Box 1, MPBL.

43. Merriam to Frank K. Mott [Oakland mayor's office], November 23, 1912, and Merriam to W. S. Gould [Oakland park board], April 14, 1913, Box 3, MPBL.

4. An Upward Trajectory

1. Two examples of Merriam's descriptive work are "The Skull and Dentition of a Camel from the Pleistocene Rancho La Brea," *University of California Bulletin of the Department of Geology* 7, no. 14 (May 24, 1913): 305–23, and "New Protohippine Horses from Tertiary Beds on the Western Border of the Mohave Desert," *University of California Bulletin of the Department of Geology* 7, no. 23 (December 22, 1913): 435–41. Merriam focused more on synthesis two years later; see "Extinct Faunas of the Mohave Desert, Their Significance in a Study of the Origin and Evolution of Life in America," *Popular Science Monthly* 86, no. 3 (March 1915): 245–64.

2. John C. Merriam, "Significant Features in the History of Life on the Pacific Coast," in *Nature and Science on the Pacific Coast*, ed. Joseph Grinnell (San Francisco: Paul Elder, 1915), 88–103.

3. Lynne Withey, *Grand Tours and Cook's Tours: A History of Leisure Travel, 1850 to 1915* (New York: Morrow, 1997), 338–40; Smith, *Pacific Visions*, 186–88.

4. Merriam to Alexander, August 20, 1915, MMSF.

5. Merriam to Matthew, July 13, 1915, MMSF.

6. Merriam to C. Hart Merriam, December 11, 1907, Box 1, MPBL; Merriam to Francis H. Bird, April 27, 1912, Box 2, MPBL.

7. Rainger, *An Agenda for Antiquity*, 117–18.

8. Despite Merriam's prodding, county officials did not develop the donated park site until the 1960s; Ray Zemen, "County Will Keep Pledge on Tar Pits," *Los Angeles Times*, November 10, 1963, C-6.

9. Merriam to N. B. Drury, November 2, 1917, Box 4, MPBL.

10. Merriam to Stock, August 2, 1916, Box 4, MPBL; Chester Stock, "Oregon's Wonderland of the Past—The John Day," *Scientific Monthly* 63 (July 1946): 64.

11. The proposal appeared as an editorial in the John Day *Blue Mountain Eagle* on December 1, 1916.

12. Merriam to Childs Frick, August 4, 1917, Box 75, JCMP.

13. Merriam to Osborn, February 13, 1917, MMSF.

14. Letter signed by Merriam, Osborn, and Grant to William D. Stephens, governor of California, August 9, 1917, cited in Joseph H. Engbeck, Jr., *State Parks of California from 1864 to the Present* (Portland, OR: Graphic Arts Center, 1980), 41–42.

15. Mather to Merriam, March 11, 1918, Save-the-Redwoods League office, San Francisco.

16. Robert Shankland, *Steve Mather of the National Parks* (New York: Knopf, 1951), 193–94.

17. Engbeck, *State Parks of California,* 42; Madison Grant, "Saving the Redwoods: An Account of the Movement during 1919 to Preserve the Redwoods of California," [New York] *Zoological Society Bulletin* 22, no. 5 (September 1919): 116.

18. Victoria Thomas Olson, "Pioneer Conservationist A. P. Hill: He Saved the Redwoods," *American West* 14, no. 5 (September–October 1977), 32–40.

19. Shankland, *Steve Mather of the National Parks,* 71; Gilbert Grosvenor, "Our Big Trees Saved," *National Geographic* 34, no. 1 (January 1917): 1–5.

20. Madison Grant, "Saving the Redwoods," *National Geographic* 37, no. 6 (June 1920): 529.

21. Engbeck, *State Parks of California,* 43; Grant, "Saving the Redwoods," *Zoological Society Bulletin,* 110.

22. Grant, "Saving the Redwoods," *Zoological Society Bulletin,* 116.

23. Grant, "Saving the Redwoods," *National Geographic Magazine,* 534.

24. Ibid., 527.

25. Drury to Mather, October 20, 1920, Box 1, RLBL.

26. Drury to Merriam, January 19, 1921, Box 1, RLBL.

27. Lon Spharler, "Newton Bishop Drury—Park System Executive" (master's thesis, Sacramento State College, 1968), 7.

28. Merriam to Drury, February 10, 1921, and Merriam to J. C. Sperry, February 10, 1921, Box 1, RLBL. Merriam by that time also headed committees on conservation for the National Academy of Sciences, the National Research Council, and the American Association for the Advancement of Science.

29. Merriam to Drury, November 2, 1917, Box 4, MPBL.

30. Robert E. Kohler, *Partners in Science: Foundations and Natural Scientists, 1900–1945* (Chicago: University of Chicago Press, 1991), 82–83.

31. Ibid., 72–75.

32. Ellis L. Yochelson, "Charles Doolittle Walcott," *NAS Biographical Memoirs* 34 (1967): 508. Some eighty-five years later, more than seven thousand people serve on study committees of the National Research Council at any one time, all on a volunteer basis. It is now the principal operating agency of the National Academy of Sciences and remains a nonprofit organization under the congressional charter that established the academy. The American Association for the Advancement of Science has grown to encompass twenty-four disciplinary sections, with its Pacific Division being the oldest and largest of the four geographic divisions, boasting roughly twenty-seven thousand members.

33. Kohler, *Partners in Science,* 84–87.

34. Alexander to Wheeler, March 5, 1919, MMSF; Verne A. Stadtman, *The University of California, 1868–1968* (New York: McGraw-Hill, 1970), 365.

35. Stadtman, *University of California,* 239–53.

36. Howard S. Miller, *Dollars for Research: Science and Its Patrons in Nineteenth-Century America* (Seattle: University of Washington Press, 1970), 166–81.

37. Kohler, *Partners in Science*, 63.

38. Merriam to Walcott, May 17, 1920, MMSF.

39. "Annie Montague Alexander: Benefactress of UCMP," biographical narrative portion of the finding aid for the Alexander Papers, University of California Museum of Paleontology, Berkeley, 1998, 2.

40. Merriam to Barrows, September 3, 1920, Box 3, JCMP.

41. "Annie Montague Alexander," 2; Barrows to Alexander, March 14, 1921, UCMP Web site, www.ucmp.berkeley.edu/archives (accessed January 29, 1999).

42. John C. Merriam, "Annual Report on the Work of the Department of Palaeontology, University of California, for the year ending June 30, 1920," 3, MMSF.

5. Redwoods and Research

1. Rosalie Edge (1938) and Paul Sears (1964) quoted in Stephen Fox, *John Muir and His Legacy: The American Conservation Movement* (Boston: Little, Brown 1981), 334.

2. James M. Goode, *Best Addresses* (Washington, D.C.: Smithsonian Institution Press, 1988), 151–57.

3. A much more detailed description of the administration building is in Sue A. Kohler and Jeffrey R. Carson, *Sixteenth Street Architecture* (Washington D.C.: Commission of Fine Arts, 1988), 289–315.

4. Andrew Carnegie, "The Gospel of Wealth," *North American Review* 148, no. 391 (June 1889): 653, 657–62.

5. Barbara Howe, "The Emergence of Scientific Philanthropy, 1900–1920," in *Philanthropy and Cultural Imperialism,* ed. Robert Arnove (Bloomington: Indiana University Press, 1982), 31.

6. Ellis L. Yochelson, *Charles Doolittle Walcott, 1850–1927* (New York: Columbia University Press, 1967), 491–92.

7. Ellis L. Yochelson, "Mr. Carnegie's Chairman," in *Carnegie Evening 1996* (Washington, D.C.: Carnegie Institution of Washington, 1996), 7.

8. John C. Merriam, grant application (1905), Box 1, MPBL.

9. Kohler, *Partners in Science*, 19–23.

10. John C. Merriam, "The Carnegie Institution of Washington," in *Forschungsinstitute, ihre Geschichte, Organisation und Ziele,* ed. Ludolph Brauer et al. (Hamburg: Paul Hertung Verlag, 1929); see also *Published Papers and Addresses of John Campbell Merriam* (Washington D.C.: Carnegie Institution of Washington, 1938), vol. 4, 2504–6.

11. John C. Merriam, "Fellowships," *Carnegie Institution of Washington Year Book* 22 (1923), 12.

12. John C. Merriam, "The Quarter Century Mark," *Carnegie Institution of Washington Year Book* 26 (1927), 5–6.

13. Merriam to Alexander, May 5, 1922, Box 3, JCMP. A letter to Alexander written more than a year earlier (April 15, 1921) emphasized the same theme.

14. Merriam to Buwalda, February 8, 1923, Box 30, JCMP.

15. Merriam to Stock, June 15, 1923, Box 169, JCMP.

16. Ralph Chaney, "John Campbell Merriam," *Year Book of the American Philosophical Society,* 1945, 383–84.

17. Harold C. Bryant, "John Campbell Merriam—A Biography," 16, MMSF.

18. See Ralph Chaney, "Quantitative Studies of the Bridge Creek Flora," *American Journal of Science,* 5th ser., 8, no. 44 (August 1924): 127–44, and Chaney, *A Comparative Study of the Bridge Creek Flora and the Modern Redwood Forest* (Washington D.C.: *Carnegie Institution of Washington,*1925). Subsequent discovery of living *Metasequoia* species in China led to a revision of the original assumption about fossilized coast redwood at Bridge Creek; see Chaney, *The Ancient Forests of Oregon* (Eugene: Oregon State System of Higher Education, 1956), vi, 26–33. Chaney unfortunately time-averaged his samples and thus combined an oak-sycamore forest, a *Metasequoia* swamp, and an alder-dominated woodland into one composite. He thus missed a detailed series of long-term events more significant than his comparison with the modern Muir Woods.

19. John C. Merriam et al., "The Pleistocene Rattlesnake Formation and Fauna of Eastern Oregon, with Notes on the Rattlesnake and Mascall Deposits," paper 3, publication 347 (Washington, D.C.: Carnegie Institution of Washington, 1925), 43–92; John C. Merriam and Chester Stock, "A Hyaenarctid Bear from the Later Tertiary of the John Day Basin of Oregon," paper 3, publication 346 (Washington D.C.: Carnegie Institution of Washington, 1927), 39–44.

20. John Buwalda, "Paleontological and Geological Investigations in the John Day Region of Eastern Oregon," *Science* 66, no. 1701 (August 5, 1927): 135–36.

21. Merriam to Buwalda, August 6, 1927, Box 30, JCMP.

22. Buwalda to Merriam, August 11, 1927, Box 30, JCMP.

23. Thomas R. Cox, *The Park Builders: A History of State Parks in the Pacific Northwest* (Seattle: University of Washington Press, 1988), 32–41.

24. Kent to Drury, August 25, 1921, Carton 1, RLBL.

25. Minutes of [Save-the-Redwoods League] Annual Meeting, September 8, 1925, Carton 1, RLBL.

26. John C. Merriam, "Messages to the Council, Save-the-Redwoods League, 1922," in *Highest Uses of the Redwoods* (San Francisco: Save-the-Redwoods League, 1941), 3.

27. Earl Pomeroy, *In Search of the Golden West* (New York: Knopf, 1957), 127.

28. Drury to Merriam, May 10, 1924, Carton 1, RLBL.

29. Engbeck, *State Parks of California,* 44–45.

30. Drury (quoting Merriam) to Kent, March 26, 1923, Carton 1, RLBL.

31. Drury to Merriam, May 27, 1925, Carton 2, RLBL.

32. Drury to Merriam, April 30, 1925, and May 29, 1925, Carton 2, RLBL.

33. Merriam to Drury, June 3, 1925, Carton 2, RLBL.

34. Newton B. Drury, "Outline of Projects of the Save-the-Redwoods League," August 25, 1927, MMSF.

35. Merriam to Drury, May 12, 1924, and October 9, 1926, Cartons 1–2, RLBL.

36. Paul Redington et al., "Report on Investigation for Proposed Redwood National Park, California, [1921]," 14–30, MMSF.

37. Greeley to Drury, August 15, 1922, Carton 1, RLBL.

38. Drury to Merriam, May 8, 1925, Carton 1, RLBL.

39. Merriam, Minutes of Annual Meeting, Save-the-Redwoods League, September 8, 1925, Carton 2, RLBL.

40. Redington, "Report on Investigation," 30–34.

41. Willis Jepson and W. A. Cannon, "Two Scientists' Views on Bull Creek Flat," in *Saving the Redwoods 1924–1925* (Berkeley: Save-the-Redwoods League, 1925), 25.

42. Merriam to Drury, [1921], Carton 1, RLBL.

43. John C. Merriam, "Scientific Research Applied to Reforestation," in *Saving the Redwoods 1924–1925,* 27–29; Minutes of Annual Meeting, Save-the-Redwoods League, September 8, 1925, Carton 2, RLBL.

44. Drury to Merriam, August 11, August 27, October 14, and November 1, 1926, Carton 2, RLBL.

45. Robert Shankland, *Steve Mather of the National Parks* (New York: Knopf, 1951), 184–88.

46. John C. Merriam, "Parks as an Opportunity and Responsibility of the States," *State Recreation* 2, no. 4 (August 1928): 10–15. He gave the address on June 6, 1928.

47. Thomas R. Dunlap, *Nature and the English Diaspora: Environment and History in the United States, Canada, Australia, and New Zealand* (New York: Cambridge University Press, 1999), 21–45.

48. John C. Merriam, "The Cave of the Magic Pool," *Scribner's Magazine* 82, no. 3 (1927): 272; republished, with some revisions, as "The Meaning of a Fragment," in Merriam, *The Living Past* (New York: Charles Scribner's Sons, 1930), 3–26.

49. John C. Merriam, "Recent Cave Explorations in California," *American Anthropologist,* 2nd ser., 8 (April–June 1906): 221–28.

50. John C. Merriam, "The Story of a Leaf," *Scribner's Magazine* 81, no. 2 (February 1927): 130.

51. Ibid., 132.

52. Merriam to Lawrence C. Merriam, October 21, 1925, and Merriam to Greeley, November 16, 1925, MMSF.

53. Merriam to Drury, November 29, 1927, Carton 2, RLBL.

54. Merriam, "Forest Windows," *Scribner's Magazine* 83, no. 6 (June 1927): 733–37.

55. Drury to Merriam, February 3, 1928, Carton 2, RLBL.

56. E. P. Meinecke, *[A Report upon] The Effect of Excessive Tourist Travel on the California Redwood Parks* (Sacramento: California State Printing Office, 1928), 12.

6. Interpreting the National Parks

1. Earl Pomeroy, *In Search of the Golden West: The Tourist in Western America* (Lincoln: University of Nebraska Press, 1990), 199–211; Hal K. Rothman, *Devil's Bargains: Tourism in the Twentieth-Century American West* (Lawrence: University Press of Kansas, 1998), 144–53.

2. John C. Miles, *Guardians of the Parks: A History of the National Parks and Conservation Association* (Washington, D.C.: Taylor and Francis, 1995), 13–24.

3. Miles, *Guardians of the Parks,* 44–48.

4. Barry Mackintosh, "Interpretation in the National Park Service: A Historical Perspective" (Washington D.C.: National Park Service History Division, 1986), 10.

5. Stephen T. Mather, *Report of the Director of the National Park Service* (Washington, D.C.: Government Printing Office, 1926), 8–9.

6. Stephen T. Mather, *Report of the Director of the National Park Service* (Washington, D.C.: Government Printing Office 1920), 113.

7. John C. Merriam, "The Responsibility of Federal and State Governments for Recreation," *National Parks Bulletin* 7, no. 49 (March 1926): 5–8.

8. Ibid.

9. Ibid.

10. Ibid.

11. Mather, *Report of the Director,* 1926, 7–8.

12. Albright to J. E. Haynes, Acting Director, Yellowstone Museum, February 9, 1926, Box 3, JCMP.

13. Robert S. Yard, "Historical Basis of National Park Standards," *National Parks Bulletin* 10, no. 57 (November 1929): 5; also cited in Miles, *Guardians of the Parks,* 73–74.

14. Yard to Merriam, July 1, 1926, p. 3, Box 186, JCMP.

15. National Parks and Education announcement [February 1927], Box 186, JCMP.

16. John C. Merriam, "Ancient Footprints in the Grand Canyon," *Scribner's Magazine* 79, no. 1 (January 1926): 77–82. Also titled "Footprints in the Path of History" and reprinted in Merriam, *The Living Past* (New York: Charles Scribner's Sons, 1930), 101–2.

17. John C. Merriam, "Elements Involved in Appreciation of Nature," May 10, 1932, Carton 3, MS Misc., file (2), MPBL/A. Interview with Harold C. Bryant and Newton B. Drury by Amelia Fry, "Development of the Naturalist Program in the National Park Service," ROHO, 1964, 23–24.

18. Merriam to Charles W. Merriam, April 11, 1928, MMSF.

19. Merriam to Charles W. Merriam, April 30, 1928, MMSF.

20. Merriam to Charles W. Merriam, June 16, 1928, MMSF.

21. U.S. Department of the Interior, *Extract from Report by the Secretary of the Interior Related to the National Park Service* (Washington, D.C.: Government Printing Office, 1928), 3; Robert Shankland, *Steve Mather of the National Parks* (New York: Knopf, 1951), 262.

22. John C. Merriam, "Suggestions Regarding Educational Program of Grand Canyon," in *Reports on Studies of Educational Problems in National Parks* (Washington, D.C.: Privately printed, 1929), 20–23; also in *Published Papers and Addresses of John Campbell Merriam,* vol. 4 (Washington, D.C.: Carnegie Institution of Washington, 1938), 2207–8.

23. John C. Merriam, "Memorandum Concerning Function of National Parks," October 17, 1928, MMSF.

24. Stephen T. Mather, *Report of the Director of the National Park Service* (Washington, D.C.: Government Printing Office, 1918), 273–74.

25. "Report of Educational Committee," in Horace Albright, *Report of the Director of the National Park Service* (Washington, D.C.: Government Printing Office, 1929), 12–13.

26. Ibid.

27. Bryant to Cramton, February 24, 1931, Box 26, JCMP.

28. Merriam to Bryant, August 30, 1930, Box 26, JCMP.

29. Edwin McKee, "The Coconino Sandstone—Its History and Origin," in Publication 440 (Washington, D.C.: Carnegie Institution of Washington, 1933), 78–115.

30. John C. Merriam, "Relation of Aesthetic to Scientific Study in an Educational Program at Crater Lake," memorandum of June 14, 1931, MMSF.

31. Merriam to Merel S. Sager, National Park Service, July 29, 1930, MMSF.

32. John C. Merriam, *A Brief Guide to the Parapet Views, Sinnott Memorial, Crater Lake National Park* (Washington, D.C.: Carnegie Institution of Washington, 1933), 1–2.

33. John C. Merriam, "Crater Lake," memorandum of May 18, 1931, MMSF.

34. Merriam to Ansel Hall, June 14, 1931, Box 88, JCMP.

35. Dick Neuberger, "Art and Science to Join Experiment This Year," *Oregonian* (Portland), November 15, 1931; Worth Ryder, "Report of Survey of Crater Lake National Park," August 1932, MMSF.

36. Merriam to Bryant, April 11, 1936, Box 26, JCMP.

37. Hall to Merriam, September 30, 1932, Box 88, JCMP.

38. Bill Belknap and Frances Spencer Belknap, *Gunnar Widforss: Painter of the Grand Canyon* (Flagstaff, AZ: Northland Press, 1969), 38–39.

39. John C. Merriam, "Human Values in Primitive Nature," preface to "Protection and Use of the Primitive," by Robert Sterling Yard, ca. 1932, MMSF.

40. John C. Merriam, *Parks: National and State* (Washington, D.C.: W. F. Roberts, 1932), 7–8.

41. Norman Hinds, "The Educational Program at Grand Canyon National Park," Box 26, JCMP.

42. Merriam to Buwalda, January 4, 1933, Box 29, JCMP; Merriam to Arno Cammerer, Director, National Park Service, December 27, 1934, MMSF.

43. Merriam to Buwalda, January 4, 1933.

44. Yard to Merriam, January 12 [1933], Box 186, JCMP.

7. A Voice for Wilderness

1. John C. Merriam, "National Policy on Historical Sites and Monuments," December 28, 1933, MMSF.

2. Merriam to Cammerer, December 27, 1934; Cammerer to Merriam, January 14, 1935, MMSF.

3. Drury to Merriam, January 29, 1934, Box 58, JCMP.

4. Merriam to Drury, November 16 and November 26, 1934, Carton 2, RLBL.

5. Merriam, untitled memorandum, transmitted November 16, 1934, Box 123, JCMP.

6. Barry Karl, *Charles E. Merriam and the Study of Politics* (Chicago: University of Chicago Press, 1974), 233–38.

7. Susan R. Schrepfer, *The Fight to Save the Redwoods: A History of Environmental Reform, 1917–1978* (Madison: University of Wisconsin Press, 1983), 74; T. H. Watkins, *Righteous Pilgrim: The Life and Times of Harold L. Ickes, 1874–1952* (New York: Henry Holt, 1990), 552–53.

8. Merriam to Buwalda, October 12, 1933, Box 29, JCMP.

9. Lawrence Merriam to John C. Merriam, May 10, 1933, MMSF.

10. Lawrence Merriam to John C. Merriam, May 17, 1935, MMSF.

11. John C. Merriam to Charles E. Merriam and John C. Merriam to Lawrence Merriam, both dated May 20, 1935; Charles E. Merriam to John C. Merriam, May 27, 1935, all in Box 123, JCMP.

12. John C. Merriam to Charles E. Merriam, May 24, 1935, Box 123, JCMP; John C. Merriam to Lawrence Merriam, May 24, 1935; Lawrence Merriam to John C. Merriam, May 27, 1935; John C. Merriam to Charles E. Merriam, May 28, 1935, all MMSF.

13. Drury to Merriam, February 19, 1937, Box 58, JCMP.

14. Merriam to Drury, February 25, 1937, Box 58, JCMP.

15. Merriam to Buwalda, October 12, 1933, Box 29, JCMP; Merriam, "Memorandum Regarding Organization of National Parks," February 26, 1936, Box 58, JCMP.

16. Stephen T. Mather, *Report of the Director of the National Park Service* (Washington, D.C.: Government Printing Office, 1924), 37.

17. Yard to Grinnell, September 18, 1926, Box 186, JCMP.

18. Merriam to Mather, October 25, 1927, Box 10, File 201-11, Yosemite National Park Library; Linda Wedel Greene, *Historic Resource Study, Yosemite National Park,* vol. 2 (Washington, D.C.: Government Printing Office, 1987), 729–30.

19. Alfred Runte, *Yosemite: The Embattled Wilderness* (Lincoln: University of Nebraska Press, 1990), 153–59.

20. Merriam to Buwalda, July 2 and July 29, 1932, Box 29, JCMP.

21. Buwalda to Merriam, September 30, 1933; Merriam to Buwalda, October 12, 1933, Box 29, JCMP.

22. Merriam to Buwalda, May 27, 1935; Buwalda to Merriam, June 7, 1935, Box 29, JCMP.

23. Merriam, preface to "Protection and Use of the Primitive," [1935], typescript, MMSF.

24. Merriam to Buwalda, June 17, 1935, Box 29, JCMP.

25. John C. Merriam, "Relation of Landscape Student to Problem of Protecting Primitive," July 30, 1935, Carton 1 (JCM Writings 1930–), RLBL.

26. John C. Merriam, "Memorandum Regarding Yosemite," September 4, 1935, MMSF.

27. John C. Merriam, "Memorandum Regarding the Primitive," August 24, 1935, MMSF.

28. Ibid.

29. Yard to Merriam, February 12, 1935, Box 186, JCMP.

30. Quote from Marshall to H. C. Anderson, October 24, 1934, Marshall Papers, Bancroft Library, cited in James M. Glover, *A Wilderness Original: The Life of Bob Marshall* (Seattle: The Mountaineers, 1986), 177–78. Glover notes that Marshall's views matched those of Yard, who envisioned an organization dedicated to preserving the primitive in both national parks and the national forests.

31. Robert S. Yard, "The Man Who Wants to Merge National, State, and Municipal Parks," [August 1936], Box 186, JCMP.

32. Yard to Drury, August 25, 1936, Box 186, JCMP.

33. Yard to Henry Baldwin Ward, September 28, 1936, and Yard to Merriam, December 22, 1936, Box 186, JCMP. Quote from Cammerer presented as a policy statement in a paper published as "A Review of the Year in the National Parks," *American Planning and Civic Annual* (Washington, D.C.: American Planning and Civic Association, 1937), 55.

34. Arno Cammerer, "Standards and Policies in National Parks," *American Planning and Civic Annual* (Washington, D.C.: American Planning and Civic Association, 1936), 17–18; G. Frank Williss and Harlan D. Unrau, *Administrative History: Expansion of the National Park Service in the 1930s* (Washington, D.C.: Government Printing Office, 1983), 154.

35. In the social science context, values and value orientation furnish justification for the tasks and outputs of the organization; Ben W. Twight, *Organizational Values and Political Power: The Forest Service versus Olympic National Park* (University Park: Pennsylvania State University Press, 1983), 137–38.

36. Ronald A. Foresta, *America's National Parks and Their Keepers* (Washington, D.C.: Resources for the Future, 1984), 26–27.

37. Alfred Runte, *National Parks: The American Experience* (Lincoln: University of Nebraska Press, 1987), 103–12. For discussion of concessions in relation to Park Service operations during this period, see Peter Blodgett, "Striking a Balance: Managing Concessions in the National Parks, 1916–1933," *Forest and Conservation History* 34, no. 2 (April 1990): 60–68.

38. Lane [Yard and Albright] in *Report of the Director of the National Park Service* (Washington, D.C.: Government Printing Office, 1918), 275.

39. Miles, *Guardians of the Parks,* 57–58; Hal K. Rothman, "A Regular Ding-Dong Fight: Agency Culture and Evolution in the NPS-USFS Dispute, 1916–1937," *Western Historical Quarterly* 20, no. 2 (May 1989): 151–52.

40. C. J. Buck, "Recreational Planning in the National Forests," March 30, 1927, Arthur L. Peck Papers, Oregon State University Archives, Corvallis; Leon F. Kneipp, "What Shall We Call Protected Recreation Areas in the National Forests?" *American Civic Annual* (Washington, D.C.: American Planning and Civic Association, 1929), 34–36.

41. Leon F. Kneipp, "The Place of Wilderness in American Life," n.d. [1926], Box 190, JCMP.

42. Kneipp to Merriam, October 19, 1926, Box 109, JCMP.

43. John C. Merriam in "Facets of Wilderness," *[U.S. Forest] Service Bulletin* 10, no. 50 (December 20, 1926): 5, Box 109, JCMP.

44. Erik Lawrence Weiselberg, "Ascendancy of the Mazamas: Environment, Identity, and Mountain Climbing in Oregon, 1870 to 1930" (Ph.D. diss., University of Oregon, 1999), 360.

45. Remarks of William B. Greeley at the hearing conducted in Portland, April 15, 1927, 66–69, SCML; Foresta, *America's National Parks,* 28.

46. Mount Hood Committee report to the Secretary of Agriculture, August 30, 1928, SCML.

47. Weiselberg, "Ascendancy of the Mazamas," 366; Frank A. Waugh, "Mount Hood and the National Forests," *American Civic Annual* (Washington, D.C.: American Planning and Civic Association, 1931), 51.

48. Olmsted et al., *Public Values of the Mount Hood Area,* Senate Document 164, 71st Congress, 2nd Session (Washington, D.C.: Government Printing Office, 1930); William C. Tweed, *Recreation Site Planning and Improvements in National Forests, 1891–1942,* FS-354, November 1980 (Washington, D.C.: Government Printing Office, 1981), 14.

49. R. Y. Stuart, Chief, to all district [regional] foresters, March 11, 1929, Box 109, JCMP.

50. Kneipp, quoting Merriam, in Amelia R. Fry et al., "Land Planning and Acquisition, U.S. Forest Service," ROHO interview, 1964–65, 117; Kneipp repeated the same rationale without naming Merriam in "What Shall We Call Protected Recreation Areas in the National Forests?" *American Civic Annual,* 1929.

51. Yard to Merriam, August 12, 1932, Box 186, JCMP.

52. Merriam to Sawyer, December 23, 1935, Box 157, JCMP.

53. John C. Merriam, "Parks as an Opportunity and Responsibility of the States," *State Recreation* 2, no. 4 (August 1928): 10–15.

8. Building State Parks

1. John C. Merriam, "Parks as an Opportunity and Responsibility of the States," *State Recreation* 2, no. 4 (August 1928): 10–15.

2. Ibid.

3. Frederick Law Olmsted, Jr., *Report of State Park Survey of California* (Sacramento: California State Printing Office, 1929).

4. Charles E. Beveridge et al., comps., *The Master List of Design Projects of the Olmsted Firm, 1857–1950* (Boston: National Association for Olmsted Parks, 1987).

5. Amelia Roberts Fry and Susan Schrepfer, "Newton Bishop Drury: Parks and Redwoods, 1919–1971," ROHO interview, 1972, 195–97; Engbeck, *State Parks of California,* 68–72; Corinne L. Gilb, "William E. Colby: Reminiscences," ROHO interview, 1954, 64–67.

6. Lawrence C. Merriam to John C. Merriam, December 16, 1934, MMSF.

7. John C. Merriam, *The Highest Uses of the Redwoods: Messages to the Council of the Save-the-Redwoods League, 1922–1941* (San Francisco: Save-the-Redwoods League, 1941), 18–20.

8. Lawrence C. Merriam, "General Plan for a Protection Study of the Bull Creek–Dyerville Tract," November 28, 1931; Lawrence Merriam to John C. Merriam, March 3, 1932; Lawrence C. Merriam, "Memorandum for the Save-the-Redwoods League," December 23, 1932; Lawrence Merriam to John C. Merriam, January 4, 1933, all MMSF.

9. A graduate student, Lincoln Constance, who had worked as a ranger-naturalist at Crater Lake National Park in 1931, did most of the work on the botanical study. Jepson subsequently used it as a starting point for his leaflet printed and distributed by the Save-the-Redwoods League called *Trees, Shrubs, and Flowers of the Redwood Region.*

10. Duncan McDuffie et al., "Recommendations of Committee on Preservation of Redwood Groves," Carton 1, Colby file, RLBL.

11. Merriam to Buwalda, July 29, 1932, Box 29, JCMP.

12. Francis McComas quoted in Fran Ciesla et al., eds., *Point Lobos State Reserve: A Living Museum* (Carmel, CA: Point Lobos Natural History Association, 1983).

13. Chester Stock, *Rancho La Brea: A Record of Pleistocene Life in California* (Los Angeles: L.A. County Museum of Natural History, 1972), 60.

14. Thomas H. Macbride, *Point Lobos* (1916), C-A 285, Carton 5, Bancroft Library, University of California, Berkeley; Drury to Merriam, October 1, 1926, and Caroline Hunter to Drury, October 4, 1926, Carton 2, RLBL.

15. Drury to Merriam, September 13, October 5, October 29, 1932, and Raymond B. Fosdick to Merriam, November 21, 1932, Carton 2, RLBL; Fry and Schrepfer, "Drury: Parks and Redwoods," pp. 305–6; Engbeck, *State Parks of California,* 62.

16. Lawrence C. Merriam, "Memorandum for Mr. Newton B. Drury Regarding the Proposed Point Lobos State Park," September 14, 1932, MMSF.

17. Merriam to Drury, October 22, 1932, Carton 2, RLBL.

18. Merriam to Drury, January 28, 1933, Carton 2, RLBL.

19. Fry and Schrepfer, "Drury: Parks and Redwoods," 306–7; Chapin Hall, "What Goes On?" *Los Angeles Times,* November 6, 1937.

20. [John C. Merriam], "Point Lobos Studies: Values of Primitive Nature," in *Carnegie Institution of Washington Yearbook 35* (Washington, D.C.: Carnegie Institution of Washington, 1936), 365–66.

21. Ibid. Wagener also thought that perhaps the salt spray at the headlands had a therapeutic effect on the native cypress; Fry and Schrepfer, "Drury: Parks and Redwoods," 367, 453.

22. Merriam, *Highest Uses,* 32.

23. Hall, "What Goes On?" See also Fry and Schrepfer, "Drury: Parks and Redwoods," 212.

24. Merriam to Buwalda, January 11, 1932; Cammerer to Merriam, January 8, 1936; Merriam to Cammerer, January 11, 1936, all MMSF.

25. Howel Williams, *The Geology of Crater Lake National Park, Oregon; with a Reconnaissance of the Cascade Range Southward to Mount Shasta* (Washington, D.C.: Carnegie Institution of Washington, 1942). The popular forms of the study are *Crater Lake: The Story of Its Origin* (Berkeley: University of California Press, 1941) and *El Lago Crater: Historia de su origen* (Mexico City: Instituto PanAmericano de Geografía e Historia, 1942).

26. Edison Pettit, "Why Is Crater Lake So Blue?" *Carnegie Institution of Washington, News Service Bulletin* 4, no. 4 (1936): 37–44.

27. John C. Merriam, "Crater Lake: A Study in Appreciation of Nature," *American Magazine of Art* 26, no. 8 (August 1933): 357–61. He remained encouraged by the volume of materials received from the University of Oregon investigators in 1940; Merriam to Drury, June 28, 1940, Carton 3, RLBL.

28. Merriam to Bryant, April 11, 1936, Box 26, JCMP; Ansel F. Hall, "Exhibit Layout Plan for Interior Exhibit Room, Sinnott Memorial," April 6, 1937, MMSF.

29. Merriam to Buwalda, August 10, 1938, Box 29, JCMP. For more detail, see Stephen R. Mark, "A Study in Appreciation of Nature: John C. Merriam and the Educational Purpose of Crater Lake National Park," *Oregon Historical Quarterly* 103, no. 1 (Spring 2002): 98–123.

30. Frank F. Bunker, "Office of Publications," in *Carnegie Institution of Washington Yearbook 35* (Washington, D.C.: Carnegie Institution of Washington, 1936), 380–85. Designed in an art moderne style, the auditorium commemorates Elihu Root, who died in 1937. It features an impressive mural by J. Monroe Hewlett that depicts astronomers and geographers gazing at maps of the earth and heavens; Sue A. Kohler and Jeffrey R. Carson, *Sixteenth Street Architecture* (Washington D.C.: Commission of Fine Arts, 1988), 295–98.

31. Staff Members and Research Associates, *Cooperation in Research,* publication 501 (Washington, D.C.: Carnegie Institution of Washington, 1938). Articles by John Buwalda, Ralph Chaney, Newton Drury, and Chester Stock related directly to Merriam's work, both in paleontology and preservation.

32. John C. Merriam, "Memorandum Regarding Research Program of John C. Merriam as President-Emeritus of the Carnegie Institution," January 9, 1939, CIWF.

33. John C. Merriam, "Paleontology, Early Man, and Historical Geology," in *Carnegie Institution of Washington Yearbook 38* (Washington, D.C.: Carnegie Institution of Washington, 1939), 301–10.

34. Merriam, *Highest Uses.* The only other publication related to the study was derived from Merriam's annual message to the league in 1942; John C. Merriam, "The Redwoods and the War," *Living Wilderness* 8, no. 1 (May 1943): 15–18. His manuscript titled "Human Values of the Redwoods" (n.d., MMSF) never made it into print.

35. Tilden to Merriam, February 26, 1940, Carton 3, RLBL.

36. Merriam to Tilden, February 28, 1940, Carton 3, RLBL.

37. John C. Merriam to Lawrence Merriam, March 5 and April 5, 1940; Charles Merriam to Lawrence Merriam, April 13, 1940, all MMSF.

38. John C. Merriam to Lawrence Merriam, April 19 and May 14, 1940; Charles Merriam to Lawrence Merriam, April 25, 1940, all MMSF.

39. Fry and Schrepfer, "Drury: Parks and Redwoods," 350–52, 666.

40. Malcolm Merriam to Lawrence Merriam, November 6, 1940; Malcolm Merriam to Charles Merriam, November 12, 1940; Charles Merriam to Malcolm Merriam November 15, 1940; John C. Merriam to Charles Merriam, January 9, 1941, all MMSF. A summary of the trip to South America appeared in "Pan American Gains Related," *Los Angeles Times,* May 28, 1941.

41. John C. Merriam to Lawrence Merriam, January 11, 1941; Buwalda to Lawrence Merriam January 26, 1941; Lawrence Merriam to Malcolm Merriam, February 15, 1941, all MMSF. An article about the ceremony appeared in the *Los Angeles Times* on February 21, 1941, in the Society section.

42. John C. Merriam to Lawrence Merriam, March 5 and August 5, 1940; Lawrence Merriam to John C. Merriam, June 14, 1942, all MMSF.

43. Merriam to Vannevar Bush, Carnegie Institution president, September 11, 1941, CIWF. The idea had its origin several years earlier, as part of Merriam's discussions with State Parks Superintendent Samuel Boardman; Merriam to Boardman, August 20, 1938, Box 21, JCMP.

44. John C. Merriam to Lawrence Merriam, June 24, 1941, MMSF; Minutes of CEPOP meetings, June 15 and November 21, 1942, John Day Fossil Beds State Park files, OPRD.

45. Boardman to Henry F. Cabell, Chairman, October 21, 1942, Ax 100, Box 3, SCUO; Boardman to Sawyer, May 22, 1943, Ax 100, Box 3, SCUO. Merriam to Boardman, July 19, 1943, OPRD; W. D. Langille, "John Day Fossil Beds, A State Park of the Yesterdays" (typescript), May 12, 1948, 2, and "The Painted Hills: A Unique State Park of Wheeler County," November 4, 1948, both OPRD.

46. Merriam to Stock, August 25, 1938, Box 169, JCMP. Merriam to Boardman, July 28, 1943, with enclosures, OPRD. Merriam, "Relation of J. C. Merriam to Continuing Activities in Study of the John Day Region," Box 3, MS Misc., MPBL/A. E. P. Leavitt to [National Park Service] Regional Director (Lawrence Merriam), January 17, 1946, MMSF. The closest to a popular account that might have aided visitors appeared within a year of Merriam's death;

Chester Stock, "Oregon's Wonderland of the Past—the John Day," *Scientific Monthly* 63 (July 1946): 57–65.

47. John C. Merriam to Charles Merriam, November 12, 1940, MMSF. R. W. Leighton, CEPOP chairman, to Frederick M. Hunter, Chancellor, May 26, 1943, OPRD. Chaney, CEPOP Meeting, September 23, 1943, OPRD. Luther S. Cressman, *A Golden Journey: Memoirs of an Archeologist* (Salt Lake City: University of Utah Press, 1988), 410.

48. Cressman, *Golden Journey*, 410–11. Howel Williams gave the first lecture in 1946; see the foreword in his book *The Ancient Volcanoes of Oregon* (Eugene: University of Oregon Press, 1948), v–vii.

49. Boardman to Henry F. Cabell, October 21, 1942, Ax 100, Box 3, SCUO.

50. Merriam to Boardman, October 9, 1934, Carton 2, RLBL.

51. Drury to Merriam, November 23, 1934; Merriam to Drury, November 16, 1934, Carton 2, RLBL.

52. Merriam to Boardman, August 21, 1934, and January 28, 1938; Boardman to Merriam, April 28, 1936, and July 5 and December 29, 1938, all in Box 21, JCMP.

53. Boardman to R. H. Baldock, Chief Highway Engineer, March 11, 1941, Ax 100, SCUO.

54. Booklets such as the one by Merriam called *A Living Link in History* were in wide circulation by 1935; "Uncle of President Struck by Beauties of Redwoods," *Eureka Times,* July 24, 1935. Merriam and Drury began discussing the need for such devices even before the dedication of Humboldt Redwoods State Park; Drury to Merriam, July 31, 1930, and Merriam to Drury, November 24, 1930, Carton 2, RLBL.

55. Merriam to Drury, December 1, 1943, MMSF (notation on Drury's copy to Lawrence Merriam). Earlier in the year Merriam wrote to one of his correspondents, "While in Oregon I am practically considered an Oregonian"; Merriam to Alan Eaton, March 30, 1943, Carton 4, Misc. folder, MPBL/A.

56. John C. Merriam, "Paleontological, Geological, and Historical Research," in *Carnegie Institution of Washington Yearbook 43* (Washington, D.C.: Carnegie Institution of Washington, 1944), 190–96.

57. John C. Merriam to Charles Merriam, July 3, 1944, MMSF; John C. Merriam, "Relation of J. C. Merriam to the Continuing Activities in Study of the John Day Region," August 5, 1944, Box 3, MS Misc. (2), MPBL/A.

58. Aubrey Drury, "Minutes [of the] Annual Meeting of the Board of Councilors of the Save-the-Redwoods League," August 31, 1944, MMSF; biographical note to 1944 file, Carton 3, RLBL.

59. Newton Drury, "Recreation and the National Parks" [November 1945], in *American Planning and Civic Annual* (Washington, D.C.: American Planning and Civic Association, 1950), 10.

60. Mark W. T. Harvey, *A Symbol of Wilderness: Echo Park and the American Conservation Movement* (Albuquerque: University of New Mexico Press, 1994), 31–35.

61. Jon M. Cosco, *Echo Park: Struggle for Preservation* (Boulder, CO: Johnson Books, 1995), x–xv.

62. Horace Albright, "National Parks in the Postwar Period," *American Planning and Civic Annual* (Washington, D.C.: American Planning and Civic Association, 1943), 75–81.

63. Drury to Merriam, [September] 1944, Carton 2, Drury folder, MPBL/A.

9. What Nature Means

1. John C. Merriam, *The Garment of God: Influence of Nature in Human Experience* (New York: Scribner's, 1943), 36.

2. John C. Merriam, "An Abyss in Time," in Merriam, *The Living Past* (New York: Charles Scribner's Sons, 1930), 91–92. The passage is repeated in *The Garment of God,* 153.

3. Attributed to Socrates and quoted by Freeman Tilden, *Interpreting Our Heritage* (Chapel Hill: University of North Carolina Press, 1957), 100.

4. Merriam, *The Garment of God,* 15–16.

5. John C. Merriam, "Influence of Nature on Thought and Life," n.d., 8, Carton 3, MS Misc., file (2), MPBL/A; "John Campbell Merriam," autobiographical typescript dated September 1, 1944, 12–13, MMSF; Merriam, *The Garment of God,* 7–8.

6. Merriam to Drury, April 9, 1928, Carton 2, and (as quoted) "Elements Involved in the Appreciation of Nature," typescript dated May 10, 1932, Carton 2, MPBL/A.

7. Merriam, *The Garment of God,* xii.

8. John C. Merriam to Charles E. Merriam, December 19, 1944; John C. Merriam to Lawrence Merriam, December 29, 1944, and February 26, 1945; John C. Merriam to Charles W. Merriam, January 5, 1945, all MMSF.

9. Charles Merriam to Lawrence Merriam, April 12 and 25, 1945, MMSF.

10. A. W. Meads to Lawrence and Charles Merriam, August 7, 1945, MMSF; "Merriam Rites Set for Friday," *Berkeley Daily Gazette,* October 31, 1945; "Dr. Merriam Dead; Paleontologist, 76," *New York Times,* October 31, 1945.

11. Ralph Chaney, "John Campbell Merriam, 1869–1945," *Yearbook of the American Philosophical Society 1945* (Philadelphia: American Philosophical Society, 1946), 381–87; Chester Stock, "John Campbell Merriam, 1869–1945," *Science* 103, no. 2677 (April 19, 1946): 470–71, and "Memorial to John Campbell Merriam," *Proceedings of the Geological Society of America* (July 1947), 183–97.

12. Newton Drury, "The Debt of Conservation to Dr. John C. Merriam," *American Forests* 51, no. 12 (December 1945): 597, 621–22.

13. Albright to Drury, December 12, 1945, RG 79, Drury Papers, National Archives, Washington D.C., quoted in Schrepfer, *The Fight to Save the Redwoods,* 55.

14. Merriam, *The Garment of God,* 132–34.

15. Joseph Sax, *Mountains without Handrails: Reflections on the National Parks* (Ann Arbor: University of Michigan Press, 1980), 103–5.

16. Foresta, *America's National Parks and Their Keepers,* 56–69.

17. Greene, *Historic Resource Study, Yosemite National Park,* vol. 2, 611.

18. Harold Bryant, "The Beginnings of Yosemite's Educational Program," *Yosemite Nature Notes* 39, no. 7 (July 1960): 165.

19. George Robinson, "Freeman Tilden, 1883–1980," in William H. Sontag, *National Park Service: The First Seventy-five Years* (Philadelphia: Eastern National Park and Monument Association, 1990), 50.

20. References to an unknowable divine force are particularly evident in Tilden's later work, such as *The Fifth Essence* (Washington, D.C.: The National Park Trust Fund Board, n.d.) and "Vistas of Beauty," in *Interpreting Our Heritage*, 2nd. ed. (Chapel Hill: University of North Carolina Press, 1967). Shelley is quoted in Merriam, *The Garment of God*, 16.

21. Barry Mackintosh, *Interpretation in the National Park Service,* (Washington, D.C.: USDI-NPS, History Division, 1986), 49–51. Mission 66 began in 1956 and was promoted by Wirth and the Park Service as a ten-year effort to prepare for the fiftieth anniversary of the agency's 1916 establishment.

22. It was nominated through a survey that largely focused on rustic architecture in the national park system; Laura Soulliere Harrison, *Architecture in the Parks: National Historic Landmark Theme Study* (Washington, D.C.: Government Printing Office, 1986), 99–121.

23. John C. Merriam, "Paleontological, Geological, and Historical Research," in *Carnegie Institution of Washington Yearbook 1943–44* (Washington, D.C.: Carnegie Institution of Washington, 1944), 196.

24. Stephen R. Mark, *Floating in the Stream of Time: An Administrative History of John Day Fossil Beds National Monument* (Seattle: National Park Service, 1996), 227. The paleontologist Ted Fremd convened the 2001 North American Paleontological Congress Symposium at Berkeley that honored the centennial of Merriam's seminal paper on the John Day Basin: John C. Merriam, "A Contribution to the Geology of the John Day Basin," *University of California Bulletin of the Department of Geology* 2, no. 9 (April 1901), 269–314. Proceedings of this symposium will appear in the journal *Paleobios.*

25. John C. Merriam to Lawrence Merriam, February 24, 1944, MMSF. Richard West Sellars, *Preserving Nature in the National Parks: A History* (New Haven: Yale University Press, 1997), 145–48.

26. Luther S. Cressman et al., *Early Man in Oregon* (Eugene: University of Oregon Press, 1940), and Cressman, *Archaeological Researches in the Northern Great Basin* (Washington, D.C.: Carnegie Institution of Washington, 1942).

27. George C. Ruhle, Park Naturalist, [1946], justification for Merriam Point, to the U.S. Board of Geographic Names, MMSF.

28. The proposed trail and observation station at Merriam Point stayed on the park's master plan until 1953. By that time, both CEPOP members (E. P. Leavitt and George C. Ruhle) had departed from Crater Lake National Park. Howel Williams subsequently named a submerged cone in Crater Lake for Merriam, again citing Merriam's importance to the interpretation of the park; Williams, "The Floor of Crater Lake, Oregon," *American Journal of Science* 259 (February 1961): 82.

29. The monograph Merriam wanted the league to fund finally appeared as an anthology; see Reed F. Noss, ed., *The Redwood Forest: History, Ecology, and Conservation* (Washington, D.C.: Island Press, 2000).

30. John C. Merriam, *A Living Link in History* (San Francisco: Save-the-Redwoods League, 1978). Other pamphlets in the series included Ralph Chaney, *Redwoods of the Past;* Emmanuel Fritz, *Story Told by a Fallen Redwood;* and Willis Jepson, *Trees, Shrubs, and Flowers of the Redwood Region.* A fifth was added some years later: John B. Dewitt, *California Redwood Parks and Reserves* (San Francisco: Save-the-Redwoods League, 1982).

31. G. Pascal Zachary, *Endless Frontier: Vannevar Bush, Engineer of the American Century* (New York: The Free Press, 1999), 84.

32. Newton Drury, "Transmuting Science into Conservation," in Staff Members and Research Associates, *Cooperation in Research,* publication 501 (Washington, D.C.: Carnegie Institution of Washington, 1938), 753–63.

33. Tilden, *Interpreting Our Heritage,* 26–39.

34. William S. Barton, "Mt. Wilson's Unknown Man," *Los Angeles Times,* July 25, 1937, and Lawrence C. Merriam, Jr., interview with the author, May 25, 2002.

35. Freeman Tilden, *The National Parks: What They Mean to You and Me* (New York: Knopf, 1951), and *The State Parks: Their Meaning in American Life* (New York: Knopf, 1962).

36. Merriam to Drury, January 16, 1941, MMSF.

Further Reading

Staff at the Carnegie Institution of Washington compiled most of Merriam's published writings in a four-volume set, *Published Papers and Addresses of John Campbell Merriam,* to mark his retirement from the Carnegie Institution in 1938. These volumes are organized under general headings (paleontology, education, and nature), but the collection lacks a contextual framework or an introduction, which might have placed Merriam and his contemporaries in the broader contexts of early-twentieth-century science and preservation. Chester Stock's "Memorial to John Campbell Merriam," which appeared in the *Proceedings Volume of the Geological Society of America* published in July 1947, includes a full bibliography, along with a biographical sketch aimed at piquing interest in his mentor's legacy. He also concluded the Carnegie Institution testimonial volume of 1938, *Cooperation in Research* (Washington, D.C.: Carnegie Institution of Washington, 1938), with "John Campbell Merriam as Scientist and Philosopher," an essay that should be read in conjunction with the penultimate piece, "Transmuting Science into Conservation," by Newton B. Drury.

Barry Karl's biography of Merriam's brother Charles, *Charles E. Merriam and the Study of Politics* (Chicago: University of Chicago Press, 1974), is probably the most accessible reference about life in nineteenth-century Hopkinton. A lot can be inferred from it about how the brothers differed, particularly in regard to their formative years and influences. Barbara Stein's work on Annie Alexander, *On Her Own Terms: Annie Montague Alexander and the Rise of Science in the American West* (Berkeley and Los Angeles: University of California Press, 2001), furnished some reasons why a strained relationship developed between Merriam and his benefactor. Robert Rainger, by contrast, directed his attention toward how paleontologists fit into the institutional values of American science during the early twentieth century in the opening of his book *An*

Agenda for Antiquity: Henry Fairfield Osborn and Vertebrate Paleontology at the American Museum of Natural History (Tuscaloosa: University of Alabama Press, 1992). Robert Kohler likewise illuminated the early growth of philanthropic foundations like the Carnegie Institution of Washington with *Partners in Science: Foundations and Natural Scientists, 1900–1945* (Chicago: University of Chicago Press, 1991). No one has explored Carnegie Institution operations during Merriam's presidency in a comprehensive way, though a booklet by Ray Bowers, *Mr. Carnegie's Plant Biologists: The Ancestry of Carnegie Institution's DPB* (Washington, D.C.: Carnegie Institution of Washington, 1992), supplies a helpful summary of the issues and key personalities in one department during that period.

The thrust of this biography is, of course, Merriam's role in the creation and management of parks and the preservation of nature. National parks and their history have fueled an especially rich literature from the 1970s onward, covering both individual units and themes such as development, the role of American Indians in parks and preservation, or that of scientific research. Merriam's place in this emerging body of work, however, has largely been limited to glancing references. A book by John C. Miles, *Guardians of the Parks: A History of the National Parks and Conservation Association* (Washington, D.C.: Taylor and Francis, 1995), serves as probably the lone exception: the author places Merriam in the role of advisor to the more central figure of Robert Sterling Yard.

Publications on the history of state parks are not as numerous as those on national parks, but it would be hard to ignore Merriam's shadow in the redwoods. Susan R. Schrepfer's *The Fight to Save the Redwoods: A History of Environmental Reform, 1917–1978* (Madison: University of Wisconsin Press, 1983) represents the first real attempt to use Merriam's papers stored in the Library of Congress. Although by comparison cursory, *State Parks of California from 1864 to the Present* (Portland, OR: Graphic Arts Center, 1980), by Joseph H. Engbeck, Jr., is more sympathetic toward Merriam and his protégé Drury. Considerably less attention has been paid to Merriam in Oregon aside from my account of his founding role for two antecedent state parks in the John Day Basin. That is discussed as part of my administrative history documenting the background, founding, and management issues of the John Day Fossil Beds National Monument, established in 1975. I paraphrased Merriam by calling it *Floating in the Stream of Time* (Seattle: National Park Service, 1996), though like many (if not most) contributions to what is sometimes called the "gray literature" of government publications, I avoided using anecdotes that can convey so much about key personalities like Merriam. Thankfully, many anecdotes are preserved in the form of interviews given by Harold Bryant, Ralph Chaney, Newton Drury, and Loye Miller. Conducted by staff in the Regional Oral History Office at the University of California's Bancroft Library, these transcripts can still be ordered from the Bancroft and are available in a small number of university libraries.

Perhaps the finest tribute paid to Merriam came posthumously from a colleague as part of Freeman Tilden's classic *Interpreting Our Heritage* (Chapel Hill: University of North Carolina Press, 1957). Some of the ideas the two men discussed years before appear in the book, one that thousands of aspiring naturalists and historians have since read. It is a magnificent guide that discusses how to reach people through a park setting, one sure to appeal to anyone curious about how those "higher values" (as Tilden and Merriam called them) form the essence of that intangible thing called heritage.

Index

Text:	10/13 Galliard
Display:	Galliard
Compositor:	Sheridan Books, Inc.
Printer and binder:	Sheridan Books, Inc.